A Hermeneutics of
Poetic Education

A Hermeneutics of Poetic Education

The Play of the In-Between

By Catherine Homan

LEXINGTON BOOKS
Lanham • Boulder • New York • London

Published by Lexington Books
An imprint of The Rowman & Littlefield Publishing Group, Inc.
4501 Forbes Boulevard, Suite 200, Lanham, Maryland 20706
www.rowman.com

6 Tinworth Street, London SE11 5AL, United Kingdom

Copyright © 2020 The Rowman & Littlefield Publishing Group, Inc.

Paul Celan's, "Sprachgitter." In: id., Sprachgitter. © S. Fischer Verlag GmbH, Frankfurt am Main 1959 and Paul Celan's, "Tübingen, Jänner." In: id., Die Niemandsrose © S. Fischer Verlag GmbH, Frankfurt am Main 1963. pg. 24, appear courtesy of S. Fischer Verlag GmbH, Frankfurt am Main.

Chapter 4 includes revised portions of "The Play of Being and Nothing: World, Earth, and Cosmos in Eugen Fink," which appeared in *Philosophy Today* 63, no. 1 (2019): 35–54. https://doi.org/10.5840/philtoday201967255.

"Todtnauberg," "In den Flüssen," "Weggebeizt," aus: Paul Celan, Die Gedichte. Kommentierte Gesamtausgabe in einem Band. Herausgegeben und kommentiert von Barbara Wiedemann. © Suhrkamp Verlag Frankfurt am Main 2003. Alle Rechte bei und vorbehalten durch Suhrkamp Verlag, Berlin.

Paul Celan, Von Schwelle zu Schwelle © 1955, Deutsche Verlags-Anstalt, München, in der Verlagsgruppe Random House GmbH.

All rights reserved. No part of this book may be reproduced in any form or by any electronic or mechanical means, including information storage and retrieval systems, without written permission from the publisher, except by a reviewer who may quote passages in a review.

British Library Cataloguing in Publication Information Available

Library of Congress Cataloging-in-Publication Data Available

Library of Congress Control Number: 2019954144

ISBN: 978-1-4985-9444-8 (cloth)
ISBN: 978-1-4985-9446-2 (pbk)
ISBN: 978-1-4985-9445-5 (electronic)

For Zack

Contents

Acknowledgments	ix
Abbreviations	xi
Introduction	1
1 Aesthetic Education and the Roots of Poetic Education	21
2 Poetry as Teacher of Humanity	59
3 Play, *Paidia*, and *Paideia*	95
4 Becoming Who We Are: A Conversation	129
Conclusion: The Play of the In-Between	165
Bibliography	181
Index	191
About the Author	203

Acknowledgments

This book provides an account of learning how to listen and to speak with one another, and I owe a great deal to those who have engaged in these lessons and conversations with me. Zack Hamm has been at my side through the entire process. This text would not be what it is without his rigor, generosity, keen eye, and patience. He has helped me to see what I otherwise could not. Karolin Mirzakhan provided critical insights, advice, and humor from the earliest stages through to the finish. We think the same thoughts. Becca Longtin and Sam Timme have continuously been both devoted friends and interlocutors.

Many thanks go to those teachers and mentors who instilled in me a great appreciation for language and philosophy. They have modeled the transformative power of dialogue and what it means to be a teacher and a scholar. I thank in particular Victoria Carlson-Casaregola, Jeanne Schuler, Rudi Makkreel, and John Lysaker. I offer special thanks to Lorie Vanchena for sparking my love of German. I am grateful to my fellow philosophers at Mount Mary University, Jennifer Hockenbery Dragseth and Austin Reece, for their wisdom and dedication to the discipline and to liberatory education. My students have also taught me in many ways what it is to learn through conversation.

A theme throughout this project is friendship, which I have had in abundance throughout this process. Of my St. Louis friends and family, who make me feel at home more than anyone, I thank Katie Luner, Rachel Smith, Angela Smith, and Rose McNamee. I would also like to thank, among many, those who have leant support and insight, including Jim Conlon, Shawnee Daniels-Sykes, Mara Drogan, Laurel End, Jessica Elkyam, Claudia Farrow, Al Frankowski, Julia Haas, Christopher Hudspeth, Helga Kisler, Jennifer Kontny, Robert Matthews, Kathy Nieman, Celcy Powers-King, Don Rappé,

Mark Rusch, Julie Tatlock, Stephanie Toumanoff, Wendy Weaver, and Kristin Whyte.

I appreciate the many opportunities to share these ideas at meetings of the *Society for Phenomenology and Existential Philosophy, Society for Philosophy of Creativity, Philosophy at Play*, and *Wisconsin Philosophical Association* and in print in *Philosophy Today* and the *Journal of Speculative Philosophy*. I remain delighted by these philosophical communities and the questions, conversation, and insights they foster.

Grateful acknowledgment is made to Suhrkamp for permission to reprint "Todtnauberg," "In den Flüssen," "Weggebeizt," aus: Paul Celan, *Die Gedichte. Kommentierte Gesamtausgabe in einem Band*. Herausgegeben und kommentiert von Barbara Wiedemann. © Suhrkamp Verlag Frankfurt am Main 2003. Alle Rechte bei und vorbehalten durch Suhrkamp Verlag Berlin. Paul Celan's, "Sprachgitter." In: id., *Sprachgitter*. © S. Fischer Verlag GmbH, Frankfurt am Main 1959 and Paul Celan's, "Tübingen, Jänner." In: id., *Die Niemandsrose* © S. Fischer Verlag GmbH, Frankfurt am Main 1963. pg. 24, appear courtesy of S. Fischer Verlag GmbH, Frankfurt am Main. "Sprich Auch Du" appears courtesy of Deutsche Verlags-Anstalt. Paul Celan, *Von Schwelle zu Schwelle* © 1955, Deutsche Verlags-Anstalt, München, in der Verlagsgruppe Random House GmbH. Thanks, as well, to the Hilma af Klint Foundation for use of af Klint's painting, "Group IX/UW, No. 25, The Dove, No. 1, 1915" as the cover image. Chapter 4 includes revised portions of "The Play of Being and Nothing: World, Earth, and Cosmos in Eugen Fink," which appeared in *Philosophy Today* 63, no. 1 (2019): 35–54. https://doi.org/10.5840/philtoday201967255. I am grateful to the editors of *Philosophy Today* for permission to include that material. Special thanks to Jana Hodges-Kluck at Lexington Books for her care and enthusiasm as an editor, as well as to Sydney Wedbush for editorial support. I am grateful to the anonymous reviewer secured by Lexington, whose incisive comments and encouragement helped expand my thinking in new directions.

My greatest thanks go to my parents, Ken and Sharon, for cultivating a language of nurture and love and for creating the conditions for people to be good. Their dedication is behind every word in this text. I am so indebted to them and to Mary, Betsy, Ken, Dan, and Maggie for their unflagging support and humor and for their constant invitations to play.

Abbreviations

CELAN

CP *Collected Prose*. Translated by Rosemarie Waldrop. Manchester: Carcanet Press Limited, 2003.
G   *Die Gedichte*. Edited by Barbara Wiedemann. Frankfurt am Main: Suhrkamp, 2005.

FINK

EC   *Existenz und Coexistenz: Grundprobleme der menschilchen Gemeinschaft*. Würzburg: Königshausen & Neumann, 1987.
HS   and Martin Heidegger. *Heraclitus Seminar, 1966/67*. Translated by Charles H. Seibert. Evanston: Northwestern University Press, 1993.
NFW *Natur, Freiheit, Welt: Philosophie der Erziehung*. Edited by Franz-Anton Schwarz. Würzburg: Königshausen & Neumann, 1992.
PSW *Play as Symbol of the World and Other Writings*. Translated by Ian Alexander Moore and Christopher Turner. Bloomington: Indiana University Press, 2016.
SM   *Sein und Mensch*. Freiburg im Breisgau: Karl Alber, 1977.
WE   "Welt und Endlichkeit." In *Sein und Endlichkeit: Vom Wesen der menschlichen Freihei*t. Edited by Riccardo Lazzari. Freiburg im Breisgau: Karl Alber, 2015.

GADAMER

GC   *Gadamer on Celan: "Who Am I and Who Are You?" and Other Essays.* Translated by Bruce Krajewski and Richard Heinemann. Albany: State University of New York Press, 1997.
GR   *The Gadamer Reader: A Bouquet of Later Writings.* Edited by Richard E. Palmer. Evanston: Northwestern University Press, 2007.
LL   *Language and Linguisticality in Gadamer's Hermeneutics.* Edited by Lawrence Kennedy Schmidt. Lanham, MD: Lexington Books, 2000.
RB   *Relevance of the Beautiful and Other Essays.* Edited by Robert Bernasconi. Cambridge: Cambridge University Press, 1986.
TM   *Truth and Method.* Translated by Joel Weinsheimer. New York: Continuum Publishing Group, 2004.

HEIDEGGER

BT   *Being and Time.* Translated by Joan Stambaugh. Albany: State University of New York Press, 1996.
EHP   *Elucidations of Hölderlin's Poetry.* Translated by Keith Hoeller. Amherst: Humanity Books, 2000.
PLT   *Poetry, Language, Thought.* Translated by Alfred Hofstadter. New York: Harper & Row, 1971.

HÖLDERLIN

EL   *Essays and Letters.* Edited by Jeremy Adler and Charlie Louth. London: Penguin, 2009.
H   *Hyperion and Selected Poems.* Edited by Eric L. Santner. New York: The Continuum Publishing Company, 1990.
SA   *Grosse Stuttgarter Ausgabe. Sämtliche Werke.* Edited by Friedrich Beissner. 8 Vols. Stuttgart: Kohlhammer, 1943–1985.

KANT

C3   *Critique of the Power of Judgment.* Translated by Paul Guyer and Eric Matthews. Cambridge: Cambridge University Press, 2000.

NIETZSCHE

BoT *The Birth of Tragedy and Other Writings.* Edited by Raymond Geuss and Ronald Speirs. Translated by Ronald Speirs. Cambridge Texts in the History of Philosophy. New York: Cambridge University Press, 1999.
GS   *The Gay Science.* Translated by Walter Kaufmann. New York: Vintage Books, 1974.
WP   *The Will to Power.* Translated by Walter Kaufmann. New York: Vintage Books, 1968.

SCHILLER

AE   *On the Aesthetic Education of Man in a Series of Letters.* Translated by Elizabeth M. Wilkinson and L.A. Willoughby. New York: Oxford University Press, 1982.
NSP "On Naive and Sentimental Poetry." In *Essays.* Edited by Walter Hinderer and Daniel O. Dahlstrom. Translated by Daniel O. Dahlstrom, 179–260. New York: Continuum Publishing Group, 2005.

Introduction

In a letter to Immanuel Niethammer in 1796, Friedrich Hölderlin writes that he wishes to identify the principle that would both explain and dispel the divisions of subject and object, self and world, reason and revelation (EL 67–68). Referencing Friedrich Schiller, he sets himself the task of writing the "New Letters on the Aesthetic Education of Man," although he will never complete this task. In these letters, he explains, he would "go on from philosophy to poetry and religion" (68). Furthermore, as he writes to his brother, Karl Gok, in 1799, while the general interest in philosophy and politics is important, it still "falls far short of being sufficient for the education of the nation" (121). He strives to foster a Germany that is free politically, intellectually, and poetically.[1] He begins his essay, "The Standpoint from which we should consider Antiquity," with the claim that we, that is, Germans, dream of education, yet have none. We dream of originality and autonomy, yet have none (EL 246). We have only appropriation. Instead of giving form to new things, we rely on the things that the ancient Greeks and Romans formed themselves. This is at odds with our primordial [*ursprüngliche*] drive "to take what is rough, untutored, child-like, rather than a shaped material, in which he who wishes to create form will find the ground already prepared" (EL 246). For Hölderlin, not only are we born from an unformed unity, we also have a drive to give form to what is formless. We have a drive to cultivate. An education that would be sufficient both for contemporary Germany and for our drive to create must necessarily be rooted in art, specifically poetry.

Hölderlin refers to Immanuel Kant as "the Moses of our nation" (EL 120), leading Germany toward a philosophy of its own time and thus toward its own education. Kant views education as the perfecting of humanity not only in terms of cognition, but also in terms of morality through the development of freedom and autonomy. In aesthetic experience, says Kant, we experience the free play of the faculties as we move from subjective experience to universal judgments. This free play quickens [*beleben*] "the mind by opening up for it a view into an immense realm of kindred presentations" (C3 5:315). Through this play, aesthetic experience yields a feeling of freedom that prompts further cultivation of autonomy, that is, a movement of the finite self away from necessity and toward freedom. Schiller, building on Kant's theory, calls for aesthetic education, play, and beauty, offering them as antidotes to alienation insofar as the aesthetic harmonizes the individual and allows her to be fully human. In play, the human feels herself simultaneously as matter, sensible, and as form, rational and free. Beauty, as the "consummation of [her] humanity" (AE 103), unites life and shape. Although humans treat "the agreeable, the good, and the perfect" (105) with seriousness, they *play* with Beauty, suggesting something fundamentally unserious in this activity that "makes all the world happy" and whereby "each and every being forgets its limitations while under its spell" (217). Importantly, "it is only through Beauty that man makes his way to Freedom" (9). Thus, for both Kant and Schiller, aesthetic experience and play serve as stepping stones to the development of rationality and autonomy. Hölderlin, however, seeks to invert their approach: rather than progressing from aesthetic taste to moral universals, he wants instead to move from reason to the harmonizing, utopic nature of poetry.

Hölderlin claims that, because these accounts of aesthetic education relegate aesthetic experience to play and frivolity, they do not take seriously enough the harmony of poetry that allows not an escape from, but a return to oneself. Kant's free play relies on a dualism between subjective and objective, freedom and necessity, self and world. Schiller's play harmonizes, but does not dispel, dualisms between matter and form, necessity and freedom. This unification is, for Hölderlin, not a genuine unification. In play, he explains, all are "united in that everybody forgets themselves and the vital particularity of each is held back" (EL 122). In other words, because play marks a departure from the everyday, it harmonizes through self-distancing. Poetry, conversely, does not require forgetting ourselves, but rather awakens us to ourselves and expands our horizons. He writes to his brother, "[Poetry] unites people if it is genuine and has a genuine effect, it unites them with all their manifold suffering and happiness and aspiration and hope and fear"; it allows them to "form a live, intricately articulated, intense whole" (122–23). By preserving all these manifold differences and divisions, poetry unites not by dissolving divisions, but precisely by maintaining them. Hölderlin believes that discussions of the synthesis or union of subject and object reverse the order of things. It is not that harmony of subject and object is made possible by poetry; rather, it is only because there is a primordial unity that anything like subjects and objects can appear. It is poetry that gives us access to this already existing unity.

We have an intuition of this unity, but cannot fully conceptualize it. This union occurs, moreover, not through reason or logic alone, but through a fundamentally poetic logic (EL 325).[2] Philosophy is not supplanted by poetry, but rather is reidentified as its complement; poetry is itself a kind of thinking. Poetry offers a glimpse into this totality by presenting this original ground by which inner and outer, individual and community, finite and infinite, foreign and familiar appear. Furthermore, other discussions of the influence of art on education take for granted the significance of art and poetry without attending to what these, particularly poetry, are in their essence (138). So long as poetry is considered only as external appearance, it remains a distraction. For Hölderlin, however, poetry, is serious, unifying, and intimate; it organizes and harmonizes humanity into an alternating whole of self and other, inner and outer, free and contingent. Poetry, properly understood, is the *"teacher of humanity"* (155).[3]

Although Hölderlin does not complete his new aesthetic education, from his account we can glean some central themes of how poetry would be the teacher of humanity. Rather than aesthetic education, I take Hölderlin to be calling for a *poetic* education. By this, I mean first, that such an education must respond to the elemental groundlessness of human existence, thus rejecting any essential distinctions between subject and object, self and world. In Hölderlin's discussion of a new aesthetic education, we easily see the etymological connections between *Bild*, as image or form, *Bildung*, as education or cultivation, and *Bildungstrieb*, as formative or cultivating impulse.[4] On Hölderlin's understanding of *Bildungstrieb*, there is an "original communal ground" for existence, yet this ground is itself groundless (EL 247). Because the ground is undifferentiated and formless, it gives rise to existence but cannot itself pre-figure or determine that existence. The formative drive is spontaneous, springing forth toward cultivation. We are made for art, for images, and possess the impulse to create and form, so education would be cultivation of that impulse. Hölderlin draws together both the natural and social, thus rejecting any clear distinction between human and nature. Whereas Kant and Schiller see education and upbringing as overcoming natural drives toward the cultivation of reason, thus separating the two sides of "rational animal," Hölderlin views education as fulfilling our nature.

Second, such an education would be poetic. Hölderlin writes "In Lovely Blueness" that "Poetically / the human dwells upon this earth" (EHP 115). Thus, if education is a cultivation of who we are, it must respond to this poetic dwelling. Although philosophy and politics are important for education, they frequently reduce human relations to duty and law, leaving little space for actual human harmony. Poetry, conversely, forms what is unformed and draws our attention to the originary unity, the primordial foundation, in which we are all equal. The poet, through creative reflection, expresses the mood of "the original living feeling" and thus, in the reflective totality, and allows the finite word to appear "as an infinite in the infinite, as a spiritual whole in the living whole" (EL 295). A poetic education is thus fundamentally creative and gives form to what is new.

Third, because poetic education is this creative giving shape, the role of tradition in education is not static, but dynamic. In a letter to Casimir Ulrich Böhlendorff in 1801, Hölderlin presents a paradox: "in the process of civilization [*Bildung*] what we are actually born with, the national, will always become less and less of an advantage" (EL 207). This is because in education, we frequently overlook that which is native to us, instead appropriating what seems choiceworthy from another. Such appropriation would be mistaken for two reasons. First, it would deny Germans' own formative impulses to create new things. Second, it assumes that the Germans could adopt the same vantage point as the Greeks, when, in reality, the Germans of Hölderlin's time had nothing in common with them (207). Yet, that does not mean that our education should jettison those other traditions. Instead, education must draw on both what is familiar and what is foreign: "For this reason, the Greeks are indispensable to us. Only it is precisely in what is proper to us, in the national, that we shall never match them because as I said, the *free* use of what is our *own* is hardest of all" (208). Whereas the education of Germany inherited the ancients, and thus created little new, the ancients themselves did act on creative impulse. In a letter to his brother in 1799, Hölderlin laments the German condition marked by a lack of elasticity, drive, and creativity that proceeds through uncritical devotion (120). The panacea for the Germans would be poetry, as creative and uniting. We cannot dwell poetically or become who we are by appropriating what has preceded us. Rather, we must create anew in our own way, using tradition as a model for how to think about and respond to what is our own. Thus, our attitude toward the past would not be nostalgia, but transfiguration. As attuned both to what is foreign and what is familiar, education is also a kind of conversation that requires our listening both to tradition and to our own current age in order to give voice to that identity.

Fourth, this education, despite being anchored in art and poetry, is not an escape from reality or unserious play precisely because it requires the use of what is one's own. Recall that Hölderlin argues against play because it is a diversion predicated on abandoning particularity. Here, Hölderlin seems to be concerned about the ways in which Kant and Schiller link play and art. For Kant and Schiller, play is serious as rule-bound, but they view play as a largely contentless and frivolous break from the everyday. Kant speaks of the free play of the faculties in an aesthetic experience; Schiller sees play as the harmonizing activity between sense and form. In these accounts, play primarily describes a spontaneous movement of the faculties enabled by abstracting from everyday life. Moreover, both Kant and Schiller see play as separation from necessity and thus as a form of freedom. For Hölderlin, however, poetry cannot be this break because it is the very basis for community and cannot be separated from life. We experience freedom not by separating off our conditionedness, but by relating ourselves, as finite, to the infinite shared ground of existence. Thus, poetic education must be a return to, rather than a departure from, that shared life.

The aim of this book is to take seriously the task that Hölderlin initiates. For Hölderlin, the poetic marks a harmony between the self and world achieved not through domination or mastery, but through receptivity to a primordial unity (EL 146). Moreover, the poetic presents a challenge to philosophy because it is concerned with the limits of what can be said. How do we speak about the primordial ground or the infinite or the world totality in language that cannot be fully conceptualized? What is curious about Hölderlin's discussion, though, is the way in which poetry is pitted against play, seriousness against frivolity. I contend that we fulfill this task of creating a poetic education not by eschewing play as Hölderlin suggests, but rather by recognizing play's central role in education. In fact, Hölderlin's rejection of play relies on a misunderstanding of the nature of play. Based on the account of play I outline below, I maintain that Hölderlin's account is playful through and through.

This project follows the phenomenological and hermeneutic approaches of Eugen Fink and Hans-Georg Gadamer in turning toward play, poetry, and being in the world with others. Both Fink and Gadamer share Hölderlin's wariness of traditional metaphysics, which presupposes a dualism between subject and object without first thinking the totality that allows such distinctions in the first place. Drawing on Hölderlin's understanding of poetry as world-disclosive, as the "teacher of humanity" (EL 342), these accounts suggest not an aesthetic, but a *poetic* education. I argue that poetry specifically allows the disclosure of this world and what exceeds us, but in a way that never fully lays bare its subject. Instead, poetry requires our attunement to this ambiguous revealing, a holding open of both what is said and what is not. Education, then, requires a cultivation of this preservation of what is other to us. Instead of the cultivation of subjective taste, education is the cultivation of listening and conversation. Such education is itself a form of poetic understanding. My project responds thus to two main questions: (1) How are we to understand education as poetic? and (2) How is such an education playful and liberatory?

I will give more thorough accounts of poetry, play, and education in the following chapters, but here I would first like to make a few prefatory remarks about each and the methods by which I engage them. In the first part of this book, I focus on what distinguishes a poetic education. Whereas Kant and Schiller identify mastery through reason as central to aesthetic education, Hölderlin instead makes attunement through finitude primary. Thus, a poetic education would not view education as an overcoming of nature, but as developing an attunement to nature, as part of that primordial ground of existence, in our finitude. Writing to his brother, Hölderlin explains "I have presented you with the paradox that the artistic and creative impulse [*Kunst- und Bildungstrieb*] with all its modifications and varieties is actually a service human beings render unto nature" (EL 136). For Hölderlin, *Bildungstrieb*, or the formative drive, emerges out of that "original communal ground" (247) and begins as raw and childlike. We are, says Hölderlin, born for art, which is not imitation or appropriation of that which already exists, but a forming of something new. These possibilities of creation are both articulated in and modeled by poetry. Poetry, as understood by Hölderlin, strives toward articulating what cannot be fully said. It opens toward the infinite while at the same time reaching toward its own finitude. As oriented toward both what we are and what is beyond, poetry bears witness. Whereas the aesthetic is marked by judgment, the poetic is characterized by formation.

In his *Elucidations of Hölderlin's Poetry*, Heidegger dwells on a fragment of Hölderlin's poetry where he speaks of the "unpoetic" (148). The unpoetic would be, says Heidegger, something unrestrained, unpeaceful, or unbound. The poetic, however, is finite and recognizes itself as such.[5] It engages limits but does not seek to surpass them. The poetic marks a kind of dwelling and letting be. Heidegger writes,

> Poetic conversation exercises the language in the presentation of what is abiding, and thus bestows on the poet the free use of his capacity, so as to remain in what is proper to him. Such conversation is good. In it, one kind of remembrance encounters another. In their encounter, the harmony of the same thoughts, and thus their belonging together, is experienced as an enduring friendship. (EHP 149)

This friendship is marked by a belonging together, a resting in the other, a harmony of remembrances. Such conversation is good. It is joyful. What is proper to the poet is this kind of orientation to the other, yet it is not a covering over. Insofar as there is peace, rest, and harmony, there is also strife, unease, and disruption. The poetic, though, remains with this.

In ". . . Poetically Man Dwells . . ." Heidegger draws from Hölderlin to assert that "Dwelling occurs only when poetry comes to pass and is present, and indeed in the way whose nature we now have idea of, as taking a measure for all measuring" (PLT 224). Similarly, in *Elucidations* Heidegger explains,

> the poetic is the finite, which submits itself to the limits of its destiny. The poetic is what is peaceful in thoughtful rest which bans all strife. The poetic is the

bond which binds together all that is unbound. The poetic is what is retained in the bond and the measure, that which is full of measure. In whatever direction it goes, the poetic does not want to surpass the limits, the rest, the bond, the measure. (149)

What would be such measuring? Heidegger tells us that "The taking of measure is what is poetic in dwelling. Poetry is a measuring" (EHP 219). This poetic measuring is not the coffeespoons of Prufrock. The nature of measure is not calculation, it is not even number. It is, though, an orientation toward limits.

The poet Paul Celan, informed in many ways by both Hölderlin and Heidegger, frequently engages themes of limits and liminality. Celan draws our attention to how language, and poetic language specifically, requires a particular orientation toward self, other, and the world and can point us toward futures yet unrealized. In his reception speech for the Georg Büchner Prize in 1960, Celan explains that language is always on the way as it moves toward directions yet unknown: in setting out from itself, the poem thereby encounters itself and what is other. Between these poles of self and other, there lies the meridian, which draws the two poles together in a space of encounter. Celan traces the topography developed through this crossing between the poles of the meridian, suggesting that poetry inhabits spaces both our own and not. As not our own, poetry introduces possibilities of freedom, of doing otherwise.

By turning us to ourselves as other, though, poetry also introduces what is our ownmost. Rather than representing something else, Celan explains, poetry speaks itself. In directing us to its own linguisticality, the poem also speaks the limits of language as such. Celan suggests, "The poem holds its ground at its own margin" (CP 49). The poem speaks itself as "still here," freed from external verification. As still here, the poem opens up a site of encounter between self and other, but also between the poem and itself. The poem is a form of address, like "a letter in a bottle thrown out to sea" (35). The movement of the poem is restless as it does not find its completion in either pole, but rather is poetry insofar as it is on the way. At the same time, the poem tarries with, attends to, the dates of what it encounters. Poetry, as the in-between, is fundamentally liminal in this traversing between past and future, self and other, imagined and realized, said and unsaid.

In this speech, Celan also describes poetry as an *Atemwende,* a turning of breath. Poetry, its own exhalation, its own speech, turns our breath. The poetic word, as initiating this turn and exhalation, is fundamentally attuned to alterity. Yet, this alterity is not any generic otherness. Rather, it is the other as You, the one who addresses me, who allows the very possibility of my speaking in return. Poetry shows language not as medium, but as language in itself. In speaking itself, the poem becomes an I and, simultaneously, speaks on behalf of another. Turning us to one another, the poem becomes a conversation, addressing the poet and reader alike. Gathering us into it, the poem points toward "open, empty, free spaces" where we also encounter ourselves.

Poetic education reclaims the corporeality of the self through the corporeality of language itself. Language, as dialogical and corporeal, is a living voice that resists any kind of mastery, cognitive or otherwise. For Gadamer, all language gives us access to the world, but what distinguishes poetry is the way it "bears witness to our own being."[6] Through our participation with the work, we catch sight of ourselves in new and different ways, and in this way poetry is so singularly transformative. For Celan, poems "are encounters . . . a kind of homecoming" in which we project ourselves both toward what is other and toward ourselves.[7] Yet, for Celan especially, the poem is never fully at home. Instead, it is the constant movement of the meridian, between the poles of self and other, presence and absence.

Gerald Bruns explains that poetry responds to the uncanniness of life and language as a whole "where (again) what is uncanny is not simply the corporeality of language as such but the way in which this corporeality reorients our relation to language (not to say the world) by turning us into listeners rather than speakers. In poetry the corporeality of language addresses us."[8] The poetic word calls us into dialogue with it. Gadamer wonders whether in our current era of destabilization and unrest "there still exist such a conjoining of words, wherein everyone could be at home."[9] What is different about the poets of our era is that they must necessarily speak more quietly. Thus, "The question is not whether the poets are silent, but whether our ear is acute enough to hear."[10] As we find ourselves fatigued by noise, the poet holds open space for the softest of voices or what is left unsaid. The poem fundamentally resists totalization. It demands responsibility. The significance of the poetic word is that it reminds us that all relationships, as made possible in and through language, likewise resist full conceptualization or mastery.

Poetic education is the cultivation of this attunement, this sort of letting be in friendship, the holding open of what is other. Heidegger explains, "man is capable of poetry at any time only to the degree to which his being is appropriate [*vereignet*] to that which itself has a liking for man and therefore needs his presence. Poetry is authentic [*eigentlich*] or inauthentic [*uneigentlich*] according to the degree of this appropriation [*Vereignung*]" (PLT 228). This authentic appropriation is possible because the poem allows us also to encounter ourselves. Poetic dwelling is thus related to what is appropriate, to what is one's own, but not as a property might be one's own. It is not the case that we *have* a poetic education, but that we are educated, we undergo something, and we are educated only insofar as we actively attune ourselves to this encounter.

Despite Hölderlin's misgivings, I argue that in poetic education, play maintains a central role, especially because play is itself groundless. However, play in poetic—as opposed to aesthetic—education is not supplanted, but complemented by reason. Like poetry, play possesses its own logic, yet this logic is at times ambiguous. Play is at once seemingly frivolous and serious, real and non-real, human and non-human, free and bound, rational and irrational. Furthermore, play applies to an extremely large number of situations. We talk of child's play, of language games, of the play of light on the water, of the play of chance, and so forth. Similarly, the behaviors and objects engaged and experienced in play are always also engaged and experienced in non-play. We all play, but are frequently unable to point to exactly what it is we are doing. Yet, despite its fundamental ambiguity and conceptual inaccessibility, play remains incredibly rich and meaningful. Play is not ambiguous because it has too little to say, but rather because it has too much.

For Gadamer, play often has no purpose, but that does not mean it is not serious. Play is not an escape from reality, but a mode of engaging reality in a different way. Play differs from other activities particularly by its "as if" character. When we play, we play as if we are something. In so doing, we take seriously the play-space and the activity at hand. The space shapes play, but it does not strictly determine it. Even if a child is playing make-believe, for example, and the rules seem entirely arbitrary or capricious, she grows upset when others refuse to follow the rules she sets out. She takes it seriously while they do not.

By taking the play seriously, the players intend the play for its own sake, rather than merely as a goal for something else. For this reason, there is no separating the form from the performance, the play from the player. As Gadamer notes, "the purpose of the game is not really solving the task, but ordering and shaping the movement of the game itself" (TM 107). In play, we negotiate between the limits before us and our own free movement.

In Gadamer's autobiographical reflections, he remarks, "I sought in my hermeneutics to overcome the primacy of self-consciousness, and especially the prejudices of an idealism rooted in consciousness, by describing it in the mode of 'game or play.' For when one plays a *game*, the game itself is never a mere object; rather, it exists in and for those who play it, even if one is only participating as a 'spectator'" (GR 23). To play is to engage in that play in a way responsive to its to and fro movement. The self is at stake in a participatory way, not in the mode of self-consciousness. Whereas many thinkers, such as Schiller, place seriousness against play's frivolity, Fink and Gadamer alike remind us that play is actually serious. The opposite of play is not seriousness, but not taking part, not taking play seriously. Through play we are transformed as we engage in possibilities that we could not otherwise access.

So far, we have said that play occurs in time and space; play opens up a space for itself; play takes up from everyday life in terms of objects, actions, and relations, although the content of play does not directly mirror the content of the everyday; as such, play is fundamentally creative and meaning-making. Because play is spontaneous and not prescribed, it is groundless. It grounds itself through being played. While there are concrete scenes and particular playspaces, the event of playing cannot be determined prior to its being played. In play, there is always a leeway [*Spielraum*] in place for the player to respond. Because play cannot be predetermined, the player must be open and responsive to the other players and the play as it happens. The game cannot happen if one strives to master it. Instead, play is a matter of spontaneity and creativity. Even when one plays by herself, one must respond in concrete ways to the development of the play. However, because play has these particular contours and is situated in a particular place, it is certainly not the case that anything goes. One cannot play in any generalizable or abstractable way and play is not solipsistic. Lastly, in part because of its fundamental ambiguity, play resists conceptualization, yet it is not devoid of knowledge or content. Rather, play is also always a movement of understanding, but because there always remains something more to be said and understood, it evades the mastery of the concept.

Our experiences of art and poetry are emblematic experiences of play. The play of the work opens up a space for the spectator to participate and be transformed through the experience of the work. Gadamer notes that poetry and art require interpretation precisely because of their ambiguity; there is always a leeway [*Spielraum*] for poet and reader alike. The work presents to us a world that both is and is not our own. Art, he claims, "begins precisely there, where we are able to do otherwise" (RB 125). By affording us the possibility to do otherwise, art is a moment of freedom. If we stand before the work and participate in the playspace opened before us, we have no choice but to allow ourselves to be transformed. Poetry needs this. Play is not a flight from, but a return to ourselves in a serious way.

Yet, this playspace of ambiguity does not belong exclusively to poetry. Rather, says Gadamer, "The ambiguity of poetic language answers to the ambiguity of human life as a whole, and therein lies its unique value. All interpretation of poetic language only interprets what the poetry has already interpreted" (RB 71). Thus, poetry points to the fundamental ambiguity of human life that requires our playful participation. Play teaches us that we cannot understand ourselves as fixed and static or as determined from the outset.

Play fosters development by providing opportunities for self-recognition and relations to the world in new ways. Because play, art, and education enable these opportunities, they are also essentially instances of freedom, characterized by creativity, conversation, and self-formation. Play provides,

I argue, a significant way of understanding the incalculable and relational nature of education as well as the groundlessness of development. Play, as Gadamer explains in *Truth and Method*, is a model for practical understanding and dialogue. Because education is a matter of speaking and listening, of conversation, and because conversation is a form of play, then we can say that education is also a form of play. What is at play in education, I will argue, is a response to abyssal freedom, where freedom is not something that a subject possesses, but an orientation toward the groundlessness of being. Freedom is not an escape from necessity or contingency. Rather, we are free precisely through our responsibility to others and through an orientation toward our own conditionedness.

In this account of poetic education and play, we find neither Kant's rational, autonomous agent nor Schiller's free citizen in the aesthetic state. Although Gadamer credits Kant with providing a rich account of the way that experiences of art and beauty, as feelings of freedom, enliven moral life, he remains concerned that Kant's aesthetic education can yield only a Kantian subject, namely one that relies on abstracted principles and a mastery of her animal nature through reason. Gadamer calls instead for an understanding of education that allows for the particularities and the incalculability of life to come to the fore. Moreover, Fink and Gadamer also establish parallels between the approaches of contemporary pedagogy, which they argue embraces a scientific mindset that pits theory against practice and prizes mastery, and moral theory, which centers humans as rational animals. On their accounts, both pedagogy and moral theory champion an adult, rational, autonomous agent. We find similar claims in Friedrich Nietzsche's wariness of scientism and morality, in bell hooks' argument that education should be a site of resistance, dialogical, and healing, or in Gloria Anzaldúa's call for a transformative education that preserves a person's in-betweenness. Although there are significant differences in these accounts, at bottom, each suggests a turn toward education as embodied, intersubjective, affective, dialogical cultivation.

I contend that an account of poetic education provides an implicit account of persons as hermeneutic subjects. This hermeneutic subject should not be understood as a subject over against objects. Instead, a hermeneutic subject is a being fundamentally conditioned by language and with others. Rather than constrained by this conditionedness, it is only on the basis of this concrete life and situatedness within language, tradition, ritual, and social practices that there can be anything like a self. On this account, being in the world is being with others in a robust, shared way, undergirded by language. Heidegger claims just this when he says that we are conversation (EHP 58). This self is simply one who is able to create and understand shared meaning in relation with others, although this need not be appear in the same way for all beings we would consider persons.[11] This may suggest that to be a person requires one to be a language user, but for me this remains an open question, particularly if language is here meant only as a prescribed mode of communication. Following Jean Grondin, who characterizes linguisticality as "the quite general capacity to mean something by something and to communicate it" (GR 422), I suggest we understand the self as one who participates in the play of linguisticality. Because this poetic education is anchored in linguisticality and conversation, the self is fundamentally a self with others and the world. If education is the development of self-understanding, meaning, and relationships, rather than the development of autonomy, then we must understand those responding to the task as participants, as *Mitspieler* in this meaning making. Fink argues, for example, that what characterizes the human is an awareness of the self as finite in relation to the infinite. Rather than *animal rationale*, we are *ens cosmologicum*: a cosmological being. To be human is to respond to that totality, the cosmos, that surpasses us. Whereas the aesthetic education of Kant and Schiller relies on the aesthetic distanciation or disinterestedness, poetic education, as self-development, thus emphasizes vulnerability, relationality, and an orientation toward that which exceeds us.

By turning us into listeners, a poetic education calls us to responsibility, to openness and hearing. Because responsibility is playful, as the to and fro movement between self and other, it also entails a kind of vulnerability. To be vulnerable is to remain open to what surpasses us, but not simply as a kind of mental or physical attunement. Rather than being passive to potential harms, vulnerability is the capacity to respond, to care, and to risk. Such responses are not merely theoretical, rational, or independent, but fundamentally embodied and shared. There can be no responsibility without others and without vulnerability.

This vulnerability occurs in different registers. In Celan's work, we find it through the refrains of "Do you hear me?" "still here," and "Do not split the No from the Yes." Poetry is an act of remembrance. As the turning of breath, the poem attunes itself to what is left unsaid. It calls us to respond to what stands before us. For Celan, this response cannot be thought separately from the Shoah. While vulnerability is part of what it means to be human, we should not minimize the way in which this vulnerability was exploited. Celan's works reflect these different senses, pointing to the vulnerability of language that could be manipulated into "murderous speech" (CP 35). Still, even if language helps make it possible, what remains after the horrors of Auschwitz is language (35). Despite every abuse of language that provided the grounds for the murder of millions, language and meaning remain. Yet, this act of remembrance cannot be the rehabilitation of old or more pure meanings. Rather, it is a form of bearing witness, a listening to both what is said and unsaid that continue to speak, even in silence. Remembrance, then, as bearing witness, attends to the particular and is dialogic in the site of encounter between self and other. Our relation to tradition, as indicated by Hölderlin, cannot be wholesale reappropriation. Rather, tradition requires us to respond creatively to what stands before us.

It is precisely this sense or remembrance, especially in regard to Hölderlin, that presents a tension in the tradition of philosophical hermeneutics informed by Heidegger's approach to language and poetry. Heidegger turns to Hölderlin, particularly in the 1930s and '40s, for resources to resist the totalizing forces and machination issued by metaphysics. Heidegger charges Plato with collapsing Being into essence and ushering in metaphysics, that is, the metaphysics of presence that abandons rather than attends to Being. The poetic, which does not depend on presence and resists totalization, allows for a measuring that is not calculation and is attuned to finitude. At the close of his 1934/35 lecture course, *Hölderlin's Hymns "Germania" and "The Rhine"*, Heidegger dwells on Hölderlin's letter to Böhlendorff discussing the free use of the national. Heidegger interprets the "national" as the task given to the German people,[12] thus agreeing with Hölderlin that the Germans cannot merely be Greeks, but instead must achieve what is their ownmost: "The hour of our history has struck. We must first take what has been given us as endowment into pure safekeeping once again, yet only so as to comprehend and take hold of what has been given as our task—that is, to question our way forward and through it."[13] The task is thus, against the totalization of metaphysics, to think the question of beyng, that is, to think poetically.

In Heidegger's work, however, this turn is particularly pernicious as it suggests that *only* the Germans have this task. Throughout the recently published *Black Notebooks*, we find recurring, undeniable themes of anti-Semitism and the sense that the Jewish people are necessarily excluded from this identity of German. Heidegger describes the Jews as the ultimate metaphysicians; they are essentially "calculative" and participate in the machination of metaphysics and modern technology that results in the loss of history, and thereby also the loss of beyng.[14] Because machination is totalizing and fully consuming, it leads to self-annihilation. Because the Jews are, according to Heidegger, "worldless," there is no possibility of being in the world, so there is no possibility for *Dasein*. Moreover, it seems that, unlike the animal that is merely world-poor, the Jew, worldless like the stone, is the enemy of *Dasein*. In *Sein und Wahrheit*, the lecture course from 1933 over Heraclitus's Fragment 53, Heidegger states that the enemy, *Feind*, of *Dasein* is parasitically attached to the *Dasein* of a people. Those who seek to protect against this enemy must bring the enemy to light with the goal of "total annihilation."[15] Here Heidegger does not explicitly link the Jews with the enemy or contend that annihilation is necessarily physical annihilation, but his *Black Notebooks* do suggest that he sees the Jews and Judaism as a threat to those tasked with the safekeeping of beyng. Thus, the task of "we," the Germans, not only excludes the Jews, but also seems predicated on their very annihilation.

The question confronts us: If Heidegger, whose work is foundational for the tradition of philosophical hermeneutics, cannot be separated from his anti-Semitism, does that also mean that the tradition and approaches of hermeneutics are inseparably bound up with commitments to annihilation? In other words, if hermeneutics is anchored in bearing witness to what is other, how do we come to terms with the elements of the tradition that not only refuse to recognize, but expressly reject the other? I admit that there is no easy answer, but contend that hermeneutics itself offers ways to respond to these concerns while still disavowing anti-Semitism and racism. Indeed, hermeneutics requires us to confront these issues. While one option might be to excise Heidegger from the conversation, to no longer include his contributions, I believe this approach is wrongheaded for two reasons. First, doing so rejects our own responsibility for confronting the troubling legacy of Heidegger and anti-Semitism in the broader philosophical tradition. As Donatella di Cesare writes,

> Getting rid of Heidegger, however, would mean getting rid of the difficult questions he has raised, and, above all, erasing the question (perhaps the most complex of all) concerning the responsibilities of philosophers toward the Shoah. If one defines Heidegger's reflections as "pathological," then in so doing one also effectively participates in the continued setting of Nazism apart from philosophy—as if Nazism were a "folly" outside reason, outside history.[16]

The *Black Notebooks* thus require us to engage critically with this tradition and to examine our own part in it. To ignore or excise Heidegger is a failure to bear witness. Second, hermeneutics reminds us that meaning cannot be reduced to intention or psychological state. Moreover, tradition is dynamic. Heidegger's contributions to developments in twentieth century thinking, including that of Gadamer, Fink, and Celan, are extensive, but we cannot reduce these ideas to Heidegger's own. We can draw on his insights regarding language and the self while also moving beyond these insights and disavowing his other philosophical and political commitments.

Philosophy, as Gadamer conceives it, is itself a mode of interpretation: meaning is anticipated, determinations are perceived, and concepts are understood through dialogue against the backdrop of historically effected concepts. To philosophize is to engage in conversation and to develop a comportment and sensitivity to what is other. Hermeneutics sets itself an educative task as it is always a learning to listen. We do not encounter the world in a neutral or objective way, but from a particular position shaped by tradition, culture, and meaning. For Gadamer, all understanding begins with particular prejudices, but these prejudices do not imperil understanding. Rather, they are what enable us to encounter the world as meaningful, to see something *as* something. Understanding always takes place within a particular horizon of meaning. Through interpretation, understanding, and engaging the other, these prejudices are challenged and developed and the horizons of meaning join as the fusion of horizons [*Horizontverschmelzung*] (TM 305). Gadamer has been widely criticized for this expression because it sounds as if the particular parts are fused or melted together, thus obfuscating or obliterating any difference.[17] However, what Gadamer means by this term is rather that a shared, joint horizon develops. For example, a joint may be fused together. This does not mean the separate pieces of the joint are melted together. Rather, they are held together through the fusion and form a joint. So, while forming a whole, the parts are still discernible from one another. On Gadamer's account, too, our encounters with others develop shared meaning and understanding, but this shared understanding is dynamic and not as static as a fused joint might suggest.

What hermeneutics requires is an unflagging devotion to listening and self-reflection. Thinkers such as Gloria Anzaldúa, María Lugones, and bell hooks speak of and through identities that have been systematically marginalized in the history of philosophy, including in the tradition of philosophical hermeneutics. Their voices and experiences push us to bear witness and to critically examine what is meant by "we" and what counts as tradition in the first place. These thinkers offer rich accounts of selfhood, rooted in language and with others, that do not rely on the dualisms of metaphysics. Instead, each seeks to cultivate an identity that understands ambiguity not as a threat, but as central to that identity. For example, in some ways like Heidegger, Anzaldúa strives to develop a new consciousness that does not keep her prisoner in the way the subject-object dualism does.[18] Instead, she calls for a new *nepantla* identity that situates itself as receptively and creatively embodied in the in-between of the self and with others. Anzaldúa and others show how we can develop hermeneutics, which has its true locus in the "in-between" (TM 295) in a more liberatory way.

Still, this reconsideration of tradition must be done with care. We do not create a liberatory hermeneutics by merely adopting the other into our own sense of tradition. Rather, when we approach the other through an openness in listening, then all prejudices we have remain subject to change. As figures like Anzaldúa show us, because she preserves her liminal identity, she resists being fully appropriated by the tradition of philosophy and instead invites others to understand her in her own terms. The task is to think along with, and at times, beyond one's partner. My aim is to converse with these and other thinkers in this text both to seek to understand them and myself, but also to open up new possibilities and horizons for understanding the self that is at stake in poetic education.

In the first part of this book, I examine in what a poetic education would consist. Chapter 1 focuses on the historic roots of aesthetic education found specifically in Kant, Schiller, Shaftesbury, and Hölderlin. I argue that whereas Kant and Schiller locate reason as central to aesthetic education, Shaftesbury and Hölderlin instead make finitude primary. Both Kant and Schiller correctly recognize the contribution of art and beauty for development, but their accounts rely on subject-object dualisms and over emphasize rational judgment. In Hölderlin's epistolary text, *Hyperion*, we see a robust turn toward the primacy of finitude, particularly in relation to nature. Rather than surmounting nature, education as *Bildung* is the creative giving form of oneself in relation to nature. Yet, because we are finite, we constantly struggle to articulate our relation to the infinite. Poetry, though, speaks both the finite and infinite together. I offer a reading of the often-overlooked character of Diotima that shows her as a model for a poetic attunement toward the finite self and what surpasses her. Because Kant and Schiller seem to equate aesthetic experience with frivolous play, Hölderlin remains concerned that their accounts do not provide for this serious attunement toward finitude. I suggest that although Hölderlin correctly replaces the overly subjective approaches of Kant and Schiller by demonstrating the ways we communally inhabit language, he mistakenly understands play as antithetical to this position.

Chapter 2 continues to develop this account of poetic attunement by following Celan's work closely in order to consider how language, and poetic language specifically, requires a particular orientation toward self, other, and the world. Informed by Gadamer's interpretation of Celan, I focus on the relationship between language and memory, considering how poetry can point us toward futures, a utopia, yet unrealized. For Celan, poetry is the movement between self and other, between foreign and familiar, that resists totalization. As this movement that opens up a site of encounter, poetry bears witness. It teaches us to listen both to what speaks out loud and in silence and to offer our response in return. Such a response cannot be the product of calculation or judgment, but rather arises from an active comportment toward the other. Celan's poetry is particularly instructive in its relation to tradition. His works are deeply informed by both Hölderlin and Heidegger, yet, as mindful of dates, he cannot separate these thinkers from the events of the Holocaust. Heidegger's *Black Notebooks* and his exchanges with Celan, while focused on poetry, prove the danger of separating philosophy and poetry from concrete, particular human dates and experiences. Our relation to history cannot be one of abstract destiny. By offering us a language that continues to speak and to listen, Celan offers us a way to critically engage these traditions while also moving toward futures both foreign and familiar.

Drawing on this movement back and forth between I and You, foreign and familiar, past and future, chapter 3 identifies this liminal to-and-fro as play. Although Hölderlin jettisons play is his account of poetic education, Gadamer and Fink show that play is serious and emblematic of poetic formation. Play, as a groundless space of the in-between and encounter between foreign and familiar, opens up spaces to do and imagine otherwise. Thus, play is fundamentally concerned with freedom. Hölderlin's interpretation relies on a long tradition that sees play as sometimes instructive for education, but still relegates play to childhood or frivolity. In Plato, for example, we see that the guardians of the city must control and properly guide play in order to inculcate children with the proper virtues. Aristotle writes that leisure, but not play, is necessary for the development of virtue because leisure allows for contemplation whereas play does not. Kant and Schiller view play as merely on the way to reason. Against these accounts of play, I argue that play provides the bridge, rather than stepping stone or detour, between poetry and education. This does not mean, however, that we should reject these traditional accounts out of hand. Instead, following the to and fro movement of play, I move back and forth across the history of philosophy to argue that a reinterpretation of these accounts suggests a richer, more serious account of play than might appear at first glance. Thus, this chapter aims to model the playful attunement toward and conversation with tradition.

Chapter 4 turns to Nietzsche, Fink, and Gadamer to see more explicitly how play might provide us a way of moving away from the dualisms presupposed by "traditional metaphysics." I argue that a more robust sense of play, which is not merely the behavior of a subject but rather an ontological stance in the world, requires a more robust sense of language and space. Language is not an abstract form of communication, but a lived inhabiting of meaning. Yet, as we have seen, this inhabiting is multiplicitous and ambiguous. As Celan, Lugones, Anzaldúa, hooks, and others explain, language has consistently been used to oppress, marginalize, and even murder. Yet, language, by always having more to say and requiring us to listen, affords creations of new meanings that preserve these multiplicitous selves. These thinkers engage in emancipatory projects that invite understanding, but also resist total appropriation. The movement between self and other, the liminal space of play, fosters resistance, transformation, and liberation. By playing along in these dialogues, we become who we are through the conversation that we are.

NOTES

1. Gosetti-Ferencei, *Heidegger, Hölderlin, and the Subject of Poetic Language*, 182.
2. Hölderlin writes in "Notes on the *Antigone*" that "Just as philosophy always treats only one faculty of the soul, so that the representation of this *one* faculty makes a whole, and the mere connection between the *parts* of this faculty is called logic: so poetry treats the various faculties of a human being, so that the representation of these different faculties makes a whole, and the connection between *the more independent parts* of the different faculties can be called rhythm, taken in a higher sense, or the calculable law" (EL 325).
3. The author of this text, "The Oldest-System of German Idealism," is contested. The fragment appears in Hegel's handwriting, but has been attributed to Schelling as well as Hölderlin. Despite its contested authorship, the fragment does appear to have originated in conversations among Hegel, Schelling, and Hölderlin, and, according to the editors of the *Frankfurter Ausgabe*, the text closely resembles Hölderlin's "On Religion."
4. Hölderlin uses *"Erziehung"* for education in this passage. In German, *Erziehung* generally connotes upbringing or character development whereas *Bildung* more often describes cultivation, culturation, formation, or maturation. The terms are not infrequently used interchangeably. In Hölderlin's description of aesthetic education, particularly in relation to his sense of the formative impulse, education seems to connote both upbringing as well as cultivation.
5. In ". . . Poetically Man Dwells . . .," Heidegger states that "Dwelling can be unpoetic only because it is in essence poetic . . . Thus it might be that our unpoetic dwelling, its incapacity to take the measure, derives from a curious excess of frantic measuring and calculating" (PLT 228).
6. Gadamer, "On the Contribution of Poetry to the Search for Truth," 115.
7. Celan, 53.
8. Bruns, "The Remembrance of Language: An Introduction to Gadamer's Poetics," 8.
9. Gadamer, "Are the Poets Falling Silent?" 74.
10. Gadamer, 78.
11. By person, I mean neither merely one who has certain properties, such as reason or self-consciousness, although a person likely will have capacities for such things, nor one who belongs to the category of human beings. Indeed, it may be possible to speak of nonhuman animals as persons. I am also wary of using the term person in a normative sense to indicate those who warrant certain kinds of considerations, for this would narrow the scope of considerations too greatly. My aim here is not to establish any sort of criteria to strictly delineate personhood or to determine what obligations we have to others, but to point to how a conception of personhood is at stake in education and to contend that a reconsideration of personhood may require us to reconsider our educational practices.
12. Heidegger, *Hölderlin's Hymns*, 264–65.
13. Heidegger, 266.

14. Heidegger writes, for example, "One of the most concealed forms of the gigantic, and perhaps the oldest, is a tenacious facility in calculating, manipulating, and interfering; through this facility the worldlessness of Judaism receives its ground." *Ponderings VII-XI*, §5, 76.

15. Heidegger, *Sein und Wahrheit*, 91.

16. Di Cesare, "Heidegger's Metaphysical Anti-Semitism," 182.

17. See, for example, Bernasconi, "'You Don't Know What I'm Talking About': Alterity and the Hermeneutic Ideal," Fleming, "Gadamer's Conversation: Does the Other Have a Say?" and Caputo, *Radical Hermeneutics*.

18. Anzaldúa, *Borderlands / La Frontera*, 80. This approach of putting figures like Anzaldúa into conversation with Heidegger is very much informed by Mariana Ortega's *In-Between: Latina Feminist Phenomenology, Multiplicity, and the Self.*

Chapter 1

Aesthetic Education and the Roots of Poetic Education

The turn in eighteenth century German thought toward understanding *Bildung* as fundamentally aesthetic in nature is largely influenced by Anthony Ashley Cooper, Third Earl of Shaftesbury. In his work, *Characteristicks of Men, Manners, Opinions, Times*, Shaftesbury draws on neo-Platonic sources to argue for nature's essential harmony, which is designed by a Creator and resonates with the natural goodness of humans.[1] This harmony is discoverable through an attunement to beauty through a shared common sense, or the *sensus communis*. This idea becomes quite important for later figures, such as Kant and Schiller, but what is distinctive about Shaftesbury's account is that this common sense is not just a formal capacity for judgment, but, as Gadamer suggests, a social virtue, more of the heart than of the head (TM 22). In attuning ourselves to beauty, we simultaneously attune ourselves to others. The aim of aesthetic education, according to Shaftesbury, is not merely the cultivation of taste or appreciation for beauty, but the formation of a political utopia.

Kant's views on education share this political element, particularly emphasizing the relationship between the *sensus communis* and self-development. In his lectures on pedagogy, Kant suggests that "Human beings can become human beings only through education [*Erziehung*]. They are nothing save what education makes of them."[2] There Kant suggests that through this process of education and enculturation, animal nature is turned into human nature. Because humans are rational, they are destined to live in society and to cultivate, civilize, and moralize themselves through art and science. To move away from animal tendencies toward becoming human is their destiny.[3] Whereas animals need no cultivation and act on their powers and instincts, humans require care, discipline, and instruction to become fully human. Kant sees education as the mode of moving toward the perfection of humanity, not only at the individual, but also at the species level. Furthermore, Kant sees this perfection through education as progress toward moral perfection, and therefore also toward freedom and autonomy.

Like Kant, Schiller points to the significance of art and aesthetic experience. Both situate the education of individuals squarely within the community. We find that education is central for Kant to the *sensus communis* or kingdom of ends, and for Schiller to political participation and citizenship. Their understanding of the relationship between education and play further demonstrates their emphasis on community. For example, Kant writes, "In addition, the expressions 'to *know* the world' and 'to *have* the world' are rather far from each other in their meaning, since one only *understands* the play that one has watched, while the other has *participated* [*mitgespielt*] in it."[4] Pragmatic knowledge, which is more than theoretical knowledge, requires participation, citizenship in the world. Schiller remarks that the aesthetic state is the highest state for in it all are equal, free citizens. Because Beauty is essential for the aesthetic state, and because humans play only with Beauty, play would also be imperative in fostering equality and a shared civil society.

Both Kant and Schiller claim that the cultivation of humanity through beauty is essential, but while Shaftesbury emphasizes the lived, felt quality for such cultivation, reason and self-mastery are more primary for Kant and Schiller. Both aim toward political utopias, drawing again on the *sensus communis*, but at times it is difficult to determine whether such utopias are intended to be actual or are regulative ideas that, while important and approachable, remain directly unattainable. For Shaftesbury, however, the *sensus communis* is not hypothetical, but actual, and provides the ground for a more robust political unity.

In the following, I will argue that returning to Shaftesbury's account allows a clearer picture of how an understanding of human finitude informs a project of aesthetic education. Shaftesbury initiates not only an important turn toward nature, beauty, and art, but also a more robust sense of education as self-cultivation and the felt attunement toward all-encompassing, but also incomprehensible nature. Whereas Shaftesbury sees aesthetic education as developing out of nature, Kant and Schiller argue that education overcomes our animal nature. As such, their conception of education risks promoting liberation from, rather than freedom for the world. In other words, their accounts suggest education requires separating the human from her embodied particular existence rather than cultivating an attunement to that situatedness. Although Kant and Schiller both recognize the significance of nature and the limits of human understanding, particularly in reference to tragedy and the sublime, they neither point to the limits of language as such nor center discussions of death in their thinking. Therefore, their accounts of education do not fully treat the human as finite. Furthermore, despite the emphasis on both art and play, aesthetic experience is frequently seen as a stepping stone to rational development and play as a means of developing self-mastery rather than valuable in its own right.

In many ways, Hölderlin's contributions might be seen as continuations of those elements of Shaftesbury's project that were less emphasized in Kant and Schiller, such as a reconsideration of Greek philosophy and the conception of humans belonging to a primordial unity with nature. Where Hölderlin moves this project forward is specifically in his attention to the relationship between poetry and tragedy. Hölderlin argues that the language of poetry is uniquely able to simultaneously speak the particular and the universal, the familiar and the foreign. The poet shows us the limits of what can be said, thus presenting the very tension between human and nature. Although nature is intelligible and accessible, the totality of nature as such resists articulation in finite expression. Hölderlin sees tragedy as the prime example of poetry. Tragedy demonstrates the essential, irreducible play between the vulnerability and fragility of human life and the simultaneous drive to create a beautiful life in that fleeting existence. In this way, language and death become central concerns. Tragedy allows us to bear witness to ourselves in our complex nature. What is witnessed, though, is not a simple harmony, but an irreducible play that cannot be completely harmonized.

Hölderlin's poetic and philosophical works provide the foundations for what I deem poetic education. What is significant for poetic education, rather than aesthetic education, is that nature is not to be supplanted by reason, but rather preserved as the basis for meaning and development. Furthermore, in poetic education, the community precedes the individual, such that the individual can understand herself only insofar as she is already embedded in relationship with others and the world. To know the self is to recognize one's finitude in relation to what surpasses us, human and otherwise. By requiring vigilance to what is other than ourselves, poetic education requires us to develop a learning to hear and an ethics of conversation. In this exploration of Hölderlin's works, I focus on his epistolary novel, *Hyperion*, for two reasons. First, in *Hyperion*, we see a clear picture of *Bildungstrieb* as the creative giving form through art and poetry to the unformed, nature. On Hölderlin's understanding of *Bildungstrieb*, there is a primordial ground of existence, yet this ground is itself groundless. Because the ground is undifferentiated and formless, it gives rise to existence but cannot itself pre-figure or determine that existence. The formative drive is spontaneous, springing forth toward cultivation.[5] The novel, which centers on death, demonstrates how *Bildungstrieb* also holds in tension the finite, particular human in relation to the eternal totality of nature. Poetic education is developed through an attunement to an irreducible play between familiar and foreign, thus requiring a holding open to what is other than the self. Second, by focusing on the often-overlooked narrative of Diotima in *Hyperion*, I seek to model the aims of poetic education, namely of listening for voices that have been covered over and allowing nature and silence to speak themselves. By attending to the vegetative metaphors characterizing Diotima, we also gain a stronger sense of a positive vulnerability that is not equated with passivity or weakness, but is rather a creative play between activity and passivity, receptivity and transformation.

EDUCATION AND FREEDOM IN KANT AND SCHILLER

Both Kant and Schiller claim that education is fundamentally connected to freedom and that art plays a particularly central role in human development. Insofar as to be human is, according to Kant and Schiller, to be moral and rational, then human development is an essentially moral project. Furthermore, freedom, on their accounts, is achieved when one becomes human, that is, when one is no longer fettered by the impulses of our animal nature.

In Kant's writings we are frequently reminded that we have a duty to raise ourselves above our animality and move toward humanity, thereby becoming capable of setting goals for ourselves.[6] Indeed, "The human being is the only creature that must be educated [*erzogen werden muss*]. By education we mean specifically care (maintenance, support), discipline (training) and instruction, together with formation [*Bildung*]. Accordingly, the human being is first infant, then pupil, and then apprentice."[7] Because humans are "raw" when born, they require the help of others to develop reason. As each generation educates the next, the human race moves more and more toward perfection; education is guided by "the idea of humanity." This perfection can never be achieved by the individual, only by humanity as such.

Kant recognizes here a tricky duality—humans possess reason, unlike animals, and yet they are also not beyond the bounds of nature:

> But since education partly teaches the human being something and partly merely develops something within him, one can never know how far his natural predispositions reach. . . . Perhaps education will get better and better and each generation will move one step closer to the perfection of humanity; for behind education lies the great secret of the perfection of human nature.[8]

Education must align itself with this nature, not work against it. Education is meant to develop what nature has given. One instinct humans possess is the instinct for freedom. In order to attain this freedom, humans must discipline themselves against caprice and instead subject themselves to the commands of reason, thus becoming autonomous. Kant suggests, moreover, that since children are more disposed toward the animal, they are incapable of being moral agents, and must be educated through a kind of moral midwifery so they can develop into humans.[9]

A difficulty for this account of human development is not only that it maintains the picture of humans as rational animals, but also that it precludes contributions from those, such as children, who have not achieved this level. Moreover, while Kant grants that all humans have the capability of becoming cultivated, he believes that some humans, that is, anyone neither white nor male, possess fundamental characteristics that prevent them from becoming fully cultivated and also fully rational.[10] Despite Kant's apparent commitment to universalism and cosmopolitanism, his lectures on anthropology and geography present a contradictory attitude. Although Kant says very little about race in his lectures on pedagogy, except for the necessity of getting rid of "savagery" by means of training, works such as "Observations on the Feeling of the Beautiful and the Sublime," (1764) "Of the Different Races of Human Beings" (1775), and "Lectures on Physical Geography" (1792), among others, make clear that the "perfection of humanity" is possible only for white Europeans. Kant claims in the "Physical Geography" lectures, for example, that "Humanity has its highest degree of perfection in the white race. The yellow Indians have a somewhat lesser talent. The Negroes are much lower, and lowest of all is part of the American races."[11] Perfection in other races is foreclosed because race is, for Kant, immutable, and those of particular races have natural dispositions that might be adapted, but not overcome. In the notes for his lectures on anthropology, he remarks, "The Negro can be disciplined and cultivated, but is never genuinely civilized. He falls of his own accord into savagery."[12] Similarly, he claims, "The race of the American cannot be educated. It has no motivating force, for it lacks affect and passion. They are not in love, thus they are also not afraid. They hardly speak, do not caress each other, care about nothing and are lazy."[13] In "Anthropology from a Pragmatic Point of View," he also claims that the Jews, "the Palestinians living among us" are a "nation of cheaters."[14] Although some scholars suggest that Kant's attitudes toward women and people of color are peripheral or indicative of his personal, rather than philosophical, attitudes, works by Robert Bernasconi,[15] Donatella di Cesare,[16] Emmanuel Eze,[17] Dilek Huseyinzadegan,[18] Jennifer Mensch,[19] and Charles Mills[20] convincingly show that such distinctions are dangerous or, at the very least, disingenuous. Providing an overly sanitized interpretation of Kant unburdens contemporary thinkers from their own responsibilities of dealing with the legacies of racism and sexism and risks perpetuating pernicious ideas.[21]

Indeed, it is the separation from lived experience that renders Kant's picture of moral development problematic in the first place. It is not reason itself that is the issue, but that his picture of the human as rational animal hinges on divorcing rational nature from animal nature in order to develop into a full human. And, because Kant aligns animality more with Africans and Native Americans, moral development, as this separating off the human from the animal, is reserved for Europeans. Furthermore, becoming human seems to require separating off from other humans, too. In Kant's pedagogical writings, the community seems to take priority, but in his writings on morality and judgment, despite his appeals to the kingdom of ends or *sensus communis*, this more robust sense of intersubjectivity is replaced by the more formal sense of community as hypothetical participants. On the one hand, embodiment seems overly determined. For example, skin color determines mental capacity. On the other hand, embodiment seems unimportant as actual relations are supplanted by formal ones. As the human becomes autonomous, he creates greater distance not only from his natural, animal self, but also from others.

We find similar themes of freedom, the *sensus communis*, and development in Kant's *Critique of Judgment*, as well as many of the same tensions at stake in his theory of education. For Kant, a judgment of taste is subjective, but still universal. What provides this universality is the idea that a judgment of taste requires the agreement of everyone. For Kant, this is the *sensus communis*: "a faculty for judging that in its reflection takes account (a priori) of everyone else's way of representing in thought, in order as it were to hold its judgment up to human reason as a whole" (C3 5: 293). Since only cognition can be universally communicable, it is the free play of the cognitive powers and their harmony that holds for everyone.

Here the imagination is productive, spontaneous, and free, although this freedom still obeys a lawfulness since it remains connected to definite forms. Kant writes, "It is this feeling of freedom in the play of our cognitive powers, a play that yet must also be purposive, which underlies that pleasure which alone is universally communicable although not based on concepts" (C3 5: 307). This play yields a feeling of freedom, which initiates the quickening of the moral subject.[22] This play is not frivolous, but productive and meaningful. Furthermore, our judgment of taste always maintains a playful "as if." We judge *as if* everyone would assent to our judgment. We must interpret nature *as if* nature has a higher meaning and intention (C3 5: 302). Furthermore, our judgment of fine art requires that we see it *as if* it were free from chosen rules *as if* it were a product of nature (C3 5: 306). Thus, play is bound up with the capacity of imagining oneself as connected to something greater.

Although the presentations of the imagination are non-conceptual, this movement of the free play is able to "quicken [*beleben*] the mind by opening up for it a view into an immense realm of kindred presentations" (C3 5: 315). Furthermore, the spirit animates [*beleben*] the mental powers. As Rudolf Makkreel explains, "[Spirit] is not merely lively or playful, but enlivening in a creative way."[23] Thus aesthetic experience is enlivening; as creative it exceeds and intensifies, through this play of freedom and finitude, what the subject was before. For example, Dennis Schmidt explains that "At that point in the disclosure of the finitude of experience, Kant says that a sudden transformation takes place in the subject and that this experience of alterity, which is not the representation of otherness but the disclosure of alterity *in* and *as* one's own limits, imparts an alteration that is the 'quickening' of an ethical sense."[24] Schmidt locates this alterity as the subject's own, as one experiences her finitude and her limits, but the recognition of others is also already implicit in the recognition of one's own alterity. Schmidt perhaps suggests more than Kant tells us, especially since for Kant the feeling of freedom and enlivening remain primarily on the level of mental life, yet the fact remains that in this text Kant locates key features of development, namely the incalculability and the motivation of feeling that result from play. Unfortunately, however, Kant denies play any cognitive import and leaves it as a merely subjective experience, devoid of any substantive understanding. Similarly, I maintain that this appeal to community is flawed since the relation to the community is only ever imagined, so it remains only at the level of the subject and her cognitive faculties.

While Schiller follows Kant's practical philosophy, particularly regarding morality and freedom, Schiller seeks to give even greater prominence to beauty. What is particularly striking about Schiller's *On the Aesthetic Education of Man* is how infrequently any reference to education actually appears. Mentions of *Erziehung* or *Bildung* appear only a handful of times. Although Schiller does not provide a precise educational program, his account of aesthetic development echoes Kant's insistence on the cultivation of reason and distancing from animal desires.

In the Second Letter, Schiller explains his motivation as seeking to understand what place an account of political freedom and reason has in the current political climate of upheaval and tyranny (AE 7). Part of the problem, he suggests, is that people have become alienated from themselves. On the one hand, a person finds herself compelled by reason alone, marked by the form drive. On the other, she finds herself ruled by her feelings, marked by the sense drive. Without a harmony between these two drives, she remains at odds. As alienated, she cannot be free, and thus cannot develop into a moral person. Schiller asserts the necessity of a third dimension, namely the aesthetic, characterized by the play drive, that will enable a person to achieve a totality of character. Schiller thus claims that the move to political freedom must first be aesthetic, "because it is only through Beauty that man makes his way to Freedom" (AE 9).

Schiller suggests in the Fourteenth Letter that the play drive constrains the psyche both mentally and physically: "it will, therefore, since it annuls all contingency, annul all constraint too, and set man free both physically and morally" (AE 97). Thus, the play drive is able to mediate between drives that cannot otherwise combine. We find in Schiller an account similar to Kant's, insofar as he, too, suggests education is unique to humans, and conceives of education as a move away from the natural or animal dimension. Education performs a harmonizing and emancipatory function insofar as the human is thus freed from both perpetual variation and perpetual stasis. Play provides the equilibrium between sense and form. Although Schiller claims that, in play, the human is fully so because the natural and rational parts are in equilibrium, he also argues that rather than harmonizing nature and morality through beauty, humans instead progress from nature through beauty to morality and freedom. Schiller does remark that that the physical stage cannot simply be passed over, for then there would be no possibility for the rational stage. Instead, the movement is much more akin to one of Hegelian sublimation. Thus, while the stages are seen just as that, stages, the moments remain preserved in the total progression.

The object of play is in fact Beauty, and it is here that Schiller draws the connection between the aesthetic and play. He questions why we speak of "mere play" when it is really play that harmonizes the drives. Rather than mere play as frivolous, it is the other way around: "the agreeable, the good, the perfect, with these man is merely in earnest; but with beauty he plays . . . Man only plays when he is in the fullest sense of the word a human being, and he is only fully a human being when he plays (AE 105–107). Beauty, like play, mediates between the distinct elements of a person since she contains elements of both. Thus, Beauty does not prioritize form over matter, but seeks the harmony of these two distinct realms. This allows for sensuousness and reason to be active at the same time and thus achieve aesthetic determinacy that avoids the pitfalls of negative sheer indeterminacy or negative sheer determinacy.

Still, however, Beauty remains much more closely aligned with form than content. Schiller contends that form, rather than content, is the marker of a truly fine work of art, "for only through the form is the whole man affected, through the subject-matter, by contrast, only one or other of his functions" (AE 155). In creating, the artist must "make his form consume his material" (AE 156–157). Thus, although Beauty is supposed to achieve a harmony between form and content, it is achieved and motivates through form alone. The reason for this, according to Schiller, is that beauty is equated with freedom and freedom can never have sensuous expression.

Despite the apparent preservation of the physical and the aesthetic, Schiller conceives of human freedom and perfection almost exclusively in terms of rational and moral perfection. Indeed, the first step toward becoming human is to recognize oneself as something other than the world, as a subject over against objects. It is here that freedom arises since this distance of the world allows the human to give shape to her life, while animals or other objects cannot so long as they remain immersed in their worlds. At times Schiller suggests that freedom is the acquisition of reason through education, and so freedom would be the result of human cultivation. Rather than created by nature, freedom is created by humans. Moreover, freedom in this sense is anything without constraint, such as the free play of the aesthetic. At other times, freedom is made possible by nature as lawgiver. As Schiller explains, freedom arises through giving form to what is formless: "Man is superior to every terror of Nature so long as he knows how to give form to it, and to turn it into his object" (AE 185). Humans give shape to and become the lawgivers of nature. While nature enables freedom, only by turning nature into an object for humans do humans become free.[25]

Because Schiller views aesthetic freedom as enabling political freedom, it seems he must have something in mind beyond the free play of ideas, yet it remains unclear in his text how these senses of freedom do or do not hang together.[26] What does remain consistent in Schiller's description of freedom is that education is emancipatory. Because aesthetic education provides a productive tension between the formal and the sensuous, it frees us from the dominance of either impulse. He writes, for example, "As soon as two opposing fundamental drives are active within him, both lose their compulsion, and the opposition of two necessities gives rise to freedom" (AE 137). In other words, freedom is precisely not the dissolution of either drive, but rather the preservation of the composite. This suggests that political freedom requires aesthetic freedom, the harmony of drives, yet in what that would consist remains to be discovered.

In his "Kallias" letter to Christian Gottfried Körner, Schiller more clearly articulates that freedom is the ground of beauty as the possibility for sensuous expression and that freedom prescribes its own limits. This has some practical effect insofar as beauty is the symbol for how one ought to be: "For this reason, the realm of taste is a realm of freedom—the beautiful world of sense is the happiest symbol, of how the moral one shall be, and every beautiful natural being outside of me is a happy citizen, who calls out to me: Be free as I."[27] In this passage, Schiller suggests that the aesthetic and the natural share the project of orienting the human toward moral freedom. Schiller claims that nature, which provides us with the power of becoming human, is our first creatress and beauty, which also allows us to become human, is thus our second (AE 147–49). Schiller thus identifies beauty and nature alike as providing the capacity or condition for humanity. This orientation is, moreover, made possible through the symbol, recalling Kant's discussion of beauty as symbol of morality in §59 of the *Critique of the Power of Judgment*. There Kant claims that beauty gives the law to itself and pleases without concept.

Indeed, in discussing artfulness in relation to Kant in a later letter, Schiller writes that "the beautiful is merely a symbol of the completed and perfect" that, as purposive, gives itself the law.[28] He describes the beautiful moreover as that which "can thus not be recognized, but must be brought out—or *felt*."[29] Thus more than reason alone in the move toward morality, there remains a dimension that is primarily *felt*. There is a feeling of freedom, as well as a feeling of connection to those other citizens, natural and human, of the world, and ultimately, a feeling of life.

Schiller speaks of the feeling of life that occurs in experiences of art, describing it is lofty, free, and full of power and vigor. When "we have surrendered to the enjoyment of genuine beauty, we are at such a moment master in equal degree of our passive and of our active powers" and can easily turn to seriousness, play, repose, or movement (AE 153). Although here Schiller speaks of surrendering to beauty and opening oneself to what surpasses and transforms, this vulnerability very quickly turns to a form of self-mastery and has its resolution in reason, as mastery or domination. This is even more the case as Schiller claims, as we saw above, that genuine Beauty and truly beautiful works of art are so because of form, not because of content.

The triumph of form over matter may seem especially odd given Schiller's insistence on the aesthetic as the balance between matter and form. We can understand this better, however, if we recall that Schiller also sees the aesthetic as leading to the perfection of humanity and a possible future state. First, if we are concerned with the perfection of humanity and not merely the perfection of the individual, then what leads to this perfection must be universal. Matter or the sensuous cannot be universal, so it is form that speaks to all. Second, according to Schiller, beauty is equated with freedom and freedom can never have sensuous expression.

Again, Schiller believes that a person cannot become rational without first being aesthetic, which is why aesthetic education is so important, but the priority granted to the aesthetic is quickly replaced by the rational. Schiller contends beauty and nature alike provide the capacity or condition for humanity, although it appears that while nature is a necessary condition, beauty is more a necessary and sufficient condition of moving humans toward reason. Nature is thus always prior to beauty because beauty establishes distance between humans and their nature. Here again we have the idea that it is the mediating aspect of the aesthetic that allows for the necessary harmony between freedom and nature.[30] For Kant and Schiller both, while play is not strictly creative, it does turn us to creativity. Aesthetic experiences bring with them the feeling of life as well as an attunement to what surpasses us.

Although Schiller does think that the rational usurps the aesthetic, he still maintains a central role for play and art. Yet, the value of play is in service of reason rather than in its own right. Schiller contends that the human becomes free in the aesthetic state for there he is no longer under the dominion of the physical, but rather "he acquires mastery over it in himself" (AE 171). Thus, rather than receiving the law from Nature, the human becomes able to be the lawgiver by giving form to what is formless (AE 185). While Schiller insists on a greater priority of play and the connection between play and freedom than Kant does, nonetheless, his understanding of play suggests play is almost exclusively at the service of reason. The free movement of play that allows for the harmonizing of drives is quickly supplanted by rational self-mastery. Play remains at the level of feeling, devoid of cognitive content. Furthermore, as in the case of Kant, it remains unclear whether the aesthetic state is an actual community of individuals or a regulative idea. Although I agree that reason and imagination are necessary for development and education, my concern is that neither Kant nor Schiller admit a cognitive element of play or provide an account of play and aesthetic education that is robustly transformative.

In what then is an aesthetic education supposed to consist? On the one hand, Schiller equates aesthetic education with unmediated aesthetic experience. That is, through aesthetic experience, we experience beauty, and thus a feeling of freedom, and are prompted to become rational and moral. Yet, it would seem that an education consisting in something devoid of cognitive content would not be much of an education. On the other hand, Schiller suggests something a bit more radical, namely that aesthetic education is self-education through a particular stance in the world. Education here is a self-cultivation through a harmonizing of and attunement to our different drives, of giving shape to our lives. In this way, education becomes further concretized and substantial. He recognizes, too, that the cultivation of reason and morality is nigh impossible when society prevents those very things from being developed. He writes at the end of the Eighth Letter that "the way to the head must be opened through the heart. The development of man's capacity for feeling is, therefore, the more urgent need of our age, not merely because it can be a means of making better insights effective for living, but precisely because it provides the impulse for bettering our insights" (AE 53). Although Schiller recognizes that we cannot flourish by reason alone, his alternative does not move beyond mere feeling. It relies on a subjective experience that lacks much substantial content or possibility of transforming life. Furthermore, this cultivation of taste ultimately remains an independent project. Little is said about engaging with others or participating in such political communities.

So long as education is understood as a matter of taste and self-mastery of a more or less Cartesian subject, there remains little space for responsibility and vulnerability. Although such education is of subjective feelings, because these feelings are at the service of reason, cultivation leads to an almost exclusively intellectual pursuit. My purpose here is not to jettison the role of feeling, but to substantiate it by demonstrating that feeling is not merely on the way to reason. What we find in Kant and Schiller is freedom understood as freedom from the human condition through a striving for human perfection, that is, as freedom away from our natural impulses and animality. Hölderlin and later thinkers like Fink and Gadamer, however, see freedom as the condition of humanity, that is, as a way of developing who we are, including in our animal and vegetative elements, by engaging the world in meaningful ways through self-formation and through relations with others.

A RETURN TO *BILDUNG*

Like his successors, Shaftesbury understands education as aesthetic and aiming towards political unity. This political unity is made possible through a *sensus communis* wherein all are already part of a preexistent harmony not only with one another, but also with nature. Thus, unlike Kant and Schiller, Shaftesbury does not think that the political union arises because of an overcoming of nature, but rather because of a return to nature. Furthermore, on Shaftesbury's account, we act on this harmony on the basis of feeling, but because the harmony precedes the individual, it is not subjective, but intersubjective, feeling. In other words, because all are endowed with the same capacity to recognize that harmony, the feeling is shared. Returning to Shaftesbury's account of *Bildung* enables us to see those elements that drop out of the accounts of Kant and Schiller, namely an emphasis on the human as relating to rather than surpassing humanity, an actual rather than hypothetical *sensus communis*, and the preservation of feeling as complement to reason. These same elements will be essential for Hölderlin, so before turning to his account, I will outline some of the central themes of Shaftesbury's *Characteristicks of Men, Manners, Opinions, Times*.

Importantly, Shaftesbury locates morality within beauty. In "*Sensus Communis*, an Essay on the Freedom of Wit and Humor," he writes, "And thus, after all, the most natural beauty in the world is honesty and moral truth. For all beauty is truth. True features make the beauty of a face and true proportions, the beauty of architecture as true measures, that of harmony and music."[31] The good poet or painter views all of the finest examples of beauty in nature in order to form a particular idea, rather than basing their ideas off only one particular. Instead, they look to the rule in nature and other fine artworks. According to Shaftesbury, art is not created from wit or fancy, but through an attunement to that pre-existing harmony. Harmony, he says, is such by nature and is to be found throughout nature in symmetry and proportion. Similarly, "Virtue has the same fixed standard. The same numbers, harmony and proportion will have place in morals and are discoverable in the characters and affections of mankind, in which are laid the just foundations of an art and science superior to every other of human practice and comprehension."[32] Importantly, too, the finest forms of beauty are not to be found in bodies, but in souls and internal harmonies of sounds. Thus, the attunement toward inward beauty, suggesting the Cambridge Platonists' influence, creates the possibility of the *sensus communis*, or common sense.

For Shaftesbury, humans have the capacity to perceive such harmony. This capacity is not a formal capacity for judgment, but a feeling of harmony and, as Gadamer explains, a social virtue (TM 22). In "An Inquiry Concerning Virtue and Merit," Shaftesbury writes, "The mind, which is spectator or auditor of other minds, cannot be without its eye and ear so as to discern proportion, distinguish sound and scan each sentiment or thought which comes before it. It can let nothing escape its censure."[33] Like feeling the harmony present in a musical score, the mind perceives the proportion and harmony of other minds and nature. This occurs without calculation—the mind cannot be without its eye, nor can it withhold its sentiments toward these subjects—and is pre-reflective. The mind cannot withhold its assessment, and it does so without prior deliberation. Furthermore, in perception, the mind recognizes "a common and natural sense of a sublime and beautiful in things" that cannot be denied. Because this sense is common and natural, it is possible for anyone to recognize this harmony. This is not to say, though, that recognition is without reflection. Indeed, Shaftesbury claims that taste, as the perception of harmony, must be developed and educated through reflection in order to bolster an attunement to nature's harmony.

This common sense contains a decisively political element. Through this shared capacity, humans can together achieve a common civility. Shaftesbury harkens back to the ancient humanists, although some believe they display little common sense. Yet, Shaftesbury argues that we understand the "common sense of the poet, by a Greek derivation, to signify sense of public weal and of the common interest, love of the community or society, natural affection, humanity, obligingness, or that sort of civility which rises from a just sense of the common rights of mankind, and the natural equality there is among those of the same species."[34] The poets demonstrate this public spirit that arises from a shared feeling for humankind. Importantly, such shared feeling calls for political solidarity by fostering a shared public good. As Shaftesbury notes, where there is absolute power, and thus no love of virtue, there is no public good.[35] Thus, when poets are seen as lacking common sense, it is not because they are poets, but because the political situation forecloses this shared good. Because, by nature, we have the capacity to recognize virtue and the common good, we project such virtue onto our leaders, thus allowing ourselves to be deceived by tyrants. At the same time, because we always have the possibility of refocusing on that original shared good, we can resist such deception.

Because he believes that harmony precedes the individual, Shaftesbury also rejects the prominent social contract theories of the time. It makes little sense, he argues, to claim that one would act civilly and virtuously in a formed government but not in the state of nature if the mind can perceive virtue naturally. Thus, if such duties toward others do exist in the civil society, then "faith, justice, honesty and virtue must have been as early as the state of nature or they could never have been at all."[36] It would be impossible to be united in civil society but not in the state of nature because, as Shaftesbury insists in "The Moralists," all of creation is united from the start:

> Neither man nor any other animal . . . can be allowed in the same manner complete as to all without, but must be considered as having a further relation abroad to the system of his kind. So even this system of his kind to the animal system, this to the world, our earth, and this again to the bigger world and to the universe. All things in this world are united. For as the branch is united with the tree, so is the tree as immediately with the earth, air and water which feed it.[37]

Shaftesbury maintains that nature is not merely the natural human disposition, but also an organized, organic whole. Despite nature's organization and intelligibility, Shaftesbury suggests that we discover this harmony not through reason alone, but also through feeling.

TOWARD A POETIC EDUCATION

This emphasis on harmony resonates throughout Hölderlin's work as well. Influenced by the history of aesthetic education from Shaftesbury forward, Hölderlin shares the view that aesthetic and political projects can and do align, particularly in connection to the Absolute, yet he remains wary of previous attempts precisely because they fail to recognize the primacy of nature and rely on false distinctions. In his 1796 letter to Niethammer, Hölderlin writes that he seeks the principle to dispel "the conflict between the subject and the object, between our selves and the world, and between reason and revelation" (EL 68). There are a few elements here that should be noted. First, Hölderlin suggests that this principle will be discovered theoretically through intellectual intuition.[38] We do not have intellectual intuition of the self, but rather of Beauty, in which the unity of the Absolute is located. In a letter to Schiller in September of 1795, Hölderlin writes of his attempt to work out "the idea of an infinite progress in philosophy," which requires the "union of subject and object in an Absolute." Such a union is possible "aesthetically, in an act of intellectual intuition," but, "theoretically possible only through endless approximation" (62). Here we find a tension in Hölderlin's account of intuition: in the letter to Schiller, he writes that theory only achieves approximation whereas aesthetic experience allows for that intuition, yet, six months later, in that letter to Niethammer, Hölderlin writes that the principle can be arrived at "theoretically, through intellectual intuition," thus reducing the gap between the two. However, Hölderlin does affirm that an aesthetic sense is necessary, so it is not the case that intellectual intuition could be achieved sans aesthetic experience or sense.

Second, Hölderlin consistently claims in both letters is that it is not the case that the Absolute is unknowable. Rather, knowledge of the Absolute occurs through intuition, through something sensed or non-discursive. In his essay, "Being Judgment Possibility" ["*Seyn und Urtheilung*"], Hölderlin argues against Fichte that consciousness or subjectivity cannot be the most primary. Being refers to the union of subject and object and can be understood only through intellectual intuition (EL 231). Thus, while Hölderlin remains compelled, much like Fichte, by the Absolute, he disagrees with Fichte's account of the nature of the Absolute. The primordial unity of intellectual intuition cannot be located in the subject, for as soon as one speaks the self, there is a cleave between subject and object. At the very moment of articulation, the self is both foreign and familiar.[39]

Like Shaftesbury, Hölderlin finds resources in the ancient Greeks for coming to a fuller understanding both of art and the Absolute. At the same time, Hölderlin also expresses his frustration with himself as inept and inconsistent. He writes, "I stand there in the modern water like geese with their flat feet and beat my wings helplessly at the Greek sky" (EL 123). Thus, the education of Germany cannot simply be a reappropriation of antiquity. Instead, it must foster in Germans both an awareness of the original unity as well as the formative impulse to create something new. Even in his own pursuits of bringing out the natural creative powers of Germans, he finds himself more compelled by Greece with its geniality and piety. Yet, at the end of his essay, "Notes on the *Antigone*," Hölderlin writes that the native poets are to be preferred for "The native forms of our poets are nonetheless to be preferred, where there are such, because they do not just exist to explain the spirit of the age, but to hold on to it and to feel it, once it has been understood and learnt" (324). Thus, the advantage of studying the ancients is precisely because they afford a model of what creation out of the raw, childlike, and uneducated into the formed and educated looks like. By examining the ancients, we are better able to seek our own possibilities of creation.

Hölderlin returns, for example, to Heraclitus, specifically the *hen kai pan* and the play between being and nothing, "from all things one and from one thing all."[40] Via Jacobi, Spinoza's thought exerted a strong influence on

Hölderlin and other thinkers of the time, specifically its interpretation of the Absolute, the *hen kai pan*, as God. Hölderlin reflects this trend in his early writings,[41] but as he embraces a more vitalist philosophy, he draws closer to Heraclitus by affirming that this Absolute is not static, as being, but dynamic, as becoming. For Hölderlin, education can be successful only if it preserves the tension between the finite human and the originary, infinite Absolute rather than trying to dispel such tensions. The turn toward poetry marks a turn toward the limits of human knowledge and understanding.

Whereas education in Kant and Schiller suggests an optimistic development toward utopian ideals, education for Hölderlin seems instead, despite the cultivation of ideals, inescapably tragic. Certainly, Hölderlin believes that education can and should lead to greater political equality and harmony, but he remains wary of an over-emphasis on Enlightenment ideals. Although Hölderlin is influenced by Kant, particularly his *Critique of Judgment*, and Schiller's account of aesthetic education, his starting point is largely different. Rather than resolving tensions and rationally harmonizing them, Hölderlin's concept of education preserves the tensions between familiar and foreign, opening and closing, joining and separating, light and darkness, homegoing and sojourning, past and future. Hölderlin remains deeply skeptical of any subjectivist project that finds the resolution of these tensions in reason. He affirms the distinctly human significance of reason, but also maintains that reason must be grounded in something else. Thus, reason cannot be what is most primary. A new aesthetic education would be one characterized by both striving and forming the self with an orientation toward the Absolute. Here the Absolute is not a regulative ideal, standing forever on the other side of human experience. Rather, the Absolute is knowable, to some degree, through a kind of intellectual intuition. In this way, education is tragic insofar as it is a constant play between the human reaching beyond her limits toward the divine or the Absolute while also returning to her finitude. Hölderlin locates tragedy as occurring at the disorienting space between two historical epochs. There, one finds oneself caught between the richness of history and yet unseen horizons of progress, between what has already been organized that cannot be harmonized with what is yet to be articulated.[42] Thus, this tragic education is founded in poetry rather than philosophy because it is only poetry that can preserve these tensions, and therefore allow for the disclosure of the totality, of the Absolute, in finite human life.

Following this line of thought, poetic education, as this attunement to tragedy, requires an attunement toward the aporetic, originary unity. Further, the concern with tragedy illustrates the way in which education is dialogical. Although the *Bildungsromane* of the era present a young man on a journey of self-discovery against society, carrying out a fundamentally Enlightenment project, tragedy reminds us that such discovery cannot be carried out independently. Oedipus, for example, knows himself truly only because of what he learns from Tiresias. In Sophocles' *Antigone*, the translation of which becomes one of Hölderlin's main projects, we find a constant interplay between Antigone, the Chorus, Creon, and Tiresias. Although Hölderlin's *Hyperion* is not stylistically a tragedy, it bears many tragic elements, not least of which is the struggle toward harmony with nature and the self, colored in every way by finitude. Importantly, though often overlooked by commentators, Hyperion comes to know who he is not merely because he finds himself dismayed by society or struggling against the bounds of language, but also through language, specifically in conversation with Diotima. As I discuss further below, it is Diotima who first clarifies for Hyperion who he is, setting him back on the right course after his struggles with Alabanda. In Hölderlin, we find a more robust account of intersubjectivity than in Kant and Schiller, which also points to a particular challenge with his account of poetry. If it is the poet who uniquely says what is unsayable, then how does poetry not dissolve into monologue? How can poetry, as the articulation of what is inarticulable, still provide the basis for conversation?

EDUCATION AS BECOMING HUMAN

In a letter to Schiller in 1794, Hölderlin reflects on his attempts to provide an education. Referring to his pupil, Fritz von Kalb, Hölderlin writes, "To form [*bilden*] my pupil into a *human being*, such was and is my aim" (21). Moreover, the aim is to develop the "most noble faculty," reason, in his pupil as soon as possible. He continues, "Still, I must be willing, and I am. It is my will to become a man" (23). Like Kant and Schiller, Hölderlin conceives of education as the process of becoming fully human through the cultivation of reason. Becoming educated is a moral imperative because it cultivates the rational capacity necessary for moral responsibility.[43] Such an education would not be a negative education that protects against the corrupting effects of society, but an active education that drives the pursuit of better things. Not only does Hölderlin intend for his pupil to become a man, but he desires the same for himself.

Such an awakening is achieved not through philosophical argument, but through meeting the child in her own interests and pointing to future horizons. A year after his letter to Schiller, Hölderlin writes to Johann Gottfried Ebel that education cannot be imposed on the child. Rather, Hölderlin must direct his pupil toward what is choiceworthy (EL 60). To awaken the desire to strive for what is better, the educator must draw attention to great and beautiful objects, those things that direct us outside of ourselves to consider what would be better. Hölderlin's interest in Plato, particularly the *Symposium*, shines through in this sentiment, as does the influence of Shaftesbury. A true educator cannot merely force knowledge into the mind or soul of an ignorant pupil. Rather, by drawing the pupil's attention to progressively beautiful and fine objects, the educator enables the pupil to ascend into reason.[44]

We find these similar themes of education through attunement toward the beautiful and noble in Hölderlin's epistolary novel, *Hyperion*. Unlike Kant and Schiller, Hölderlin does not believe that reason requires separation from our relation to nature. Education is instead a reunion with nature and with others. Like Shaftesbury, Hölderlin remains emphatic that particular individuals cannot precede society because the unity is itself primordial. This thought of a reunion with nature, which Hölderlin develops over several works, becomes the main focus of *Hyperion*, thought to be modeled on Rousseau's *Julie*.[45] In the following, I turn particularly to *Hyperion* because it demonstrates specifically how Hölderlin conceives of the relationships among nature, art, and beauty as well as the role of language, both as conversation and through poetry, in developing a poetic education. Hölderlin further refines these ideas, especially in connection to tragedy, in later works such as *Empedocles* and his translation of *Antigone*, so a close examination of *Hyperion* will help establish the framework for understanding those later texts.

A product of his times, Hölderlin initially presents *Hyperion* as a Bildungsroman. Drawing on characterizations of *Bildung* from Wilhelm Dilthey and the influence of Shaftesbury on thinkers such as Wilhelm von Humboldt and Johann Gottfried Herder, Susan Cocalis suggests,

> The artist-hero of a *Bildungsroman* would have to be an earnest young man who finds himself in conscious opposition to existing forms of society or to his particular social class and who therefore embarks on a mission to ameliorate the situation after a period of passive exposure to the world. Such endeavors would probably only be successful insofar as they coincided with the liberal ideals of an aesthetic education.[46]

Humboldt sees education as the cultivation of the individual. Influenced by Shaftesbury, he maintains that education will have an aesthetic dimension that surpasses the political. He writes, "Nothing on earth is as important as the power and the most versatile [*vielseitigste*] cultivation of the individual, and thus therefore the first law of the true morality is: educate yourself, and second, influence others through what you are."[47] Cocalis reads this as Humboldt's privileging of the individual, stressing that the aim of education is precisely the cultivation of the individual's own powers. Humboldt does not view this as anti-social, but instead sees it as requisite for a unified civil society. Yet, as we have seen from Hölderlin, the idea that an individual could be cultivated before establishing a connection with society makes little sense.

Rather, it is only because there is an originary unity that such individuation could be possible. Dilthey, explaining the ways in which Hölderlin's *Hyperion* mirrors the *Bildungsromane* of the day and yet also moves beyond them, writes that the difference "lies precisely in the fact that the poet for the first time makes manifest the darker features buried deep in life's countenance with a power that only lived experience can provide. He attempted to interpret life in terms of itself, to become aware of the values contained in life, both for their potential and their limits."[48] Thus, while cheerful or optimistic elements delight Hyperion consistently, Hölderlin also draws our attention to the darker features of life and to the ways in which such limits and darker experiences are made manifest through language. Thus, although Hyperion does embark on a mission to ameliorate the tensions with society he experiences, he cannot simply do so through a process of maturation, nor will such dissolution of tension be total.

Hyperion opens with an eye toward these tensions. Before the preface to the text, Hölderlin quotes Ignatius of Loyola, "*Non coerceri maximo contineri minimo, divinum est.* (Not to be confined by the greatest, yet to be contained within the smallest, is divine)" (H 1). Here we see the play between unity and individuation, between the mortal and the divine. This line first appears as part of Hölderlin's "Fragments of Hyperion," published in Schiller's *Thalia* in 1794. Hölderlin introduces this passage to suggest that it "serves to designate the all-desiring, all-subjugating dangerous side of man as well as the highest and most beautiful condition he can achieve." He prefaces this by explaining,

> There are two ideals of our being: one is a condition of the greatest simplicity, where our needs are in accordance with one another, and within our powers, and with everything to which we are related, through the mere organization of nature, without our assistance. The other is a condition of the highest cultivation [*Bildung*], where this accord would come about between infinitely diversified and strengthened needs and powers, through the organization which we are able to give ourselves. The eccentric path, which the human, in general and individually, runs from one point (which is more or less pure innocence) to another (which is more or less perfect cultivation), appears, according to its essential directions, always to be the same. (SA III: 163)

On the one hand, we find the ideal of "the greatest simplicity" requires nothing of our own effort but is contained within organized nature itself. On the other hand, we find the ideal of "the highest cultivation" is achieved through our own powers and organization. As Hölderlin articulates in his discussion of *Bildungstrieb*, we have a drive to organize ourselves in the way that nature is organized, to give form to the formless through the process of creation, but this does not require choosing one ideal over the other.[49] As in the case of *Bildungstrieb*, these ideals would be harmonized through an attunement of self-cultivation toward nature. At the same time, the path toward harmonizing these ideals is eccentric; we aim not only to be part of the world, but also to be above it. The path is not straightforward, but dynamic. We might take a wrong direction or go astray, but the "essential directions" of the drive show that they derived from "this drive as having emerged from the original communal ground, from which it always emerges with its products" (EL 247). We recognize, moreover, that even in the shared ground of creativity, we place our own direction: "we feel one and united with all, be it great or small, but in the particular direction, which we take" (247). There is unity, but that unity remains full of dissonances.

This eccentric path appears in *Hyperion*, whose ending closely mirrors the beginning. Whereas with a traditional *Bildungsroman*, we might expect a more linear trajectory of progress and cultivation, Hyperion ends much in the way that he started. The closing lines of *Hyperion* reflect the opening: "Like lovers' quarrels are the dissonances of the world. Reconciliation is there, even in the midst of strife, and all things that are separated find one another again. The arteries separate and return to the heart and all is one eternal glowing life" (H 133). Here again Hölderlin draws our attention to the unity of dissonances; things that are separated are reconciled, but not dissolved. There is an Empedoclean moment here, too, as love and strife are seen as mutually held in an eternal bond. The lovers maintain their singularity, yet are joined in one union. The arteries are a distinct section of the human body, but participate in and make possible life as a whole. Furthermore, this metaphor highlights the corporeality of such joining. The unity is not merely theoretical, but felt and physical. The difference, though, between the beginning and the end is the degree of Hyperion's own self-reflection, which is made possible not only by his own growing attunement to the Absolute, but particularly through Diotima's mediation. Hyperion begins his narrative understanding that Diotima will die, but only comes to fully understand her death through the re-telling.

At the beginning of the text, Hyperion, alone on an island off the coast of Greece, laments the state of his homeland and the rubble and "vast graveyard" it is has become (H 3). He writes to Bellarmin that he has failed and that nothing belongs to him. Yet, in almost the same breath, he remarks that he senses at the same time a belonging to nature, as if the place of eternal rest, the Absolute, is opening its arms toward him. A moment later, it seems that nature has instead closed her arms. This play between foreign and familiar repeats itself throughout as Hyperion longs both for the peacefulness of childhood and a future where Greece again achieves its glory. He remains a stranger among his own people as he awaits "but one thing, a more beautiful life" (H 19).

After his disappointment with his friend, Alabanda, Hyperion longs for a return to his gardens and to nature, ultimately recognizing that the world consists "in an alternation between opening and closing, between going forth and returning" (H 29). If this is the nature of the world, then so too must it be "so with the heart of man" (29). Recovering his happiness, then, is possible not through a nostalgia for childhood or Greece as it once was, but rather through an attunement to this play of tensions. Again, such unity is achieved not by overcoming these moments of closing and opening, going and returning, but by following that eccentric path of existence. There is yet time to return to the innocence of childhood, but one finds this happiness, this "one place of rest . . . upon earth" (H 40) even when one has become old and shriveled.

But what is this *one* place of rest? Hyperion describes it as perfection beyond the stars, yet in the world; it is in both the darkness of the past and also the labyrinth of the future (H 41). This one place of rest, which Hyperion has experienced once in his life, is Beauty, the *hen kai pan*, "the name of that which is one and is all" (H 41). Beauty now names that Absolute primordial unity. Thus, beauty is set apart from human life insofar as it is the highest and perfect, but it is also recognizable as that all-encompassing unity that permeates even the darkness of the past and the depths of the earth. The repose Hyperion seeks is found not merely in the familiar or the lofty alone; rather, such repose is possible only in the tension between the familiar and the hidden, the dark and the light. This illustrates as well that beauty is not static, but dynamic.

Although Hölderlin, via Hyperion, chooses beauty, this does not mean that beauty is separable from nature or from art. Indeed, that connection becomes clearer when we consider the ways in which Diotima, as the one who leads Hyperion to beauty, is consistently described in both musical and vegetative, almost vitalist, terms. Recalling his first meeting with Diotima, Hyperion recounts how everything was blessed by her beauty. Her touch drew all things nearer and made them more beautiful. Their conversation was not one of words, but of music, for "music alone would serve: to become all music and united with each other in *one* celestial melody" (H 42).[50] Music presents a harmony of tones that reflects the dynamic rhythm of life that can be neither silenced nor stilled. To recognize beauty is to recognize the most essential rhythm and melody. The harmony of music is not that all is resolved in one chord; rather, music works by the one chord separating itself in difference. Our orientation to music is often pre-reflective, that is, we feel attuned to the rhythm of music in a way that does not require conscious deliberation. Certainly, we may reflect on music and systematize it, but, for Hölderlin, our primary orientation toward music is one of intellectual intuition.

Hölderlin's description of Diotima as a bud unfolding, ripening to the highest beauty, that divine being with whom Hyperion names heaven and earth, reflects the connection between tragedy and *Bildungstrieb*. Diotima, as the flower that blooms in beauty only to die just as quickly, represents the fragility of life. Hyperion describes Diotima's heart as "at home among the flowers, as if it were one of them" (H 45) In budding forth, she distinguishes herself from surrounding nature, but in dying, she returns to that self-same unity. As both human and divine, she and Hyperione, like Adam and Eve, name the creatures of nature and orient themselves toward the most divine, yet their mortality is inescapable. At the moment Diotima glows and tends "the all-beneficent flame," she loses herself in "the night of the woods." She is Hyperion's "sacred Lethe," that river of forgetting that allows him to forget himself (H 49).

If Diotima represents nature or represents how one responds to nature, then we find that this orientation is not only one of love, of naming, but also of hiding and forgetting. Hyperion writes to Bellarmin that he and Diotima were "*one* flower, and our souls lived in each other, like the flower when it loves and hides its tender joys in its closed cup" (H 49). Here love is the joining force that both differentiates in its union and protects what it holds. Though their love remains in this closed space, there also remains the possibility of it opening forth into unconcealment. Similarly, although Hyperion depicts Diotima as Lethe, at the moment of self-forgetting, she reminds him who he is. Hyperion's young life has been filled with mourning and longing for one moment, but Diotima, more than anyone, knows what he seeks is a "better age" and "more beautiful world" (H 54). Hyperion longs for that original unity from which he has become separated. She mirrors his own being and enables him to awaken to himself. Still, at this moment of recognition, she also recedes, sending Hyperion away from her into the world. Here again we find the eccentric path of concealing and revealing, familiar and foreign.

How should we understand these vegetative and musical metaphors in connection to poetry and education? Hyperion speaks of a longing for nobler tones that "sound again in the symphony of the world's course" and "harmony of childhood." Initially, humans, from a source of love, "grew from the happiness of the plant, grew until they ripened." They continued to grow and began to ferment, so that they now find themselves in chaos rather than harmony. Out of chaos, they long for the ideal, which has replaced nature, as they strive to return to childhood through a "rejuvenated divinity" (H 51). This rejuvenated divinity is art, for art is the first child of divine beauty. In the process of creation, the artist sets beauty over against himself and, in so doing, rejuvenates himself (H 65). Art, then, is not exclusively a process of creation, but also one of discovery. In art, humans re-create themselves through a recovery of what was hidden.

Whereas Kant and Schiller emphasize overcoming childhood through education, Hyperion demands a preservation of childhood. Although school is designed to cultivate mastery over chaos, Hyperion argues that school actually results in chaos because, in asserting mastery, it prevents this rejuvenated divinity resulting from creative acts, and so forecloses harmony. Instead, Hyperion seeks the other direction, for "the image of childhood may show him the way back from school to the perfection of nature" (H 64). Importantly, the argument here does not favor an arrested development, but rather maintains, as Hölderlin's account of *Bildungstrieb* does, that the source of development already resides within us, and returning to childhood, which lacks alienation, is not a literal return to youth, but a return to the unity with nature.

Hyperion frequently explains this unity it terms of a loving dynamic between mother and child. Nature, as mother, cares for the child, who also recognizes the self as vulnerable and dependent. This echoes Rousseau's thought that the roots of morality are in us as children, but as Hölderlin emphasizes, those roots must be actively, not passively cultivated.[51] Art, the first child of beauty, is the creative mode of organizing what is unorganized, of achieving differentiation in unity. For Hyperion, ancient Athenian art and religion, the second child of beauty, are paramount because they achieve the appropriate golden mean between human and divine. Furthermore, because the Athenians do not fall into extremes, their work reflects a sense of freedom. Hyperion argues that if one seeks to dominate, then one is actually beholden to a dogmatic extreme and not engaged in the freedom that arises from attunement and receptivity. Thus, an aesthetic education that seeks mastery of the self or otherwise is destined to be restraining rather than liberating because it rejects the insights of childhood and falls too greatly into extremes.

Most important for Hyperion, and we might also say Hölderlin, is that poetry, rather than philosophy, is the best way of returning to beauty. Moreover, there would be no philosophy without poetry: "Philosophy springs from the poetry of an eternal, divine state of being. And so in philosophy, too, the irreconcilable finally converges again in the mysterious spring of poetry" (H 66). Because poetry, as art, is the first child of divine being, that is, beauty, then philosophy is borne of poetry. Both poetry and philosophy develop out of a kind of groundlessness, springing forth from the divine, mysterious source of all. In this way, while poetry and philosophy are rooted in beauty, they cannot be strictly derived from that source. This, too, echoes the groundlessness Hölderlin calls for in his conceptions of *Bildungstrieb* and *Kunsttrieb*. Although the creative impulse belongs to the shared primordial Absolute, it becomes such only through the artist's active cultivation, which cannot be predetermined or figured. Thus, there is formation [*Bildung*] only through the active giving form to what is previously unformed.

If Hyperion's task is to create a beautiful life, then such a life can only be created in language, that is, through the poetic word. Reason, claims

Hyperion, is ancillary to poetry because poetry can speak both the one and the many in a way that propositional content cannot. Because of this, poetry also is the antidote to skepticism. Hyperion remarks, "The great saying, the hen diapheron heautô (the one differentiated in itself) of Heraclitus, could be found only by a Greek, for it is the very being of Beauty, and before that was found there was no philosophy."[52] In other words, before philosophy was beauty. The "one differentiated in itself" could not be articulated without poetry, which speaks the one and many at the same time. Reason, without beauty, is incapable of achieving anything actually reasonable. Hyperion compares pure reason to a journeyman or overseer of servants; both can follow patterns and construct things, but have little knowledge of their subject beyond this. Philosophy requires poetry if it is to attune itself to the totality of nature. Furthermore, poetry, not pure intellect, is the antidote to skepticism. The person who has felt the pure harmony of the world at least once is incapable of being a skeptic. While the skeptic may be able to find any variety of imperfections in thought, the harmony of pure beauty cannot be thought, and so cannot be subject to that skepticism. Thus, although Kant and Schiller remain large influences for Hölderlin, and traces of their thought reside in many of his texts, Hölderlin moves beyond both by locating objectivity not in pure reason or theory, but in the felt intellectual intuition of the Absolute.

As we have repeatedly seen, Hölderlin believes that theory cannot hold two thoughts together at the same time. Rather, theory attempts to dispel such tensions. In "The Ground of the *Empedocles*," Hölderlin highlights the tensions between what he calls the "organic" and the "aorgic." The organic refers to human activity as giving form to the formless whereas the aorgic marks that initially unformed nature. Though marked by contrast, these two positions do not form an absolute dualism. Although it seems like nature and art are opposed, it is instead the case that through art, nature becomes what it is, and, through nature, humans become what they are: "More organic, more artificial man is the blossom of nature; more aorgic nature, if it is purely felt by a purely organized man, purely formed and educated in his way, gives him the feeling of perfection" (EL 261). Thus, when Hölderlin speaks of humans returning to that originary unity, he does not mean that nature takes precedence over humans. Moreover, Hölderlin suggests this life is one of sentiment, of intuition, not of theoretical knowledge. To understand the relationship between the human and nature is to separate out the two in such a way that both sides, working through an excess of intimacy, become extreme versions of themselves through their opposite, only to meet again in unity. Nature, by being formed "through the creative drive and the creative powers in general [*durch den bildenden cultivirenden Menschen, überhaupt die Bildungstriebe und Bildungskräfte*]" becomes more organic, while, as creative, the human becomes "more aorgic, more universal, more infinite" (258). In other words, to know what each side, nature and human, is requires not separating each off and classifying it in itself, but understanding the reciprocal tension between both.

Although this life cannot be fully cognized by theoretical knowledge, Hölderlin maintains that we still can understand it through poetry, which itself works at the limits of knowledge. Hölderlin develops this connection between poetry and cognition more clearly in "On the Procedure of the Poetic Spirit," where he argues that poetic life is united with itself as attuned to its harmonious oppositions between matter and form, in striving and lingering, and being relaxed and taut. Furthermore, this poetic life is characterized in language and by intellectual intuition, for "Just as knowledge anticipates language, language remembers knowledge" (EL 294). Here again we find a connection between knowledge as recognition and memory.[53] Knowledge, *Erkenntnis*, intuits or anticipates language. Knowledge, prior to language, is pure sentiment repeating itself in the dissonances and tensions of life. Finding that it cannot reproduce itself internally, knowledge "goes beyond itself, and finds itself again in the whole of infinity" (295). Language is anticipated once knowledge finds itself again in that primordial unity and totality and feels itself home again. Language, he claims, remembers knowledge through an attunement to the primordial unity. Knowledge is a matter of recovering what was lost, namely an attunement to the primordial unity.

Because language provides the reflective element necessary for knowledge to reach beyond itself toward the infinite in life, language is neither finite nor infinite. Language accompanies the highest feeling, the highest infinite, according to Hölderlin, wherein the human, and the poet in particular, is returned to the original unity, but not in a simple recapitulation. Rather, there is a progression toward this return. Humans and poetry share the same destiny worked out over stages. When the human is at the stage of education where she "emerged from original childhood and struggled upwards in opposing attempts to the highest form," she began to feel herself as "an infinite spirit in infinite life" and could now begin to anticipate her identity. Similarly, the poet works in the same way and "anticipates, at the stage where he also has struggled from an original feeling through opposed essays upwards to the tone," likewise finding himself as part of the infinite. Accessing what is beyond the finite, the poet thus speaks in ways not previously available. Because language emerges out of the creative reflection, such language would not be possible except through the poet's becoming one with the infinite. Nature and art emerge as if for the first time through "the *infinite beautiful reflection*, which in its continuous limitation is at the same time continuously relating and unifying" (EL 298). Poetry, because it is born of nature, "unites [people] into a living, a thousand times divided, inward whole, for precisely this shall be poetry itself; and like the cause, so the effect" (139).

Poetry yields a harmony, not sameness. It is divided, yet whole; it speaks both the particular and the totality. The repose that poetry offers by affording this union, this antidote to alienation, is not an empty repose, but one of active, creative, harmonizing forces.

Although poetry is unifying, in many ways, the poet remains on the edge of mainstream culture, able to speak in ways that others cannot. Indeed, Hyperion is himself a hermit on an island, never fully at home with his own people. We have only his letters, not those of his interlocutors, and so find ourselves at best with only a monologic re-telling of dialogues. However, if Hölderlin is correct that we always already belong to a union, that is, that the intersubjective precedes the subjective, then some of the concerns about subjectivism this might raise are dampened. The poet does not stand in isolation, but gathers others back into that original harmony.

As gathering, the poet's actions are never fully solitary. So long as Hyperion remained on the island in isolation, he remained alienated, not only from others, but also from himself. It is only through his friendships with Adamas and Alabanda and, most especially, through his relationship with Diotima, that Hyperion comes to know himself and recognize his vocation as poet. As discussed above, Diotima tells Hyperion that he is called to live a beautiful life. Later, she tells him more specifically that he is "born for higher things" and, despite his protestations, he must go out into the world to share with others what is noblest and most beautiful. In response, Hyperion exclaims, "If the bee can make her little kingdom flourish, why should not I be able to plant and cultivate what is needful?" (H 77). He claims that nature will be the bride of a rejuvenated people, who will renew their spirits in nature such that all be united in that one divinity. To cultivate is thus not to impart self-discovered truth, but rather to bring out the divine already present in others. Furthermore, this relationship to the divine is not one sided, that is, it is not the case that humans are merely passive in the face of nature's activity. Rather, humans, too, can rejuvenate, can be creative, toward nature, which is therefore also responsive. Nature will be like a bride, joined to humans through love and an all-embracing unity, demonstrating the one differentiated in itself. For Hyperion, to be a teacher means that he would be a cultivator; thus, he is not so much a creator or teacher of wholly new things, but a gardener who draws out that divine that is already present in those he teaches.

Although Hyperion likens himself to the bee, in a letter to Karl Gok in June 1799, a few months before the second volume of *Hyperion* appears, Hölderlin argues for a difference between human and non-human animals. While non-humans might be quite content with their world, humans distinctly strive for something else. It would be nice, he suggests, to be like the deer who is connected to nature like a baby to its mother, free of anxiety and complaint. Yet, that would be unnatural for humans. Rather than satisfied with life as the deer is, the human instead feels compelled to "to accelerate nature's endless process of perfection, to complete what he has before him, and to idealize" (EL 135). Unlike non-humans, humans have an instinct, a drive to push forward and to cultivate what is yet uncultivated, to give form to the formless. To remain merely content or stagnant would be *un*natural for humans. We have gardens, for example, because we want to form a better world than the one we inherited. Thus, we find ourselves in tension: to satisfy our natural drives, we must create and give form to what is unformed, but that striving is ceaseless. Because we are finite creatures, there is no possibility to achieve complete satisfaction. At most, what can be achieved is the repose between active and passive, between love and strife, through the recognition of the particular self in response the universal totality. To recognize the self as particular is also to recognize the self as inescapably finite. Here, then, Hölderlin seems to suggest that in all our striving for creation, we must also prepare for death.

Hölderlin borrows a line from Sophocles' *Oedipus at Colonus* as the epigraph to the second volume of *Hyperion*: "Not to be born is, past all prizing, best; but, when a man has seen the light, this is next best by far, that with all speed he should go thither, whence he had come" (H 75). This line, spoken by the Chorus, occurs when Oedipus seeks refuge in Colonus, where the oracle has predicted he will die. Asserting that one who seeks a longer life is a fool, the Chorus continues, "The Helper comes at last to all alike, when the fate of Hades is suddenly revealed, without marriage-song, or lyre, or dance: Death at the end."[54] The second volume of *Hyperion* shifts from the burgeoning, budding anticipation of the first volume to themes of decay and strife, epitomized in Diotima's death. If we read *Hyperion* not only as a *Bildungsroman*, that is, as a narrative of Hyperion's development and self-discovery, but also as an account of the nature of *Bildung* itself, then this second volume provides more concretely what previous accounts of education have lacked, namely a focus on death. I argue that what distinguishes a poetic education from an aesthetic education is the centrality of tragedy. Paramount to this account is no longer merely the human as rational, but the human as finite.

THE TRAGEDY OF DIOTIMA

In November 1799, Hölderlin writes to Susette Gontard, whom he also addresses as Diotima, with the final draft of *Hyperion*. He asks for her forgiveness for letting Diotima die, but remarks that such a death was necessary (EL 163–64). Although Hölderlin suggests that he merely let Diotima die, Marlies Janz reads Diotima's death as murder.[55] Not only does Hyperion bring forth Diotima's death, but he also becomes who he is because of her death. For Janz, Diotima's downfall is precisely the same as Hyperion's becoming a subject. This is because Diotima is language; she is poetic speech. For Hyperion, Diotima mirrors what he both is and what he could become.[56] She is, "in her miraculous omniscience," able to catch every harmony and dissonance and reveal Hyperion to himself before he was even aware of them (H 50). Through Diotima's mirroring, Hyperion becomes a subject. Furthermore, he becomes a poet, and Diotima is the source of the poetic word. She leads him out of the chaos, out of fermentation, and enables him to see that "the Ideal is what Nature was," and thus that Nature can be rejuvenated (51). For Hölderlin, creative reflection yields poetry, so, insofar as Diotima opens the space for Hyperion's self-reflection, she also is language and grants Hyperion's development into poet. Although she is language, in a letter to Hyperion, she writes, "My life was silent; my death is loquacious" (122). If Diotima is language, her death speaks the most. On Janz's reading, this is because Diotima, while alive, is only ever an object, allowing Hyperion to become a subject: "Hyperion, biased in his picture of her as an always available marionette in his imagination, most blatantly denied the consideration of the mere possibility that Diotima could move beyond her receptive and passive role and become herself an active agent."[57] Indeed, Hyperion frequently describes Diotima as a marble statue, static and fragile.[58] Diotima dies when Hyperion embarks on his political quest, which marks his becoming a subject in the fullest sense. So long as her existence is the grounds for Hyperion's becoming a subject, then her death is, according to Janz, intentional because Hyperion replaces her with his political actions.

While I agree with Janz that Hyperion arguably mistreats Diotima, I also aim to offer a more expansive reading of *Hyperion* that identifies Diotima's death less as an instance of sacrifice and victimhood and more as an instance of self-preservation. This does not deny that Hyperion reduces her to a static object, but attends more to how Diotima describes herself. Diotima senses, from her very first meeting with Hyperion, that there can be no permanence to their relationship, or even to their existence. This, however, is not a cause for despair. She gently rebukes Hyperion, "The heart's flowers need gentle care. Their roots are everywhere, but they themselves flourish only in fair weather" (H 66). She parts ways with Hyperion, only for him to chase after her for more time together. Later, as they reach a summit overlooking ancient Athens, Diotima reflects that one learns to accept one's fate, good or bad, in silence. Whereas Hyperion laments what has been lost in ancient Athens—"Remind me not of time!"—Diotima attunes herself to her fate, but without resignation. Rather, she speaks of possibilities of future blossoms. When Hyperion becomes distressed by fate treating the world as a plaything, Diotima calls him to come out where it is green, into the colors of life. As they walk in the gardens, Hyperion finds himself revived by the plant life as well as Diotima's presence. In each of these instances, Diotima does not fight time, but accepts it as it passes. Furthermore, she likens the passage of time to plant life. Growth, blossoming, and decay are all necessary, and thus should not be fought, but embraced. Finally, right before she tells Hyperion what his mission is, she reflects, "There is a time for love . . . as there is a time to live in the happy cradle. But life itself drives us forth" (72). Here, she reminds Hyperion that his dissatisfaction so far has been because he has misunderstood time. He has attacked too quickly or proceeded too timidly. By returning to Athens, not in an effort to recreate Athens as it was, but rather by giving form to Athens as it is by creating art, Hyperion might finally find that equipoise he seeks.

In Diotima's final letter to Hyperion, after he has set off on his political adventure, she writes, "Little did you think to hear my swan song this year" (H 120).[59] Here, she recognizes her own decline and chastises him for not attending to her. It is not only that he did not hear her, but that he did not even think to hear her. He had already rendered her silent. Still, she does not blame him for her death. The grief she experiences in her separation from Hyperion is actually welcome insofar as grief itself becomes for Diotima a kind of creative expression, giving form to the formless. Yet, in this process, her soul grows overripe in love, unable to remain in one place. Her death is not a complete end, but another moment in the continuous cycle of growth and decay. She reflects on the life of Nature, higher than all thought, and wonders whether it would be such a loss to be become a plant: "How should I be lost from the sphere of life, in which eternal love, common to all, holds all natures together? how should I escape from the union that binds all beings together?" (H 121). Even if death is separation, it is not total separation, for all is united in love and in nature. To be like a plant is not to be weak or inhuman, but rather to participate in that eternal rhythm. This union is not the jumble of bodies on market day, but, Diotima claims, the divine spirit that is particular to each and common to all.

Diotima views her death not as a final loss nor as a murder, but as a way to preserve her life in the original primordial unity, the *hen kai pan*. As finite, we "represent perfection in mutability; we divide the great harmonies in of joy into changing melodies" and "accompany the majestic procession with dance and song in changing shapes and tones" (H 123–24). Although she joins in with these melodies and sings forth, Diotima writes, "Now let me be silent. To say more would be too much" (124). Diotima falls silent, not because she has nothing left to say, but because she has given voice to something else, namely the eternal rhythm of loving nature.

In *The Vegetative Soul*, Elaine Miller contends that, "From the very moment that Hyperion and Diotima kiss for the first time, she begins to wilt, as a flower will droop if its petals are fingered. Diotima as flower (a comparison Hölderlin explicitly makes) must bear the brunt of the confluence of desire, resistance, and love."[60] In Diotima, nature is personified. She is divine, embracing, and, as Hyperion expresses frequently, she speaks in her silence. Like Janz, Miller suggests that Diotima's death is not orthogonal to Hyperion's development, but perhaps the result of it. Yet, Miller also contends that figures such as Hölderlin offer roots of a new, feminist conception of the subject. Rather than the Enlightenment subject prized for his autonomy and reason, existing atomistically, Hölderlin's model of subjectivity, based on the vegetative soul provides a framework for understanding the subject in terms "of finitude and vulnerability."[61]

Yet, as Miller argues, finitude and vulnerability should not be taken to be the same as passivity or weakness. What the vegetative soul shows is the possibility for "transformation and renewal."[62] Plants are receptive, like the sunflower that tracks the movement of sunlight, but also grow and develop in ways that cannot be predetermined. Tree roots burst through cement sidewalks; hemlock kills. Miller draws on Irigaray's understanding of efflorescence, which suggests a kind of bursting forth or "subject-in-becoming," to consider an alternative to the traditional Western philosophical picture of the human as rational animal.[63] The flower, opening and closing, growing new shoots and dropping leaves, points to an understanding of the subject as indefinite and multifaceted.

Thus, if Diotima is a flower and represents nature, then a fuller reading would be one that does not simply stop where Hyperion does. Rather, we can read Diotima as both responsive and transformative, as holding open space for language and speaking herself. Moreover, she maintains a unique relationship to time that is neither steeped in nostalgia nor yearning for the future. Our focus should be on Diotima, rather than Hyperion, as a tragic figure.[64] As Miller points out, for Hölderlin, the tragic hero is the one who, rather than gaining consciousness, loses consciousness, and in so doing, allows what is otherwise silent to speak, giving form to the formless.[65] In "The Ground of the *Empedocles*," Hölderlin explains that the poet, attuned to the deepest intimacy in the harmony between organic and aorgic, finite and infinite, loses herself to give voice to what is silent (EL 260). In recognizing and becoming attuned to time by participating in the eternal rhythm, the poet becomes one with the eternal. The opposite of the tragic hero is one who, rather than uniting the extremes, seeks to subdue them by attaching them to a firm and lasting foundation. This opponent strives for consciousness since it is reason that will separate the extremes from one another and provide that foundation (270).[66] Although Hyperion consistently champions poetry over philosophy, he strives toward consciousness, laments the passage of time, and seeks to quiet chaos, thus not fully developing into a tragic poet himself.[67] In the case of the tragic poet, the aorgic and organic cannot be separated, for in their individuation they return to one another in a new way.[68] What had been active is now passive, subject now objective, forming now formless. To see Diotima as only a meek, sacrificial character is to see only one half of this harmony.

By giving voice to what could not otherwise be articulated or articulate, giving form to the formless, centering her finitude, and attuning herself to the primordial unity of nature, Diotima epitomizes the poetic figure. Although she does not write poetry or create art, that we know of, she creates her life. She names the flowers and animals and teaches Hyperion who he is. She reflects the play of the organic and aorgic, dying in order to live.

Earlier I presented the question of whether the poet, as uniquely capable of saying what is unsayable, falls into a monologue rather than a dialogue. Returning to Diotima as our example, we find that what most characterizes Diotima is her silence. Yet, this silence is not a failure to speak, but what allows silence itself to speak. By this, I mean that rather than mastering nature or subsuming it under a concept, she allows what it silent to present itself as it is. Even without words, nature sings forth in great melodies. She provides space for Hyperion to speak himself.

What we learn from this analysis of *Hyperion* is that education as poetic education is less the individual's self-cultivation into rational autonomy, but rather the development, through language and tragedy, of an attunement of the finite self to what surpasses us. Paying particular attention to the often-overlooked experience of Diotima offers an account of the self as responsive and transformative, as actively attuned to that which surpasses. Art and poetry provide ways of articulating what could not otherwise be articulated, such as silence, thus enabling participation in the world totality.

Recall that for Hölderlin, *Bildungstrieb* marks the particular cultivation of the self. Nature cannot be objectified or overcome. The human is driven to form, all the while aware of her finitude. *Bildungstrieb* reflects the joining and separating of life and death through the creative cultivation of the self toward both elements. A poetic education, as suggested in *Bildungstrieb*, would thus be anchored in an active cultivation toward that which surpasses and to the all-surrounding unity. Poetry, as uniquely capable of speaking and listening to this all-surrounding unity, is better positioned than political or philosophical thought that attempts to achieve such unity through reason. Thus, as suggested by both Shaftesbury and Hölderlin, an education that presupposes a social contract or champions rational autonomy is misguided from the start. Rather, to be human is always already to be a member of a community, to be part of an eternal conversation and melody.

NOTES

1. Shaftesbury, *Characteristics of Men, Manners, Opinions, Times*.
2. Kant, "Lectures on Pedagogy," 9:443.
3. Kant, "Anthropology from a Pragmatic Point of View," 7:325.
4. Kant, 7:120.
5. Johann Friedrich Blumenbach, *Über den Bildungstrieb*, 12–13. Johann Friedrich Blumenbach, responding to debates in epigenesis, develops the concept of *Bildungstrieb* to account for a certain causal organizing principle or life force in nature. This drive, distinct from other natural powers, bestows, preserves, and restores a creature's form. Whereas proponents of evolution at the time held that an organism develops by incrementally unfolding a nascent form, Blumenbach, though later modifying the concept, employs the concept of *Bildungstrieb* to explain how an organism develops a form out of an otherwise homogenous substrate. Kant adopts this concept of *Bildungstrieb* in *The Critique of Judgment* to explain the apparent connection between mechanistic and teleological accounts of nature. Yet, while Blumenbach sees this drive as actual, causal, and indicative of a Creator behind the scenes, Kant takes it be regulative; organisms act *as if* guided by a formative drive (See Richards, "Kant and Blumenbach on the Bildungstrieb: A Historical Misunderstanding," 25). We might use a teleological understanding to make sense of biological elements, but we would be wrong to use that teleology as a scientific explanation. This allows us to recognize the purposiveness of nature, which we then use to make judgments of beauty in nature. That is, the purposiveness yields objective knowledge, but does allow us to assess nature or art from a human perspective.
6. Kant, *The Metaphysics of Morals*, 6:387.
7. Kant, "Lectures on Pedagogy," 9:441.
8. Kant, 9:444.
9. Kant explains, "In the formation of reason one must proceed Socratically. For Socrates, who called himself the midwife of his listeners' knowledge, gives in his dialogues, which Plato has preserved for us faithfully, examples of how even in the case of old people, one can bring forth a good deal from their own reason" (9:477). Johannes Giesinger argues that there is a tension between Kant's views on morality and pedagogy since in order to recognize herself as a moral being, a person must also recognize herself as noumenal, that is, as free and rational, guided by the categorical imperative and *sensus communis*. This freedom in particular, however, is not discoverable by experience alone, so the child cannot have this knowledge in the natural world. If education is recognition of the self as free, and therefore as morally responsible, it is unclear how education would bring about this recognition. However, part of this tension is resolved when we recognize that insofar as Kant does believe there is an instinct for freedom, the child feels some pull toward autonomy. Giesinger, "Kant's Account of Moral Education."
10. While many of Kant's remarks on *Bildungstrieb* occur in *The Critique of Judgment*, and these would have been informative for Schiller as well, Robert Bernasconi highlights that Kant sought Blumenbach's approval not only to explain mechanical and teleological purposes, but also that "there is sufficient evidence to consider

plausible the idea that Kant was also still seeking Blumenbach's support for his concept of race, a process begun in 1788 when Kant implicitly contrasted his account of race with the notion of variety, and then somewhat gratuitously praised Blumenbach's notion of *Bildungstrieb*" (Bernasconi, "Kant and Blumenbach's Polyps," 82). On Bernasconi's reading, the notion of *Bildungstrieb* provides the explanation for natural dispositions and fixity that Kant's account of race requires. Whereas Kant's reliance on germs or *Keime* to explain race could not be empirically verified, now *Bildungstrieb* is able to explain, for example, the skin color of Blacks as indicative of nature's purposiveness (84). Because the form already exists, racial characteristics cannot be simply modified. Blumenbach himself adopts Kant's examples and integrates them into his 1797 edition of the *Handbuch of Naturgeschichte* (84). Jennifer Mensch suggests that this exchange is not based on a misunderstanding, as Richards suggests, but that Kant actively sought for Blumenbach to adopt his understanding of race. See Mensch, "Kant and the Skull Collectors: German Anthropology from Blumenbach to Kant." When Schiller and Hölderlin take up *Bildungstrieb* in their accounts of creative and artistic production, it is unclear whether Kant's commitments to race are thereby imported. Neither explicitly remarks on race, though there remain lurking attitudes wary of the Oriental other or affirmative of the superiority of the Greeks.

11. Kant, "Lectures on Physical Geography," 9:316.
12. Cited in Bernasconi, "Kant as an Unfamiliar Source of Racism," 158.
13. Cited in Eze, "The Color of Reason," 116.
14. Kant, "Anthropology from a Pragmatic Point of View," 7:206.
15. See Bernasconi, "Kant as an Unfamiliar Source of Racism," "Will the Real Kant Please Stand Up?" and "Kant's Third Thoughts on Race."
16. Di Cesare, *Heidegger and the Jews*, 32–36.
17. Eze, "The Color of Reason."
18. Huseyinzadegan, "For What Can the Kantian Feminist Hope? Constructive Complicity in Appropriations of the Canon."
19. Jennifer, Mensch. "Caught Between Character and Race: 'Temperament' in Kant's Lectures on Anthropology."
20. Charles, Mills. "Kant's *Untermenschen*."
21. My aim in including these references is not to offer gossip or to give in to a kind of tabloid philosophy. Rather, my aim is more akin to what Huseyinzadegan deems "constructive complicity." She writes, "First, we must admit that we as professional philosophers constructing and re-constructing Kantian arguments are complicit in the problems that Kant's texts exemplify. Then, we must highlight and inherit these problems as our own issues rather than disavowing them as the historical limitations of the man himself or marginal empirical claims that do not infect or inflect the rest of his philosophical system" (2). Much more can, and should, be said about these issues in Kant's work. This is beyond the immediate scope of this section, so I refer instead to the important work of the above cited scholars.
22. Schmidt, *Lyrical and Ethical Subjects*, 1.
23. Makkreel, *Imagination and Interpretation in Kant: The Hermeneutical Import of the Critique of Judgment*, 99.
24. Schmidt, *Lyrical and Ethical Subjects*, 17.

25. Although Kant couples *Bildungstrieb* and an apparent purposiveness in nature, he does not seem to ascribe this formative impulse to the genius of the artist, which gives the rule of nature to art. Because the formative drive is internal to the organism as it forms itself, the artist, though full of natural talent, remains external to the art object. Schiller, however, does ascribe this formative impulse to the artist. The artist has the divine impulse to form [*der göttliche Bildungstrieb*] (AE 59), that, if moderated appropriately by patience and tranquility, allows the artist to harmonize form and matter, thus achieving freedom. If not properly restrained, however, the impulse misdirects itself to the present and falls into debasement and unhappiness. Violetta Waibel suggests this is why we should read the formative impulse as distinct from the play impulse. She points to Schiller's Twenty-Sixth Letter, where he writes, "And as soon as the play-drive begins to stir, with its pleasure in semblance, it will be followed by the shaping spirit of imitation [*Bildungstrieb*], which treats semblance as something autonomous" (AE 195). This capacity for imitation is given with the capacity for form, but the play impulse is something that must be acquired: "In the midst of the fearful kingdom of powers, and in the midst of the sacred kingdom of laws, the aesthetic impulse to form [*Bildungstrieb*] is at work, unnoticed, on the building of a third joyous kingdom of play and of semblance" that frees humans from all constraints, physical or moral (AE 137). For Schiller, the formative impulse does belong to the human, who then acts on it to, ideally, harmonize the self toward beauty and freedom, and thus to achieve the ideal aesthetic state [*Staat*].

26. For an extensive discussion of Schiller's conception of freedom, see Beiser, *Schiller as Philosopher: A Re-Examination*, 213–37.

27. Schiller, "'Kallias, or Concerning Beauty: Letters to Gottfried Körner' (1793)," 143.

28. Schiller, 167.

29. Schiller, 143.

30. Spariosu, *Dionysus Reborn*, 55. Mihai Spariosu explains, "The play-drive occupies the same middle position in Schiller that the aesthetic judgment does in Kant, and for the same reason: while it is itself devoid of any cognitive value, it nevertheless helps Reason mediate between the realm of the concept of freedom and that of the concept of freedom." I would add that while aesthetic judgment does not have any direct cognitive content, it does have cognitive value, for it does expand our thinking and enliven the imagination.

31. Shaftesbury, *Characteristics of Men, Manners, Opinions, Times*, 65.

32. Shaftesbury, 157–58.

33. Shaftesbury, 172–73.

34. Shaftesbury, 48.

35. Shaftesbury, 50.

36. Shaftesbury, 51.

37. Shaftesbury, 274.

38. See further, Beiser, *German Idealism*, 299–301.

39. "How can I say: I! without self-consciousness? But how is self-consciousness possible? By opposing me to myself, separating me from myself, but notwithstanding this separation recognizing myself in the opposition as one and the same" (EL

231.) Hölderlin writes similarly in a letter to Hegel in 1795, that at first Fichte's work appears overly dogmatic. Fichte seems to strive to "get beyond consciousness theoretically," but because his absolute I has nothing outside of it, it can have no object. For Hölderlin, it is inconceivable to have a consciousness without an object. I cannot be the object of the absolute I because then I, as object, would be limited, not absolute, so I could then not be I (EL 48).

40. Heraclitus's Fragment 10: "συλλάψιες· ὅλα καὶ οὐχ ὅλα, συμφερόμενον διαφερόμενον, συνᾷδον διᾷδον καὶ ἐκ πάντων ἓν καὶ ἐξ ἑνὸς πάντα" in Diels and Kranz, *Die Fragmente der Vorsokratiker*, 68–69. Robinson translates, "Graspings: wholes and not wholes, convergent divergent, consonant dissonant, from all things one and from one thing all" (Robinson, *Heraclitus*, 88). Compare to Fragment 51 "(καὶ ὅτι τοῦτο οὐκ ἴσασι πάντες οὐδὲ ὁμολογοῦσιν, ἐπιμέμφεται ὧδέ τως·) οὐ ξυνιᾶσιν ὅκως διαφερόμενον ἑωυτῷ ὁμολογέει· παλίντροπος ἁρμονίη ὅκωσπερ τόξου καὶ λύρης." (Diels and Kranz 73–74). "They do not understand how, while differing from (or: being at variance), [it] is in agreement with itself. [There is] a back-turning connection, like [that] of a bow or lyre" (Robinson, 37).

41. Beiser, *German Idealism*, 391. Frederick Beiser explains, "Hölderlin agrees with Fichte that subject–object identity is the necessary condition of all knowledge; but he disagrees with him that this identity is subjective, given that subjectivity implies the possibility of self-consciousness, which involves some distinction between subject and object. In Hölderlin's view, only Spinoza's substance, pure being, expresses the pure subject–object identity that is a necessary condition of the possibility of experience itself."

42. Empedocles epitomizes this tension. In "Ground for *Empedocles*," Hölderlin explains that the destiny of Empedocles' epoch demanded neither speech or song "where the pure is still easily conceived in an idealistic presentation" nor action that immediately helps, but lays the human bare. Rather, this epoch demands a sacrifice that would dissolve the tensions of the destiny. But even in this dissolution, difference remains, for art, as the organic, forming drive, works through the aorgic. Empedocles is destined to be victim because the closer he draws to the divine, in fact the more finite he is. Although he reunites art and nature, this reunification is temporary. It cannot be fixed and permanent. Thus, the very daring reconciliation he enacts is his own downfall (EL 264–65).

43. Referring again to his pupil, Hölderlin writes that he strives make him aware of his moral freedom and capable of responsibility (EL 23).

44. Yet, such an experience was not to be had by Hölderlin with this particular pupil, Fritz von Kalb. He would be awakened, so to speak, but would then fall back into apathy and stubbornness (EL 40). Hölderlin became increasingly despondent by these circumstances, not only because he believed he failed the child and in his profession, but also because it left him no time or energy for his own education.

45. Shaftesbury was not Hölderlin's only, or even main influence. His focus is more often Rousseau, who argues for education as a passive awakening of goodness in children as a way to rehabilitate, as much as possible, the goodness and attunement to nature that was lost with coming out of the state of nature. In the early 1790s, Hölderlin is influenced by Rousseau's writings on political rights and on nature. For

Hölderlin, as in many of the other Romantic thinkers, a rejection of the modern social contract theory that views civil society or unions as secondary. In Rousseau, we find the roots of Hölderlin's insistence that morality is not a matter of overcoming nature, but indeed of returning to it. Although Hölderlin at times sets himself against Rousseau, in other regards he follows Rousseau closely, even writing three poems about him and referring to him in one as "*Halbgott*." Some of Hölderlin's wariness of Rousseau may be from the influence of Schiller and other thinkers who disregarded Rousseau as sentimental or misguided. In "On Naïve and Sentimental Poetry," Schiller claims that Rousseau looks everywhere for repose, focusing too much on the limits, rather than the possibilities, of humans: "Rousseau, the poet just much as the philosopher, tends only either to either seek nature or to avenge it on art . . . His compositions have poetic content since they treat the ideal; only he does not know how to use that content in a poetic way . . . Thus, too, in the ideal of humanity that he sets up, too much attention is paid to the limitations of humanity and too little to its capability." Schiller, "On Naive and Sentimental Poetry," 213–14. For an extensive discussion of Hölderlin's relationship to be Rousseau's thought, see Link, *Hölderlin-Rousseau*.

46. Cocalis, "The Transformation of 'Bildung' from an Image to an Ideal," 408.

47. Cited in Cocalis, 408.

48. Dilthey, *Poetry and Experience*, 336.

49. See further Larmore, "Hölderlin and Novalis."

50. This reflects what will later become of greater focus for Hölderlin, namely a shift to viewing poetry as an alternation of tones and a growing concern with music as capable of articulating what language cannot.

51. Rousseau, *Emile; or, Education*, 57–58. "Therefore the education of the earliest years should be merely negative. It consists, not in teaching virtue or truth, but in preserving the heart from vice and from the spirit of error. If only you could let well alone, and get others to follow your example; if you could bring your scholar to the age of twelve strong and healthy, but unable to tell his right hand from his left, the eyes of his understanding would be open to reason as soon as you began to teach him. Free from prejudices and free from habits, there would be nothing in him to counteract the effects of your labours. In your hands he would soon become the wisest of men; by doing nothing to begin with, you would end with a prodigy of education."

52. Warminski, *Readings in Interpretation: Hölderlin, Hegel, Heidegger*, 55. Some interpreters maintain that it is ambiguous whether only a Greek could have discovered this thought or whether the discovery of this thought is what makes one Greek. Hyperion states the Egyptians could not experience Beauty as the Greeks do because the Egyptian does not love Heaven and Earth in equal measure or living attuned to the primordial unity (67). This may also be informed by Kant who writes in the Preface to the *Critique of Pure Reason*: "Mathematics has, from the earliest times to which the history of human reason reaches, in that admirable people the Greeks, traveled the secure path of a science . . . I believe that mathematics was left groping about for a long time (chiefly among the Egyptians)" (B xi). Kant's interpretation seems to rely on speculation informed, too, by his racial prejudices.

53. See also Gosetti-Ferencei, *Heidegger, Hölderlin, and the Subject of Poetic Language*, 159–60.

54. Sophocles, *The Oedipus at Colonus of Sophocles*, 1211. This reference is similarly central for Nietzsche, certainly influenced by Hölderlin in *The Birth of Tragedy*. There he identifies Oedipus as emblematic of that Greek serenity. Oedipus at Colonus, stricken and suffering, comes to see that "unearthly serenity" of the gods. Nietzsche, *The Birth of Tragedy and Other Writings*, 47.

55. Janz, "Hölderlins Flamme. Zur Bildwerdung der Frau im Hyperion."

56. Janz, 128.

57. Janz, 138.

58. Janz, 131.

59. In an early letter to Bellarmin, recounting the fluctuations of joy and despair, Hyperion reflects on his own swan song and tones of death. He writes, "Gladly would I have woven myself a funeral wreath, but I had only winter flowers" (41). That Hyperion sang a swan song for himself is telling. He maintains the vegetative element by requiring not only flowers, but the right sort. Whereas funeral wreaths in Ancient Greece were often made from laurel leaves or myrtles, Hyperion has only winter flowers.

60. Miller, *The Vegetative Soul*, 95.

61. Miller, 16.

62. Miller, 17.

63. Miller, 188.

64. I argue this against interpretations from figures like James Luchte, who claim that *Hyperion* is a novel of failure, rather than tragedy, and that Diotima's death is pathetic, rather than tragic. He writes, "Though she dies, Diotima's death is not tragic, but pathetic, occurring at a distance. It does not reveal the infinite and her courage in the face of her meagre portion, but only her weakness, simply a modern death, without meaning" (Luchte, *Mortal Thought*, 93). Such a dismissive reading takes Diotima's narrative at face value as told by Hyperion without holding open a space for a more nuanced depiction. Indeed, such a reading perpetuates a violence to Diotima by reducing her to only Hyperion's interpretation rather than attending to how she might otherwise understand herself.

65. Miller, *The Vegetative Soul*, 115.

66. See also Miller, 116.

67. Schmidt, *On Germans and Other Greeks: Tragedy and Ethical Life*, 128–33. Dennis Schmidt reads Hyperion as a tragic figure in the sense that tragedy marks the inability to recover time and a speculative experience of the whole that is also a separation from that whole, articulated by language. Because Hyperion cannot recover Diotima, he remains plagued by their separation of time. Tragedy does not shy from this vulnerability, but celebrates it. I do not dispute this reading and think this understanding of the relationship between time and tragedy is particularly insightful. Still, I maintain that Diotima's story provides a fuller understanding of that vulnerability, particularly in relation to nature.

68. Hölderlin suggests that, in the case of Empedocles, art and nature unite through an encounter and transformation between "an excess of objectivity and of being-outside-oneself . . . in a brave, open character" and the subjective, which "assumes to passive shape of suffering." In exchanging their shapes, the subjective and objective become one (EL 270).

Chapter 2

Poetry as Teacher of Humanity

In a short speech in delivered to the Hölderlin-Gesellschaft in 1983, Gadamer reflects on Hölderlin's contemporaneity and how this poet, whom Gadamer first discovered around 1914, continues to resonate with the audience of the day. Gadamer attributes this to the idea that, "What, for Hölderlin, was speaking is perhaps the originary form of speaking in general. Speaking is the searching of words."[1] What confronts Hölderlin, what confronts all of us, is the despair of searching for expression. Gadamer describes his own attempt at speaking: "You see, I speak here in search of words because I believe in the infinity of what one fails to say and that, precisely by not succeeding, begins to be heard in another."[2] There is something excessive to all meaning, and yet we also never quite express what we intend. Similarly, in *Truth and Method*, Gadamer explains that to try to make ourselves understood "means to hold what is said together with an infinity of what is not said in one unified meaning" (TM 464). This infinity of what is unsaid is not a deficiency, but a richness belonging to the nature of speaking itself.

For Gadamer, this searching for words is what makes Hölderlin a poet for our time: although subjugated to the ideologies of Nazi Germany, which pounced on themes of homeland, blood, and soil, Hölderlin's poetry could never be fully appropriated because it always says more than could be expressed. Because Hölderlin's experience of searching for language is one shared by all, his project can be neither relegated to the era of Romanticism nor appropriated for political gain. Yet, in the aftermath of the war and the totalization of fascist thought, we have become more aware of the limits of our speech. Gadamer speaks of "the wisdom of stuttering and falling silent" and how today's poetry has become increasingly "hermetic."[3] This ceaseless challenge of articulating oneself is not a problem, but rather a kind of wisdom. The play of said and unsaid belongs to language in general, but is epitomized by the poetic word because of the poetic word's self-reflection (TM 465). The poetic word speaks, and continues to speak, precisely because it is aware of its own limitations. This, suggests Gadamer, is the legacy of Hölderlin who draws our attention to what it means to speak in the first place.

Although accused of hermetic speech himself, Paul Celan sees poetry rather as a venturing beyond. Celan was born to a German-speaking Jewish family in Bukovina in the Austro-Hungarian Empire, which later became part of what is now Ukraine.[4] His parents died in the concentration camps. Celan survived work camps and later moved to Paris, where he continued to write in German. The language through which he sought to orient himself, to win reality, was also grounds for murder of his family and community. In his speech in reception of the Bremen prize in 1958, Celan observes that the only thing remaining "through terrifying silence" and the "thousand darknesses of murderous speech," is language (CP 35). What remains is not meaning or reference, but language, the words themselves, even if that language is German, the language of Nazi terror. In response to a questionnaire from the Flinker Bookstore in 1958, Celan writes that the "I" who speaks this language, German, attempts an outline and an orientation of what is given and what is possible. Reality, he claims, "is not simply there" (15). Rather, such reality must be sought and won. In the Bremen speech, he states that poetry, as a movement of dialogue, is like a letter in a bottle cast out with the hope that it might wash ashore and return. For Celan, this means that poems are fundamentally *unterwegs*, on the way "toward something open, inhabitable, an approachable you, perhaps, an approachable reality" (35). As oriented toward this reality, poems are future oriented. Yet, as Celan also reminds us, the poem is an act of memory, of bearing witness. It preserves what cannot be lost. As such, the poem does not stand outside of time, but rather gathers time as it spans between past and future.

In "The Meridian," Celan invites us to reconsider not only the time of the poem, but also its space and place. He characterizes his exploration as "topological research" that investigates the poem as the site of encounter between the "altogether other" and the other that remains quite close (CP 48).[5] We have here two senses of the other: one wholly other and one not so distant. In choosing the language of the other [*Andere*], Celan explains that he can no longer use the word strange [*Fremd*]. Although the other is wholly so, it remains recognizable or even familiar. In speaking itself, Celan explains, the poem encounters itself as other. Gadamer describes the poem as the very embodiment of language as searching for words, searching for itself. *Unterwegs*, the poem both is and is not yet itself. This movement leaves the poem groundless and never fully at home. Yet, because the poem encounters itself as other, it remains at home, "still here" even in this groundlessness. Sending itself out toward each and every other, the poem becomes a conversation.

Although the language speaks in an unexpected way, it remains a form of address that also encounters us. The poem, then, marks a curious play not only of time—as already and not yet—but also of space as the place of both presence and absence. As the place of encounter and, as Celan suggests, a kind of breath-crystal, the poem is corporeal.

What we find in Hölderlin, Celan, and Gadamer is the idea that language, specifically poetic language, is on the way; it both exceeds and is not yet itself. Returning to Hölderlin's idea that poetry is the teacher of humanity and world-disclosive, we ask now what it would mean for poetry, as itself on the way, to be the teacher. Similarly, if education as *Bildung* is self-formation, then what role does poetry play in self-cultivation? In the following, I will argue that poetry, because it spans between past and future, teaches us that education, as self-formation, is nonlinear. Poetry discloses the world and what exceeds us, but in a way that never fully lays bare its subject. In the encounter between self and other, something always remains left to be said that resists complete understanding. Poetry, then, requires our attunement to this ambiguous revealing, a holding open of both what is said and what is not. Thus, education requires a movement and negotiation between past and future, self and other, familiar and foreign. Here again we find that the path of human life is eccentric and expansive, akin to a plant that grows in all directions.[6] Yet, such expansion is possible not because of a lack of friction, but precisely because there is an encounter with another, even if this other is the self.

Thus, whereas aesthetic education relies on a conception of the individual progressing linearly toward autonomy and developing increased capacities for making rational judgments, poetic education proposes the cultivation of an attunement to the other and the self. Rather than *technē*, we find *poiesis*. Rather than mastery, cultivation. Poetic education does not abandon rationality, however. There remains a connection between poetry and thinking: the poetic word is not at the service of philosophy, but does provide a corrective to tendencies of calculation or scientism in philosophical thought. Indeed, poetry challenges us to consider what the task of philosophy is in the first place. Rather than disinterested objectivity, we find in poetry a transformational encounter. Displacing the emphasis on cognition and self-mastery, poetry returns us to ourselves as vulnerable and finite. Furthermore, this account of poetic education maintains that the self is groundless, that is, there is nothing to ground the self but the active giving shape to oneself. Yet, such formation and cultivation are fundamentally dialogic. What is particularly the task of the poet is remembrance, and as Gadamer writes, "to keep in memory is to be human."[7] Poetry, as remembrance, thus teaches us how to remain open to what stands before and beyond us and to preserve what is other. Ultimately, poetry teaches us what it is to be ourselves.

DO NOT SPLIT THE NO FROM THE YES: THE LANGUAGE OF LIFE AND DEATH

Both Hölderlin and Celan believe that the poetic word marks a departure from all customary modes of understanding and meanings of words. Recall that, for Hölderlin, poetry emerges from a primordial undifferentiated space. The poetic word becomes such by attuning its finite self toward the infinite. Language anticipates the whole. The poet, in deepest intimacy, spans between the past and the future and opens space for language to speak itself. In this spanning, both the poet and the poem are returned to the original unity of the totality of creation as language remembers the knowledge of the living whole. The poem is at home in recognizing itself in the infinite, but, because it is particular and finite, the poem is not fully at home. What distinguishes the poetic word from that of the everyday is that the poem is aware of its limits, is aware of the infinity of searching for expression. But because language can remember, that is, because it preserves this originary harmony, it can also orient itself toward future harmonies.

This idea of homecoming and dwelling at home reflects the close link between Hölderlin and Celan. In his notes in preparation for his Meridian speech, Celan references Hölderlin's work, specifically the tension between the aorgic and the anorganic.[8] In Hölderlin, Celan sees a similar commitment to the possibility of poetic thinking and of the poetic word holding open tension between the foreign and familiar. Yet, although Hölderlin conceives of poetry as uniting, of holding tensions in play, as oriented toward finitude, he does not necessarily call poetry itself into question. Like Hölderlin, Celan views the poetic word as the emergence of language anew. For it to emerge, however, language must become unfamiliar. It must disorient and bring together the strange and strange into a new space. Because the poem is on the way toward a yet unknown reality, its language cannot be the language "which many ears seem to expect" (CP 15).

Although both poets wrote in German, for Celan, German is also a language of betrayal, of devastation. Celan explains that German poetry has become more sober, more distrustful of beauty, for it wants at once to locate its musicality in its bearing witness to the atrocities made in in its name. Whereas Hölderlin views this venturing toward language as a recovery, an unforgetting, Celan seems to worry about the very "burned-out meanings" of the poetic word. What would it mean to continue using the language of Auschwitz? Because the language of Nazi Germany defined itself in absolute concepts of home, blood, purity, and loyalty, the German language must now confront its own burned out meanings. At stake is not only the mortality of humans and the violent destruction of human life, but also the destruction of language itself. Thus, to recognize the way in which language emerges anew is at the same time to recognize the possibility of language's collapse. The poem speaks the living death of language.⁹ Celan writes of the poem holding its own margin, remaining "still there." In so doing, Celan preserves the particularity of the poetic word, thus also preserving poetry from being merely at the service of philosophical thinking. At the same time, by attending to the poem's own marginality, its own temporality and finitude, Celan further calls into question poetry's fragility and possibility of being at home.

The poem, Celan observes in "The Meridian," pays close attention "to all that it encounters" (CP 50). When the poem speaks, it is "mindful of all our dates" because what is its ownmost is time (50). In the Flinker response of 1958, he writes that poetry tries to be truthful and has become a "greyer" language (15). For language to be grayer means for it to be more nuanced, more ambiguous, or darker, yet still discernible in this shade. The poem, trying for truth, attends to the other not through more precision or scientific observation, but through mindfulness. Drawing this speech to a close, Celan remarks that poetry is "an infinite speaking [*Unendlichsprechung*] of death" (CP 52).¹⁰

Here, three lines of thought begin to crystallize around one another. First, as mindful, of dates in particular, the poem becomes both truer and grayer. There remains something ambiguous and bleak, but there also remains an identifiable moment of time. In this becoming, poetry both is and is not yet itself. As the infinite speaking of death, the poem spans finitude and infinitude, death and revival. Second, as paying close attention to all that it encounters, including itself, the poem moves toward truth. Poetry bears witness. Such truth is neither fully achievable nor possible through disinterested observation. Rather, such truth is itself under way. In this encounter, the poem speaks as a form of address to the other. That is, the poem can speak only because it listens to the other. Third, as the site of encounter of itself and the other, the poem sets up a space, a world, for the encounter. Because the encounter of the poem is underway, it is abyssal. This space cannot be prefigured, and yet it remains there. We do not know where it is or where it heads. Celan describes this encounter also as a utopia, nowhere. What does it mean for an encounter to be both abyssal and utopic? In other words, what does it mean to dwell in a place that is not home?

We find potential answers to these questions in Celan's 1948 essay on a painting by Edgar Jené. Celan begins by reflecting on some of the words he heard deep in the sea, surrounded by silence (CP 3). To find these words, he had to enter into the inner world beneath the sea's surface, beneath Jené's painting to cut through reality to find new paths. The journey toward these words deep in the sea could not be an attempt for a return to pure meaning or words as they were, regardless of time. Such a path would be dishonest. It would be unable to speak and would instead groan under false sincerity. Celan exclaims, "What could be more dishonest than to claim that words had somehow, at bottom, remained the same!" (6). To appeal to timelessness is to mistake the very temporality of such claims and to deny the history, such as the Third Reich, that gives rise to such insistences on purity, including of language. Instead, it is the recognition of the "ashes of burned-out meanings" (6) that shows how such meanings both cover and uncover our constant striving for expression. Reified meanings are "nasty lies" that render one unable to speak. The new words and figures of expression come neither from essential meaning nor from familiarity, but instead from "the marriage of strange and most strange" (6). These more primordial expressions are at first unrecognizable, but knowable. They are both strange and familiar. Jené's painting offers a path into and out of this new truth and possibility of meaning; it opens the space to dream a new future. Like the painting, the poetic word is utopic as opening itself toward silence. Out of the space of burned out meaning, the poem moves toward new possibilities that cannot be prefigured.

Although language is what remains amidst all losses, it cannot be the same as it was before. Because poetry is an act of remembrance, it is also an act of becoming, of forming. In "The Meridian," Celan suggests that poetry moves "into the uncanny and strange to free itself" (CP 44). Poetry, as language, must send itself out beyond itself in order to recover itself. The poem, as aware of itself, is mindful of dates, of its origin and destiny. But, because the poem is on the way and is not yet, the boundaries between past, present, and future are blurred. Thus, to remember, to recover, is not merely to bring the past to present view, but to reach across and beyond time.

The issue of memory, particularly the date of the 20th of January, features prominently in Celan's Meridian speech. He does not tell us what this date indicates, but it seems that he is referencing January 20, 1942, the date of the Wannsee conference where the Nazis proposed their "final solution." This date marks the very possibility of annihilation, of the end of time, the end of meaning. Yet, the 20th of January is the date at which Büchner's character, Lenz, "an 'I'," lives on, having set himself free "as an–estranged—I" (CP 46). The I, like the poem, steps beyond the self and thus into strangeness where the I encounters the self. Later, Celan suggests that every poem has its own 20th of January. Each poem is mindful of its date because the date, as the poem's ownmost, is its origin. Commemorating a "missed encounter," Celan explains, he wrote a story about a man like Lenz and finds that, in writing from "a '20th of January', from my '20th of January,' I had . . . encountered myself" (53). The date is the origin, but because we can turn toward it, the date is also a destination not yet reached. In marking, attending to, these dates, note that Celan does not merely say that it was the 20th of January. Rather it was "a" or "my" 20th of January that allows for an encounter. The date, though repeatable year after year and belonging to all poems, all encounters, remains absolutely singular. It is neither replaceable nor universal. There is a danger, though, of seeing these dates as substitutable and collapsing them into one another. The singularity of the poem marks its vulnerability. Because it cannot be replaced, its very possibility for existence is also the possibility of annihilation. Thus, for the poem to be mindful of its date is also for it to be mindful of its mortality.

But. In his reflections on "The Meridian," Derrida notes that Celan speaks this "but" three times immediately following mention of the 20th of January:[11]

> But the poem speaks. It is mindful of its dates, but it speaks. True, it speaks only on its own, its very own behalf.
>
> But I think—and this will hardly surprise you—that the poem has always hoped for this very reason, to speak also on behalf of the *strange*—no, I can no longer use this word here—*on behalf of the other*, who knows, perhaps of an *altogether other*. (CP 48)

"But the poem speaks"; "but it speaks"; "But I think . . . " The poem, absolutely singular, its own date, speaks. It does not collapse into its own individuation. In order to speak itself, to speak its particularity, the poem must be mindful of its dates, of its origin and its future. The poem speaks on its own behalf. "But" suggests that despite the very particularity of the poem's date, it cannot be reduced to that date. The poem continues to speak and to offer an encounter. Derrida explains that, in order for the poem to continue to speak, it must reach beyond its pure singularity to render itself intelligible.[12] It must efface its date, its singularity, as it encounters the date of the other. At the same time, the poem's concealed date is commemorated since it is what renders this speaking intelligible to the other. In stepping beyond itself, the poem encounters the not so distant other, the altogether other, and itself.

At the end of his speech, Celan finds that what allows for and leads to encounters is both immaterial, like language, and terrestrial, like the earth. Between poles, it "rejoins itself and on the way serenely crosses even the tropics: I find . . . a *meridian*" (CP 55). This rejoinder is not, however, to an origin or to an identical self. The movement of the meridian is as a semicircle, not a circle.[13] Returning to the self is possible only through both the projection and openness toward what is other. The poem, like the meridian, steps beyond itself and journeys toward the altogether other, but the poem's origin is not lost in this movement. Rather, because of the meridian that joins the two poles of the poem, of the already and the not-yet, the poem's encounter with the other is only possible because it remains mindful of its date. Because of this inseparability and the movement between the poles, the poem is never fully settled or at home. The poem encounters itself as other, as uncanny, and also something altogether other. Yet, the meridian, as the connective, preserves the poem in its movement. While meanings may turn to ash, to annihilation, the poem continues to speak. Celan and Hölderlin hold in common that the poetic word searches for the expression of what exceeds it, but Celan shows that we must think the possible annihilation of language even more than we have. The possibility of death cannot be separated from the possibility of life.

This sense of keeping death and life together is found in Celan's poem, "Sprich Auch Du" or "Speak You Also."[14]

Speak, you also,
speak as the last,
speak your say.

Speak—
But do not split the No from the Yes.
Give your say also the sense:
give it the shadow.

Give it shadow enough,
give it as much
as you know is dealt out to you between
midnight and midday and midnight.

Look around:
look how it leaps alive round—
at death! Alive!
Truly speaks the one who speaks Shadows.

But now shrinks the place where you stand:
Where to now, shadowstripped, where to?
Climb. Grope upwards.
Thinner you grow, more unknowable, finer.
Finer: a thread
on which it wants to lower, the star:
to swim down below, below
where it sees itself shimmer: in the swell
of wandering words.

Here we find a series of imperatives and observations. There is an I— though who this I is, we do not know—telling a You to speak, and not only to speak, but to speak on its behalf and to give it the shadow. What does it mean for You to give speech the shadow? And what would be shadow enough, in proportion to what has already been dealt out? Recall Celan's Flinker bookstore response that, for language to speak more truly, it must become grayer. This new language is "concerned with precision" and not with aesthetics. It does not try to render poetical, but rather "tries to measure the area of the given and the possible" (CP 16). Similarly, in the reflection on

Jené's painting, Celan writes of diving beneath the sea's surface to the "dark springs" to encounter language. In these remotest regions, he finds a new radiance "born from the marriage of strange and most strange." The images in this radiance, though, are not fully laid bare, but remain both veiled and unveiled. The light of the radiance is not daylight; it is inhabited by figures familiar but unrecognizable. Thus, encountering the new language requires an attunement to the shadows, to the veiling, to the unrecognizable.

To give speech the shadow, then, means to resist what obviously shines forth and instead to preserve what remains beneath the surface. The shadow is what is appropriate between the different changes of light—between the absolute darkness of midnight and absolute light of midday, cycling between either pole. Dealt between these polarities, the shadow itself is not absolute, but grows and fades. To give speech shadow enough is not to obscure speech or the truth, but rather to orient oneself toward it as the proper measure. For example, in nautical navigation, sailors track their position by observing the sun's relation to the meridian and celestial poles. By attending to the shadows crossing and the encounter with the meridian, one knows her orientation. To know one's orientation to and with language similarly requires an orientation toward the shadows. Moreover, like the sailor, the one who speaks is on the way. Here the question is not only where You are, but where You will go. The star itself wants to see its shimmering among wandering words.

In "Bread and Wine," Hölderlin writes that "clear eyes too love the shadows" (H 179). Earlier in the poem, he speaks of a divine fire that urges us to go to those open spaces so that we might "seek what is ours, distant, remote though it be!" (H 181). Here Hölderlin suggests that what is ours is that measure, which is "common to all, though his own to each one is also allotted/ Each of us makes for the places, reaches the place that he can" (178–179).[15] To find what is our ownmost, to speak on our behalf, we require an eternal measure that has been dealt out between midday and midnight. Even this eternal measure, then, is not fully laid bare. Rather, recognizing the measure requires attention to the shadows and enjoyment of night. To reach what is ours, we venture to distant places that are our own. We reach what we can, although we neither reach an ultimate destination, nor return to where we were. The poet is the one who orients herself toward her finitude to venture out into these unknown places. We might read the question "Where now, shadowstripped, will you go?" as posed to the poet. For the clear eyes that have perceived the eternal measure, where do they go when they are stripped of shade? Without shadows, the self and perhaps the measure also become unrecognizable. At the moment of speaking oneself according to that measure, the self becomes other, and must grope its way into new spaces beyond itself as words continue to wander.

The closing line of Hölderlin's "In Lovely Blueness" is "Life is death, and death a kind of life." To be alive is to be on the way to death. Because death has no end, it is not mortal; it is also a kind of life. The aim is not to dispel this tension, but to preserve it and orient oneself to it. To know what is appropriate, to be attuned to the eternal measure, then, is to hold oneself in relation to this harmony, thus reaching toward the limits of the self as mortal, but not fully surpassing that limit. For Hölderlin, there is always a precariousness to this harmony. At the same time the tension is held together, there is also a withdrawal of sense. To render familiar is thus at the same time to open space for the strange. Human life is a continuous melody of these interplays.

In Celan's poem, "Speak You Also," we see similarly that life and death are not only present together, but that life leaps where death is. The one cannot be separated from the other. A thread remains between the star in the heavens and the swell below. The more the You ventures out, loses the sense of place, and gropes upward, the more the desire arises to lower down to the depths where the self shines back. This thread of connection sheds some light on what it means to not split the No from the Yes. To speak the No is to recognize annihilation or absence while to speak the Yes is to speak life or presence. Yet, as we see in Hölderlin's idea that life is death, speaking life or presence is possible only because one at the same time speaks death or absence. Speech wanders between these two opposite poles. The Yes of life can be spoken only if one also speaks the No of death. Thus, speaking the Yes, the poem at the same time brings absence to presence, and in speaking the No, it brings presence to absence. Being is not only fully being, but also nothing, and vice versa.

In *Economy of the Unlost*, Anne Carson places the ancient Greek poet, Simonides, in conversation with Celan, tracing the ways in which negation, blank spaces, and emptiness come to presence in their works. The poet, as the speaker of memory, transforms our human relation to time.[16] The poet calls the past into the present by allowing the dead to live again. The poem and poet venture forth into yet unknown territories and terrains. This, explains Carson, is what distinguishes the poem from the painting: the poem can "render the invisible."[17] More precisely, what the poem renders is nothing. The poem is the space between being and nothing. In changing this relationship to time, the poet changes the relationship to mortality. The poet can "negate the negating action of death" because of her special view that "sees death everywhere and finds life within it, a view that perceives presence as absence and finds a way to turn the relation inside out."[18] When Celan writes "do not split the No from the Yes," he thus renders nothing visible. If nothing is now present, the field of possibilities is radically altered by transforming our relation to time and space. When the poet negates the negating action of death, she does not negate death altogether. Mortality is not overcome, but placed at the fore. What is changed, however, is what death means. As Carson observes, Celan witnessed the strange math of six million becoming zero[19] and the place of the concentration camps becomes the universe of nothing.[20] Mindful of its dates, like the 20th of January, what the poem allows is the very confrontation with that negation; the poem demands responsibility for negation.

LANGUAGE MESH: ABSENCE AND ADDRESS

The poem speaks and calls us to respond. To speak may mean to use one's mouth, but one also speaks with hands, with gestures, with organs, and, importantly, with silence. In several of Celan's poems from the *Sprachgitter* series, we see a coupling between mouths and eyes. For much of the history of western philosophy, the primacy of sight has been maintained, particularly in reference to reason, with blindness signifying ignorance. Indeed, as Plato tells us in the allegory of the cave, education is not a matter of inserting knowledge into blind eyes, but rather, "takes for granted that sight is there but that it isn't turned the right way or looking where it ought to look, and it tries to redirect it appropriately."[21] Eyes that are blind could never achieve knowledge of the truth. As the prisoner ascends from the cave, his eyes are temporarily dazzled, but ultimately what he catches sight of is the Form of the Good. Heidegger and others assert that philosophy, and especially Greek philosophy, prioritizes ocularity because of the metaphysics of presence (BT 170).[22] What it is for something to be true is for its essence or being to be present; thus, sight is a way of grasping this presence. Not splitting the No from the Yes specifically defies the metaphysics of presence. To speak the truth here means to speak both what is and what is not at once. It is to challenge what it means for anything to be present in the first place. If the poem is to be truer, it becomes so not by stripping away all contingencies or finding an eternal essence. Rather, it becomes truer by not splitting the No from the Yes. To render absence or nothing visible does not reinscribe the primacy of sight because such rendering allows only a glance, an awareness of what is at the periphery, rather than a gaze that fixes in place.

This glance is evoked in Celan's poem, "Sprachgitter"[23] or "Language Mesh":

Eyeround between the bars.

Ciliate lid
rows upward,
releases a glance.

Iris, swimmer, dreamless and dreary:
the sky, heart-grey, must be near.

Slanted, in the iron socket,
the smoking splinter.
By its lightsense
you guess the soul.

(If I were like you. If you were like me.
Did we not stand
under *one* trade wind?
We are strangers.)

The flagstones. On them,
close to each other, the two
heart-grey pools:
two
mouthsfull of silence.

The "gitter" of "Sprachgitter" can mean grille, lattice, grid, or mesh, among others. It suggests a solid object, of varying materials, penetrated by nothing. What it is for a grille to be a grille, for example, is for it to be solid, but not entirely. It is a grille insofar as negative space is present. Grilles and meshes also block or close things off. What does it mean, then, for language to be a grille or a mesh? The poem begins with eye's roundness between, though not necessarily behind, bars. Although this might at first suggest prison bars, we find the eyes are not incarcerated. They occupy the space in between. They are not fully restrained: the "lid / rows upward, / releases a glance." The iris swims, though without energy. In the eye, there remains a smoking splinter—evoking ashes of burned out meaning—that has not been fully extinguished. It still provides a sense of light, if not light itself, by which we can "guess the soul." And then, an interruption. The speaker addresses the listener, drawing them together in conversation that is at the same time a moment of alienation. We no longer stand together. We are strangers. And yet, here we are, held together in this moment of encounter. At the end of the poem, two puddles mirror the eyes and the sky, both reflecting heart-gray. But where there were eyes, we are now two mouthsfull of silence. We, strangers to one another gathered in the conversation of address, remain silent. The glance, which allows insight into the soul, renders silence.

In Celan's poem, "Tübingen, January," written three months after "The Meridian," we find a similar confluence of dates, eyes, and silences.[24] The poem also suggests Celan's ambiguous relationship to Hölderlin and his own encounters with language:

Tübingen/January
Eyes talked into
blindness.

Their—"a riddle is
the purely
originated"—, their
memory of
swimming Hölderlin's towers, gulls
whirling around.

Visits of drowned joiners to
these
diving words:

Came,
came a man,
if a man came into the world, today, with
the light-beard of the
patriarchs: he could
if he spoke of this
time, he
could
only babble and babble
over-, over-
againagain.
("Pallaksch. Pallaksch.")

The poem begins mindful of its date. January suggests again the 20th of January. The poem is also mindful of its place. Tübingen marks the place where Hölderlin lived in his final years. Yet, the next lines of the poem, "Eyes talked into / Blindness," suggest a resistance to an obvious conclusion. The meaning is not immediately visible. Charles Bambach ventures that January might also refer to Janus, the two-headed god of beginnings, looking both at the past and the future. January, Janus, marks the ambiguity of Tübingen: Hölderlin's tower standing high above the banks of the Neckar, preserved in memory and standing for a new way of Germanic poetic speaking, paired with images of drowning and submerging and the man of today who can only babble.[25] Whereas some commentators, such as Anne Carson, read this poem as "a praise of Hölderlin,"[26] this Janus face suggests Celan's relation to Hölderlin cannot be thought without also considering the ways in which Hölderlin's poetry was taken up in the Nazi regime and the ways in which the new Germanic speaking silenced more than six million. The connection between January and a river also calls to mind the death of Rosa Luxemburg, whose executed body was thrown into the Landwehr Canal in January 1919. Although Celan finds in Hölderlin a common spirit and bond, this poem points to a failure to question language, especially in terms of its historicity.

The eyes are talked into or over to [*überredete*] blindness. There is a distinction between the eyes "talked" [*redete*] into blindness and the possibility of speaking [*spräch*] that appears in the third stanza. Talking suggests everyday speech, the speech of the many that is not mindful of dates or that remains satisfied with superficial understanding or, conversely, totalization.[27] *Überreden* also connotes cajoling or persuading. As Heidegger discusses in *Being and Time*, idle talk [*Gerede*] "divests us of the task of understanding" and is a "closing off" (169). Idle talk does not necessarily intend to close off, but proceeds by acting as if everything has already been understood, and so fails to question meaning and itself. Idle talk characterizes the everyday way we engage in ordinary life, often swept along through the motions of the everyday. Because idle talk does not ask questions, it moves through a prescribed attunement toward the world. Idle talk, then, becomes particularly dangerous by precluding the possibility of criticism or resistance. Idle talk has a totalizing effect that precludes the possibility of genuine conversation and authenticity.

The opposite of idle talk would be poetic speaking. Gadamer concludes the speech given to the Hölderlin-Gesellschaft, also in Tübingen, with the idea that the kind of stammering that belongs to Hölderlin's searching for words perhaps must become the future legacy of our current age. He explains, "There is no need to wonder either that there is no widespread resonance of poetry in public, or that those who take the word of poetry to be an indispensable element of life do not crow more joyfully and serenely over the position of a poetic legacy, but rather themselves, as crowded and stammering, gaze into this our world and out into our future."[28] Speaking resists the frictionless idle talk, and indeed, idle talk affords it almost no room. Poetic speaking, though, continues to try to speak, but in ways that are mindful of dates and characterized more by silence than by vocalization.

This relationship between silence and speaking is at the center of Celan's prose poem, "Conversation in the Mountains." He presents a conversation between a Jew, who, like Büchner's Lenz, walks through the mountains, and his cousin, whom he encounters walking along the path. Though no date is mentioned in this "Conversation in the Mountains," the invocation of Lenz suggests again the 20th of January, the decision to strip everything, including life, from millions. Donatella di Cesare believes Celan also references the Shoah through his employing the disparaging term, Jew, and anti-Semitic attitudes toward Jews, such as "what does he have that is really his own, that is not borrowed, taken, and not returned?" (CP 17).[29] In "The Meridian," Celan describes Lenz as wanting to walk on his head to orient himself to groundlessness. Here, too, the cousins, Jew Gross and Jew Klein, set off as groundless as they walk out into the shadow that both is and is not theirs. Although surrounded by brilliant blooms and plants bearing the names of

Turk's-cap and *dianthus superbus*, the cousins are not named, except as having unpronounceable names, as being large or small, and as being Jews. This may at first imply that the cousins lack singularity, seen only as particular instances of a general category, but Rochelle Tobias argues that because the names remain unpronounceable, the men remain singularities because an unpronounceable, thus unspeakable, name can never be invoked for any other representation than this singular being.[30] Singularity is informed by alienation, shadows, and groundlessness; to be singular is to be both Yes and No.

The cousins, the narrator describes, have no eyes to see these blooms. Or, they do have eyes, but a moveable half veil hangs in the eyes. Every image gets tangled in the veil, "half image, half veil" (18). The cousins are surrounded by the silence of the road, of the walking stick, of the stones. Although the cousins are "windbags," they struggle to talk to one another. Their tongues stumble and their lips do not move correctly, but they must talk. The silent stones, however, do not talk, but speak. One cousin manages to say that who speaks does not talk because no one hears. To speak is to ask, "Do you hear me?" (20). The cousin repeats this phrase over and over. "Do-you-hear-me does not say anything, does not answer, because Do-you-hear-me is one with the glaciers . . ." (20). That Do-you-hear-me does not say anything does not mean that it does not speak. Rather, precisely in silence, it speaks itself. It holds itself open to an encounter with the other. It speaks like the stones. Speaking is conversation rather than monologue.

At the beginning of "Conversation in the Mountain," the cousins, with veiled eyes talked into blindness, have only idle talk and cannot make themselves understood. By the end, though, this talking has turned into speaking.[31] One cousin begins to recognize the nature surrounding them, calling the turk's cap lily and corn-salad by name, and recognizes the half-veils that remain in their eyes. Like the eyelid rowing itself northward, the veils do not entirely foreclose the possibility of sight, but allow for images, like the star, to be half-star, both itself and not. To understand and recognize is not to strip away all shadows, but to recognize the play between concealed and unconcealed. What begins as talking or repetition between two independent poles becomes conversation as the two cousins find themselves, like Lenz, on the way through the mountains, with one another: "you Gross and me Klein . . . with our unpronounceable names, with our shadows, our own and not our own, you here and me here" (CP 22).

The closing lines of this text serve as the response to the question, "Do-you-hear-me?" What the cousins recognize is the place of their encounter. The I and the You are gathered into a We, but that space of encounter is neither final nor total. This recognition begins with memory of a previous meeting and develops through the attunement to what remains unspoken. The cousins are the same insofar as they are both windbags with sticks and unpronounceable names, but they are different from one another as Gross and Klein and with their shadows their own and not. Through their wandering across the mountains, the cousins have encountered one another, but also themselves. Thus, the Do-you-hear-me is addressed as much to the other as to the self. The cousins have learned to keep the Yes not split from the No.

"Pallaksch. Pallaksch." The final line of the poem refers us again to Hölderlin. Celan writes in a letter to Ilana Shmueli, "A word of Hölderlin already appeared once in a poem of mine, 'Tübingen, Jänner.' There at the end it reads 'Pallaksch' by which Hölderlin, in the time of his madness, meant Yes and No at the same time."[32] This phrase refuses to collapse either Yes or No into the other or to separate them from one another completely. Rather than mere speechlessness, this neologism articulates what cannot be said. As such, Do-you-hear-me echoes throughout. The poem ends with a resolution of what cannot be resolved. The patriarch, who serves as prophet of the future, here is tasked with memory of the towers and of the "Pallaksch. Pallaksch." In "Tübingen, January," Celan cites Hölderlin's poem, "The Rhine": "a riddle is the purely originated" [*ein Rätsel ist Reinentsprungenes*]. The patriarch remembers this riddle. The play between *Rein-/Rhein* suggests again the coupling of origin and water. We might read this as Heraclitean—the river, as pure origin, is never self-same, but always flowing. The origin is a riddle, scarcely revealed in language. The origin is both Yes and No.

Celan's use of "Pallaksch," prompts us also to think of the connotation of *rein* in terms of the purity laws of Nazi Germany. The memory of Hölderlin's towers cannot be separated from the genocide engendered in the same language. Bernhard Böschenstein explains that Celan's poem marks a reversal of Hölderlin's. Rather than the poetic words springing forth from an unknown source, here they are plunged underwater. The origin in Celan's poem is that of a "more originary possibility of poeticizing, which now can only be remembered from out of negation."[33] The poem, as Yes and No, remains both the not yet of actualization and the not yet of destruction. The patriarch, between the poles of past and future, can only babble over and over again-again.[34] Di Cesare draws from Primo Levi to illustrate that in Auschwitz and other concentration camps, one's fate was especially dire if one did not speak the language. The guards identified those who could not speak or could not understand as babblers or barbarians, thus lacking humanity. Levi explains that those who could not communicate, could not understand or be understood, were more likely to suffer greatly and die earlier. If one is not human, then any treatment is justified. The failure to communicate with another, to make oneself understood, also means the failure of the self. Life and language are thus fundamentally connected. Even babbling remains a Do-you-hear-me, a still here, that refuses total annihilation.[35]

That the final word of Celan's poem is Hölderlin's own suggests that Hölderlin's work cannot be fully appropriated by totalizing forces. A seemingly nonsense word continues to resist. As discussed in the beginning of this chapter, Gadamer takes the search for words to be the most essential form of poeticizing. As we have seen with Hölderlin and Celan, the task of the poet is not to recover absolute meaning or provide eternal meaning. Rather, the poet is oriented toward the limits of language, searching out new words and meanings that resist such totalization. To continue speaking, one attends to what cannot be spoken. One attends to the limits of language. To continue speaking, one falls silent.[36]

In Celan's poem, *Weggebeizt* (G 180–81), these themes of speech, talk, and silence come into greater crystallization. He begins,

Etched away by the
ray-wind of your language
the manycolored chatter of the pasted on-
experienced—the hundred-
tongued lie-
poem, the noem.

Though given voice by hundreds of tongues, such a poem is no poem. Rather than *Gedicht*, it is *Genicht*: noem. The chatter of the hundred-tongued gives the illusion of illusion of insight. Decorative and ornate, such poems move on pretense. They are the poems of idle talk. As spoken by a hundred tongues, these poems also do not attend to the singular or particular, but operate in the generalities that are not really lived, but assembled or pasted on experience. At first, it seems that the noem, *Meingedicht*, is mine, yet as Gadamer suggests Celan himself clarifies, *Meingedicht* is better understood in terms of *Meineid*, a false witness or broken oath (GC 137). The hundred tongues bear false witness because they do not attend to singularity. The noem belongs to a hundred tongues because it is so general as to belong to everyone. Language, though, etches away at such superficialities. Importantly, it is *your* language that etches away with its wind. The poem continues:

Whirled
out,
free
the way through the human-
shaped snow,
the penitent's snow, to
the hospitable
glacier-rooms and -tables.

Deep
in the time-crevasse
by
the honeycomb ice
waits, a breath-crystal,
your irrevocable
witness.

Again, we find an imperative addressed to an unknown You. In this instance, You should free your way past human activity and toward the crystal of breath, deep within Time's crevasse. The coupling between breath and crystal is at first discordant. On the one hand, breath is fleeting, insubstantial, nearly immaterial. On the other hand, the crystal is a sharp presence formed over eons by the compression of carbon. In place of the flowing rivers or puddles of the other poems discussed so far, we have water solidified in ice and snow. As Gadamer suggests, time, which ordinarily flows, is here interrupted and stands frozen (GC 125). The breath, ordinarily itself fleeting, is momentarily preserved as a crystal; it waits. Michael Hamburger renders *Wabeneis* as "alveolate ice," coupling the pattern of the lungs with the breath crystal.[37] Penitent's snow, *Büßereis*, refers to the formations of snow found at high altitudes that resemble a field of figures kneeling in prayer, waiting. The ray wind of language mentioned at the beginning of the poem suggests a directionality. Here, too, Celan embarks on a topological and geological exploration. The poem digs down below the surface of everyday talk to locate this irrevocable, irrefutable witness. As the language that speaks the poem, and not the noem, the witness attends to singularity.

As we saw in "The Meridian," the poetic word bears witness by being on the way and mindful of dates. In his poem, "Ashglory," Celan concludes that no one bears witness for the witness. That poem marks, on the one hand, a memory of his childhood friend who drowned,[38] and, on the other, the ashes of those murdered in the concentration camps. In "Poetics and Politics of Witnessing," Derrida focuses at length on the multiple readings of this final line of "Ashglory." What does it mean to bear witness? What does it mean to bear witness for a witness? What does it mean that no one bears witness for the witness? Derrida reads this as perhaps the poem bearing witness to bearing witness. He cites Murray Krieger's assertion that art's role is to reveal the mask as mask.[39] In bearing witness, I ask to be believed. I cannot necessarily prove the veracity of my claim except insofar as I am believed to be a responsible witness, one who can answer for myself what I claim. To bear witness, Derrida suggests, is to claim that You must believe me. Bearing witness, then, is not an objective, disinterested claim of fact, but a claim, a plea of "I'm still here." The sense of "for" in "bearing witness for" might mean on behalf of, in place of, or in front of.[40] To say that no one bears witness for the witness is to say that none of these three meanings is possible. For those who perished in the horrors of Auschwitz, I cannot substitute witness of my own death or survival for their own or replace mine with theirs. Although death belongs to us all, each of us has our own. I cannot, must not, take death's singularity as a commodity to be exchanged. The poem, as bearing witness, in fact bears witness to the very limits of witnessing. In speaking the limits of bearing witness, the poem is silent, but this silence continues to speak. Derrida explains, "Revealing its mask as a mask, but without showing itself, without presenting itself, perhaps presenting its non-presentation as such, representing it, it thus speaks about bearing witness in general, but above all about the poem that it is, about itself in its singularity, and about the bearing witness to which every poem bears witness."[41] The poem unmasks, but does not reveal an indisputable truth below the surface. Rather, it reveals itself as a mask. The poem speaks itself, or, as Celan states in "The Meridian," it holds itself at the margins. Its speaking is a singularity of self-presentation. This is not a total presentation, but a presentation of non-presentation. Like the eyes with moveable veils, the poem allows not absolute unconcealment, but the unconcealment of the imperative to keep Yes and No not split. This singularity is also the site of solitude. Because no one else can bear witness for the poem, the poem is, as Celan suggests, lonely and in need of another (CP 49). Thus, bearing witness is a form of address. As soon as "I" am present, a "You" is invoked. To bear witness is to address another and open oneself to an answer, to responsibility.

Returning to the sense of an irrefutable witness in Celan's poem, we find the poetic word beneath the surface. The honeycomb ice, like the language mesh, is solid, yet has open spaces. The witness is irrefutable because there is no third term to verify the correspondence of the witness. Rather, the poem asks to be believed and asks to be heard. The "Do-you-hear-me [that] is one with the glaciers" (CP 20) is the address that bears witness for both the I and the You. In contrast to the idle talk that gives rise to the noem, the speaking here is a breath of stillness and silence. The breath is *your* witness because it is your language that clears away the false witnesses. Though purity connotes clearing away and crystallization of vapor, the poem speaks not because it has uncovered a pure, essential meaning. Rather, the poem speaks because it is a form of address between the I and the You, between the Yes and the No.

ATEMWENDE: POETRY AS CONVERSATION

In "The Meridian," Celan describes poetry as an *Atemwende*, a turning of breath. In this turning of breath, the poem turns toward the other. Thus, what it is for the poem to be itself is, as this turning, to at the same time be attuned to another. Poetry, its own exhalation, its own speech, addresses us and turns our breath as well. Rather than representing something else, Celan explains, poetry speaks itself. In directing us to its own linguisticality, the poem also speaks the limits of language as such. Celan states, "The poem holds its ground at its own margin. In order to endure, it constantly calls and pulls itself back from an 'already-no-more' into a 'still-here'" (CP 49). In other words, nothing grounds the poem or holds it open but itself. The "still here" is the poem's speaking, freed from external verification. By defining the poem as a turning of breath or a breath-crystal, Celan affirms that the poetic word is corporeal. It is there.

The breath-crystal is, to be sure, a metaphor that signals the corporeal "thickness of poetry."[42] But it is more than a metaphor: the breath-crystal is a symbol of poetry. To illustrate this, I suggest we look to Gadamer's distinction between a symbol and an allegory. Whereas the allegory stands for something else, the symbol refers to itself. In ancient Greece, the *symbolon* was a fragment, often one half of a token, of remembrance. In an act of hospitality, a host would break an object in two, keeping one half and giving the other to the guest. If, much later, the two or their families encountered one another again, the two fragments could be fitted together to be whole again. The symbol is thus a token of remembrance that points both to itself and to another. Furthermore, as preserving this memory, the symbol serves as the basis for recognition. For Gadamer, art and poetry are symbols because they are not merely representations of meaning, but mean something themselves. The works express themselves (RB 30–33). Referencing Valéry's comparison of the poetic word to gold coins, Gadamer explains that "the language of poetry is not a mere point that refers to something else, but, like the gold coin, is what it represents" (RB 133). Understanding a poem thus is not a matter of simply uncovering a meaning, but rather attuning ourselves to the very texture—the feeling, sound, tone, rhythm, vocality—of the poem.[43] The poem is corporeal. In presenting itself, the poem also presents what remains but is no longer present; that is, the poem presents, like one half of the *symbolon*, the other. Holding open the space for itself and the other, preserving both previous encounters and encounters yet to come, the poem bears witness. The poet, as namer of memory, serves as host.[44]

By turning us to this other who addresses us, the poem becomes a conversation, addressing the poet and reader alike. Gathering us into it, the poem points toward "open, empty, free spaces" that we venture into where we also encounter ourselves. The paths opened by the poems "are encounters, paths from a voice to a listening You, natural paths, outlines for existence perhaps, for projecting ourselves into the search for ourselves . . . A kind of homecoming" (CP 53). The poem, as a token of remembrance, allows for the recognition of the familiar in the foreign. Yet, as on the way and searching, we move toward only a kind of homecoming. What it is for the poem to be poem, as the place of encounter on new paths, is that this familiarity is never total, but it is never entirely impossible, either. Like the eccentric path described by Hölderlin, the path of the poem is a constant negotiation between familiar and strange. This uncanniness, this *Unheimlichkeit*, belongs to poetry. The poem is the mystery, the *Geheimnis* of encounter. As opening the space for the encounter, the poem reaches out for the You and initiates a moment of remembrance and recognition in the bond between the I and You. Yet, such an encounter remains partially veiled, partially concealed. This is especially the case for figures like Celan for whom German afforded both the possibility to say what otherwise could not be said and the possibility of silence, of murderous, death-bringing speech.

Celan begins his Bremen speech with echoes of both Hölderlin and Heidegger. He reflects on the etymological connection between thinking, *denken*, and thanking, *danken*. When we extend this connection to *Andenken*, remembrance, then "we enter the semantic fields of memory and devotion" (CP 33). If we follow this line of thought, then we see, too, the etymological connection to poetry, *Dichtung*. Heidegger draws together thinking and thanking in *What is Called Thinking?* to suggest that thanking is memory of what is to be thought and gratitude for what is most thought, namely being and the unconcealment of being.[45] This unconcealment is never total. What it is for truth to be unconcealed is at the same time for it to be concealed, that is, *a-lētheia*. The particular task of the poet is the naming of things, the poetic projection, that brings them into appearance.

The closing lines of Hölderlin's "Remembrance" are, ". . . But memory/ Is taken and given by the ocean, / And the eyes of love do not waver in their gaze, / But poets establish what remains" (H 267). Memory, *Gedächtnis*, is like the message in the bottle described by Celan. The poem, mindful of dates, both casts and receives the message. What remains, amid all losses, is language. The poet holds and preserves such memories. The eyes of love are not the eyes of calculation or mastery; they are not the eyes of a subject fixing objects in their essences. In other words, these eyes are not those of the Western metaphysical tradition. Rather, the eyes are eyes of love. They are relational and hospitable in holding open what is other. As discussed in the previous chapter, love, according to Hölderlin, is that joining force that holds together beings in their singularity. The poet thinks mortal thoughts and attends to love and deeds.

Since it is attuned to memory, according to Heidegger, poetic speaking is attuned to history. Poetic projection is no universal abstraction, but an "opening up of that into which human being as historical is already cast" (PLT 72). History is the appointed task of a people rather than a chronology of events. It marks the origin of the unconcealment of truth. Heidegger identifies Hölderlin as a poet who speaks the destiny of a people. Remembrance, *Andenken*, is a kind of founding because it is neither recollection of the past nor prediction of the future. Rather, the poet thinks back to the origin and concealment that allows for such unconcealment in the first place (EHP 171). The poet dwells by abiding in the secure destiny, which "has sent the poet into the essence of poetic activity, and chosen him to be the first sacrifice" (EHP 171). The poet greets this destiny and remains with it, holding open the gift and dispensation of destiny and remembrance.

This concern with time, poetic speaking, and being at home echoes in many of Celan's poems as well as in his complicated relationship with Heidegger.[46] As we have seen, the poet allows for things to make themselves present. The poet bears witness to dates and to things. Both Heidegger and Celan remain engaged in topological research, concerned with the specificity of place and space. Yet, although Heidegger consistently emphasizes the importance of preserving and sheltering, of dwelling and measuring, his insistence on destiny obscures the particularity of those very mortals or dates at stake. Similarly, although he maintains that there is a pervasive homelessness and mortality in human existence and that poetry provides a way of attuning ourselves to that homelessness, he, in ways like Hölderlin, does not fully engage the possibility of total annihilation. In other words, he does not consider what it would mean for not only the poet to be *unterwegs* or for language to be *un-heimlich*, but also for them to be fully exiled.

Celan's poem, "Todtnauberg" (G 282–83) reflects on his meeting with Heidegger at Heidegger's hut in the Black Forest in 1967:

Arnica, eye-bright, the
drink from the well with the
star-die above,

in the
hut,

into the book
—whose name did it take in
before mine? –,
the line inscribed
into this book about
a hope, today,
for a thinker's
coming
word
in the heart,

woodland sward, unlevelled,
orchis and orchis, singly

crudeness, later, in driving
clearly

who drive us, the man,
who listens in,

the half-
trodden log-
path in the high moor,

dampness
much.

This encounter between Denker and Dichter begins in healing and hope and ends in disappointment.[47] The poem, which begins "eyebright" and "star-crowned," speaks of a hope for a coming word in the heart of a thinking man. Arnica, belonging to a family of star-shaped blooms, is used as a salve for wounds and pain; *Augentrost*, eyebright or Euphrasia, has been traditionally been used to heal the eyes and poor memory. The poem explores and illuminates the landscape surrounding the hut, including different varieties of grass, the pervasive dampness, and changes in topography.

In the center of the poem stands the hut's guestbook, full of dates and names. The poet offers a brief interruption to ask about whose name was inscribed above his own. The poem reflects Celan's own entry in the guestbook: "In the cabin-book, with the view of the fountain-star, with a hope for a coming word in the heart."[48] The language of words in heart calls to mind Heidegger's interpretation of "Remembrance." The heart, Hölderlin writes, intends to hear, and such a conversation is good. In his notes for "Todtnauberg," Celan revises the poem to add, "Since we are a conversation, on which we choke, on which I choke."[49] This play on Heidegger's interpretation of Hölderlin's line "Since we have been a conversation . . ." (EHP 51) turns the unifying conversation into one that cuts off breath and prevents speaking.

For Heidegger, speaking and hearing are "co-original" and spring from the same origin of a shared world with others (57). Thus, this conversation is one conversation, unified in and as grounding that world. Thus, since the grounding of humans, since the time of all times, we have been conversation: "Both—to be one conversation and to be historical—are equally ancient, they belong together, and they are the same" (57). The conversation and history are one. Although Heidegger does not mean history as specific dates, but as a people's founding of truth, it seems to be precisely this line of thought that Celan protests. While this originary conversation is supposed to create the possibility of all conversation, Celan writes instead that it chokes; it cuts off any breath. It refuses the turning of breath. The language that Heidegger valorizes is the very language used to advance the Shoah. The urgent question of who "we" are presses in, but Heidegger does not entertain it. The question of whose history, whose name is registered, drops out.

"Todtnauberg" is full of references to the Shoah. The *Sternwürfel* evokes the Star of David that Jewish people were forced to wear. In a letter to Gisèle Celan-Lestrange, Celan explains how the *Augentrost*, the eyebright, reminds him of his time in the work camp. Furthermore, he frequently associates the high moors with the concentration camps.[50] A clue to Celan's reservations reflected in this poem is found in his mention of a hope for a coming word in the heart. The same phrase occurs in Celan's entry in Heidegger's guestbook:

In the cabin–book, with the view of the fountain–star,
with a hope for a coming word in the heart
25th of July, 1967
Paul Celan[51]

Here, Celan is mindful of dates, marking his encounter with Heidegger. The guestbook presents a log of other such encounters, perhaps marked by similar anticipations. As mindful of dates, though, the poet attends not only to those dates recorded, but also those rendered absent. The encounter with Heidegger cannot be thought without also attending to the voices of those tortured, annihilated, and silenced. That the word is coming, is *unterwegs*, means that this word is not final. As coming, it is sent out from a particular date and seeks what is other.

Returning to the Meridian speech, we find another discussion of the poetry in terms of hope. Celan writes that the poem has "always hoped" to speak on behalf of the altogether other (CP 48). This "who knows," he remarks, is all he can add to the "old hopes." The hope marks the very possibility of encounter between the self and the other, even the altogether other. Although the poem finds itself underway and lonely, it still "takes such thoughts for its home and hope—a word for living creatures" (48). In the middle space between poles, the poem holds itself open at its margins and holds its own ground. The poem endures as still here.

As holding itself open for an encounter, as a turning of breath, the poem remains hopeful. Celan explains, "Nobody can tell how long the pause for breath—hope and thought—will last." Hope and thought, *das Verhoffen und der Gedanke*, characterize this *Atemwende* as the poem heads toward the other where it can be free. As Celan further reminds us, the still-here of the poem can only come from poets who remember "their own existence, their own physical nature." Such a poem, itself corporeal, can only ever be sent forth from a particular existence. The coming word, then, is perhaps issued from Celan himself, seeking an encounter with Heidegger as wholly other. As the word continues to speak, it resonates with the sounds and the silences of "still-here." Indeed, as tending more toward silence, it cannot force itself upon the other, but must be received like a message in a bottle that might wash up "on the shoreline of the heart" (CP 35). Because such a hope for the coming word cannot be fully determined, it remains at risk.

Heidegger recognizes the risk at stake in language. In *Elucidations on Hölderlin's Poetry*, he focuses on a line from Hölderlin's verse: "That is why language, the most dangerous of goods, has been given to man . . . so that he may bear witness to what he is . . ." (EHP 51). Language is the most dangerous because it is what allows danger to appear in the first place. Language, as both clearing and concealing, allows for the human to be "exposed to something manifest: beings which press upon him and inflame him in his existence, or nonbeings which deceive and disappoint him" (EHP 55). Language never fully makes evident what is essential or what is deception, but rather allows the human to orient herself toward her situation with others. Poetic speaking springs forth from the original conversation, thus from the danger of language, that issues an original claim. Heidegger continues, "To stand under such a claim means to be able to hear. That is the essential ground of genuine saying. Saying is originally a hearing, just as a genuine ability to hear is an original re-saying (not a mere mechanical repetition) of what has been heard" (146). To say, then, is to hear and to face the risk that one has misheard. Heidegger suggests in "What Are Poets For?" that the poets are the most venturesome as those who venture to say. Such saying is also hearing, which requires an active receptivity to language and being. The poet, as cast out of ordinary life, has the most dangerous occupation. She must consistently work against illusion and common understandings without full certainty of having accomplished this task. Thus, the poet is never fully at home and finds the poetic work uncanny in both its danger and innocence.

Although Heidegger correctly identifies the poet as cast out and not at home, he fails to account for the more totalizing exile experienced by Celan and others. Such exile is not only the result of the distance from ordinary life, but the loss of intelligibility and the possibility of annihilation. If Adorno suggests that writing poetry after Auschwitz is barbaric because there is no longer a way to perform cultural criticism without replicating the totalizing forces of culture,[52] Celan's poetry is a striving to recover language from out of the ashes of burned up meanings in order to speak, to breathe, again.

In his poem, "I drink wine," Celan writes of drinking from two glasses and of plowing away at the king's caesura. The language of plowing, *zackern*, comes from Hölderlin, as is also suggested by the subsequent reference to

Pindar. Different scholars speculate on the interpretation of the king's caesura, but one common theme is that it marks the clear separation between God and humans, particularly regarding justice, following Auschwitz and the separation between Graeco-Christian Germany, Hölderlin's legacy, and Jewish mysticism, Celan's own.[53] This caesura is a wound that can be neither fully healed nor covered over. Yet, the caesura is not absolute. The poet's words, even in "Todtnauberg," hold the two sides together. Celan does not split the Yes from the No.

Celan's hope for a coming word in the heart is a hope for an attunement to the poet's own existence, own physical nature, and the poem's own corporeality. Thus, "the conversation that we are" chokes because it does not allow for this pause of breath or recognize the caesura. It does not turn toward the other. By collapsing conversation and history, Heidegger does not remain mindful of dates; he covers over the particular. Di Cesare states pointedly, "In the history of Being, there is no place for the muffled cries of the victims."[54] Heidegger's insistence on speaking and saying remains at the level of responding to language itself rather than to an actual other. The conversation fails to be a dialogue. What we have learned from the *Black Notebooks* is that although Heidegger remained publicly silent, he perceived the Germans as the real victims. Heidegger writes in *Anmerkungen I* that the Allied Forces' failure to recognize the Germans' world-willing and destiny is a far greater crime "whose magnitude could not be measured against the gruesomeness of the 'gas chambers.'"[55] In other words, the crimes committed against the Germans are greater than those perpetuated by the Nazis, from whom Heidegger distinguishes the Germans. Peter Trawny writes regarding Heidegger's silence,

> But who heard the "silent voices" of those murdered in the "gas chambers and death camps"? Who was to hear them, who wanted to hear them? Who heard the "silent voices" of the murdered Jews? Who said they had heard them? After the war, Germany was a country of silence.
>
> One could ask whether the refusal to hear the "silent voices" of these dead, in order to express what is undoubtedly owed to them—namely grief, perhaps even innocent grief—does not inevitably become a deadly silence, indeed a silencing that kills, a silent killing-once again, a killing of the dead, and in any case, the avoidance of remembering what "really" happened to the Jews. One could ask whether the refusal to express grief does not become a deadly silence. In that case, keeping silent about the Shoah would be telling enough. If not indicative of tacit consent (i.e., "consenting to the horrible"), it would be, nonetheless, a recalcitrant refusal to acknowledge the unconditional moral meaning of the Shoah.[56]

While Celan finds Heidegger's analysis of silence and the speaking of silence important, Heidegger's failure to speak, to denounce his anti-Semitism and involvement with the Nazis becomes a deadly betrayal. We could also say that Heidegger's silence actually becomes idle talk in failing to ask the questions that confront it. In Heidegger, we find the noem.

What is necessary is a more thorough hospitality that bears witness to the particularity of the guest and the possibility of hostility that requires that one risks not only language, but one's own self.[57] Celan presents this possibility of language providing shelter, of providing the dialogue with the other, that holds together both the possibility of harm and healing. Otto Pöggeler writes that Celan's experience—his exile from Bukovina, his fraught relation to his mother tongue, and his identity as Jewish—comes to be that of every poet, namely exiled without the possibility of returning home.[58] Di Cesare interprets this even more strongly as indicative of the general state of humans as cast out into the world without the possibility of returning to the origin.[59] Human existence is thus one of exposure. By not falling into totalization, the poem continues to speak after Auschwitz.

IN THE RIVERS NORTH OF THE FUTURE: TOWARD UTOPIA

What would a more thorough hospitality and hope look like? We find an example in another of Celan's poems (G 176):

In the rivers north of the future
I cast out the net, that you
hesitantly weigh down
with stone-written
shadows.

Gadamer interprets the "I" of this poem as the human who lives, as humans do, north of the future, beyond justification of the next step. To be human is to anticipate what stretches beyond us, even if that is yet unrecognizable. Furthermore, he suggests, we read this casting out as a form of hope, albeit one that is weighted with the net of expectations, by shadows and disappointments. For, "No human hoping can be optimistic, unless one's own hoping is weighted by these shadows. And, it almost appears that someone is there who would know how unfathomably much one can burden a hoping heart without allowing the hope to sink."[60] On Gadamer's interpretation, we cannot think hope without thinking despair. We cannot cast out in optimism without the possibility of collapse. Here we find that hope, as the breathturn, is dialogic.

Gadamer reads the hesitation not as indecision or doubt that challenges the fisher's confidence. Rather, to catch anything in the net, it must be weighed down, but in such a way that it does not sink. The hesitation is the caution of placing stone-written shadows carefully in order to find the weight of balance. The hesitation is the pausing of breath, the turning toward the other. In casting out, I ask the other not only, "Do you hear me?" but "Will you hear me?" My hopes are sent out like a message in a bottle that seek an encounter and bearing witness. The I cannot be successful in the casting except through the measured, the appropriate, weighing done by You.

The shadows, as stone-written, are imbued with sense. They are, perhaps, like the fragment of the *symbolon* that speak the bond of guest-friendship and the tension between stranger and friend. Although I and you could be anyone, the poem calls us to read both in their particularity. As Gadamer suggests, we could read the I as the poet who casts out in search of the true word at risk of finding instead the noem. It could also be that the I is any of us who confronts the reality of failing to be understood or succeeding in bearing witness. It is not just someone, but I and You who are at stake in this task. The net, like the language mesh, works only because it is penetrable. That is, the net is a series of interlocking open spaces; it does not split the No from the Yes. It can neither fully close off, nor can it be fully open. The net preserves what is caught without domination. The net remains vulnerable to what is beyond it and is what it is because of such vulnerability. Without the possibility of vulnerability and touch, there can be no genuine encounter.

If we read this poem as articulating the nature of poetry more generally, then we see that the poem reaches beyond itself toward the other. Celan remarks in his Bremen speech that the poem is on route and attempts to find its direction. In so doing, the poem is not outside of time. Rather, it "claims the infinite and tries to reach across time—but across, not above" (CP 34). Casting the net out into the rivers north of the future is like claiming the infinite. The poem raises itself beyond itself; it makes a claim of infinity. Yet, the poem remains within time. It reaches across time like how the net spans the depths. Both must be carefully allotted. They remain intelligible, even at the limits of articulability. Thus, at the very moment of reaching toward the infinite, the poem remains keenly aware of its finitude.

Pöggeler reads "north of the future" as suggesting the death that is yet to come and that lies beyond all sense. The poet, the I, casts out nets in the land of death and dead.[61] Pöggeler notes, it is not that the net is laden with stones, but with shadows. Shadows are what bring things and beings back to their outlines, their corporeality. To have a shadow is to be genuinely earthly and alive. To be alive is at the same time to face the shadow of death. There is a presumed "we" of the dialogue, but the we must be thought as the traversing of the meridian between two poles. Celan explains in "The Meridian" that I and You that are gathered in—often desperate—conversation, but this conversation is possible only through a form of address that also brings its "otherness into the present" (CP 50). What this otherness gives voice to is "what is most its own: its time." By casting out with You, I am able to hold life and death together at once.[62] Recalling "Speak You Also," we find again the sense of giving shadow enough, of spanning between midnight and midday and midnight. The rivers north of the future are the places where life leaps where death is; the rivers are perhaps that place where the star "sees itself gleam: in the swell / of wandering words."

The rivers north of the future might also be read in relation to the Neckar in "Tübingen/January." The river serves as a source of identity and orientation. Heidegger suggests that the spirit of the river is the poetic spirit. The poet—here Hölderlin specifically—understands the river as leading between humans and the divine as making the land fertile and allowing dwelling (EHP 120). The poet similarly stands between humans and gods, establishing a new ground for dwelling between the two. The poet does this through remembering. The river is the source, but its movement constantly draws us away from the source. Remembering the source is not simply recovering what was lost, but abiding in the traversing and flow of the river (EHP 171). In "Tübingen/January," though, we are also confronted with the possibility of drowning in that river and the sinking of language beneath the surface. Thus, the river opens possibility as well as risk; the poet bears witness to this.[63]

The river, and poet, chart both space and time. The river ventures out beyond itself as it flows, and as Heraclitus reminds us, is thus both itself and not. The river follows the topography of the land while also shaping that topography. The river's banks shift; it carves out new terrain; it floods or dries up. What we find in Celan's river is a new configuration of space and time based on this new topography. The rivers are north of the future; they have a specific location, but they are not yet. They are perhaps "as immaterial as language, yet earthly, terrestrial" (CP55). Still, the poem is mindful of its dates as the river is mindful of its origin. Although unnamed, these rivers are particular; they lie north of the future. These rivers are also the work of memory as the poem and poet search for the origin that can be witnessed but not recovered. Because such poems can be issued only from poets who are mindful of their own corporeality, their own *Kreatürlichkeit*, the river must also be particular and irreducible.

The poem, as still-here, continues to speak in language that is "actualized, set free under the sign of a radical individuation" that remains aware both of language's limits and open possibilities (CP 49). Celan tells the audience that he is undertaking topological research in the light of utopia: that open, empty free space that the poem seeks. Utopia, too, lies north of the future. It exists, but in an ambiguous way. It is the place "where all tropes and metaphors want to be led *ad absurdum*" (52). Although utopia literally means nowhere, Celan's utopia is not no*where*. Rather, it is not *yet*. It is like the coming word into the heart of the thinker, the poet, the thanker. It is both Yes and No, both I and You. In another interpretation of "In the rivers north of the future," Gadamer writes that the one casting out the net and the one weighting it build a "unitary activity" that is "between the freedom and agility of throwing and projecting, and the pull downwards to the boundary, towards the limited."[64] Thus, projecting is dialogical. The success of the casting is measured not by an absolute value, but according to the tension of the opposition and the recognition of boundaries that allow it to become "a prospect, i.e., the unreal utopia of this projecting, which reaches into the unpredictable."[65] Similarly, as Celan writes in the Flinker bookstore response, a new poetics "tries to measure the area of the given and the possible" (CP 16). This utopia, then, requires a new topological understanding as a way to chart the heights and depths of what we cannot fully know.

Celan remarks that in his topological research, he arrives at his point of departure and searches for his origin. This origin, perhaps implying Bukovina, can no longer be found. It does not exist. Instead, he finds something else, namely, the meridian. This meridian, which departs from and rejoins itself, is the path of all encounters. The meridian, then, is the clue to this new orientation as the caesura that is the turning of breath. Rather than the subjective projection of space and time as intuition or the calculation of geometric space, Celan's articulation calls for a fully embodied attunement to the world, to others, and to ourselves. This orientation is bookended by the abyss of groundless grounding and the utopia of the not yet that is on the way, with the caesura running through the middle. We set out from a particular origin and give form to ourselves as we venture out, as we cast out, with others toward what is north of the future.

It is precisely this sense of utopia that distinguishes Celan's understanding from other, more totalizing pursuits of utopia. As Pöggeler notes, all other attempts at utopias as self-contained perfections, whether in the form of the absolute poem, the classless society, or the eternal return, annihilate what is human. The utopia promised by National Socialism proved this most clearly. In bearing witness to the reality of destruction, decay, and homelessness, poetry can bring forth new realities. Interpreting Celan's poem, "Into the grooves," Gadamer writes,

> For the task of the poet is to seek the true word, not the word which comes from the usual, protective roof of every day, but the one which arrives from beyond as if it were his true home. Therefore, the poet must dismantle the scaffolding of every day words syllable by syllable. He must fight against the ordinary,

customary, obscuring, and leveling function of language in order to lay open a view of the glimmer above. That is poetry. (GC 82)

Because Celan's utopia is yet to come, because it is both present and absent, it cannot be totalized. By clearing away the burned out meanings, the poet traces new paths. The poet preserves what is human by allowing for language to continue to speak, even in silence, through dialogue between self and other.

In the forward to *Gadamer on Celan: "Who am I and who are you?"* Gadamer writes that his aim is to receive Celan's messages in a bottle, not to provide a conclusive analysis of his poems, but rather to "[bear] witness to an extended acquaintanceship" (GC 63). Importantly, for Gadamer, the truth of poetry is not the truth of propositions or correspondence, but a remembrance of language. Understanding a poem is not so much a concern with correctness, but of turning ourselves in the direction suggested by the poem and poet. Gadamer explains that the proper function of the poet is a shared saying. Because poetry is language-bound, the poet does not stand outside language, but rather moves in this shared saying to what could not otherwise be said. The poem "transcends both poet and interpreter. Both of them pursue a meaning that points to an open realm" (RB 72). Like Celan, Gadamer maintains that, as the poem measures what is given and possible and reaches toward those free, open spaces, it is also free. Those open realms demand interpretation because of their ambiguity. Such interpretation cannot "be translated in terms of conceptual knowledge" (RB 69). Instead, we must attune ourselves to the ambiguity. There is a triangulated bearing witness among poem, poet, and interpreter. As we recognize that to which the poem and poet bear witness, we also recognize ourselves.

Because the poem, and work of art more generally, has no external verification, but still stands there before us, "The work of art is an assertion, but it is one that does not form an assertive sentence, although it is telling in the highest degree" (GR 212). The word of the poet is both uncanny and familiar because "it stands over against this process [of making ourselves at home] like a mirror held up to it. But what appears is the world, not this or that thing in the world, but rather the nearness of familiarity itself in which we stand for a while" (RB 115). Indeed, it is language that gives us access to the world. Laws tell us what is right and wrong, or religious texts articulate the structures of society. Language gives the world a horizon within which we are able to dwell. As our familiarity in language grows, particularly in our mother tongues, we become more at home in the world. This familiarity is not merely of words, but of a comportment to the world. It is a mode of understanding. What is distinctive about poetry is that the poetic word "bears witness to our own being" (RB 115). The poet allows us to see what could not otherwise be seen. In so doing, we recognize that we belong to (*gehören*) the poetic conversation as listeners (*Hörer*) (GR 212).

Yet, as Celan demonstrates, our mother tongue and the horizon it structures is not neutral. Even in the language most familiar to him, Celan remains unsettled. As in Levi's description of the concentration camps, one's mother tongue becomes the basis of barbarism and dehumanization. To articulate the self requires language, and yet it is this same language that jeopardizes the self. Thus, if poetry is a mirror that reveals the nearness of familiarity, we must also understand it as revealing the searching for words and the foreign dimension of language that is both our own and exceeds our grasp.

Gadamer returns to this connection between poetry and a community of listeners in his essay, "Are the Poets Falling Silent?" There he questions whether in our age of mechanization and indirect communication the poetic word maintains any power, any currency. In an era of destabilization and unrest, of pressure for solidarity and community, "does there still exist such a conjoining of words, wherein everyone could be at home?"[66] Tracing the poems of Celan and Bobrowski, Gadamer reminds us that when we read a poem, we must enter into a relationship with the work such that we, too, are the subject of address. To know that it is I who reads the poem requires that I see myself also as a You. In Gadamer's language, we tarry with the poem in conversation. What the poet offers is respite in the quiet word of humanity for those who have cultivated this ability to listen, even for the softest of voices or what is left unsaid. By presenting us with language that continues to speak, even in ways that are indeterminate, the poet does not articulate the concepts themselves, but the possibility of concepts as a world opens before us.

As we have seen with Celan, what is the poem's ownmost is its time. Gadamer writes in "The Verse and the Whole" that "language signifies memory" and thus is "a way of confronting ourselves in which we become mindful of ourselves."[67] For Gadamer, what we are mindful of is our finitude, our dates. He explains that "we orient ourselves toward our future in expectation and hope" while at the same time, "the human state of having-been-forced-out of the living creation bounded by nature, implies a continual task of return and self-communion."[68] We are forced out beyond nature because that step beyond, that step toward the future, is one of freedom. Our task is to return to what we have been allotted. *Nomos*, he explains, is the "most profound symbol" of this task. *Nomos*, in this sense, is law, but not law a that can determine every element of human life. Rather, it is what is allotted to us; it is the measure. To be subject to this measure is human. What the poem teaches is "to submit to the measure which gives freedom."[69] Like the I who casts nets in the rivers of the north, our weighing of the nets must be appropriate. The poem specifically teaches this because "the natural and thorough rhythmization, which the reading of a poetic creation demands and transmits, articulates, and orders not only the recitation but also the breathing of the speaker."[70] The poem teaches the turning of the breath and the comportment necessary to understand what is addressing us. A return to this measure is to learn again what it is to live in poetry, that is, to attune ourselves to our finitude and to hold open space for an encounter with an other.

NOTES

1. Gadamer, "Die Gegenwärtigkeit Hölderlins," 181.
2. Gadamer, 181.
3. Gadamer, 181.
4. Bruns, "The Remembrance of Language: An Introduction to Gadamer's Poetics," 17.
5. Pöggeler, "Ach, die Kunst!: die Frage nach dem Ort der Dichtung," 89–90. Pöggeler explains, "Topological speech speaks each time from its place and its search for place; so it fits itself into that overarching and always Utopian, never-concluded '*Erörterung*' in which the conversation of history allows truth, as a way, to find utterance."
6. In the previous chapter, I suggested that plant life is both active and passive, responsive and transformative. Even invasive species, like kudzu, have to respond to their material conditions, yet the model of expansive plant life I have in mind is more like the phenomenon of "crown shyness" that occurs in some tree species. The tree expands in relation to its neighbors by leaving a small gap between its leaves and those of its neighbor. See, for example, Franco, "The Influences of Neighbours on the Growth of Modular Organisms with an Example from Trees."
7. Gadamer, "The Verse and the Whole," 89.
8. "Aorgischen" rückt: "die Autarkie des Gedichts: [. . .] = SprachKristall—Gitter → Anorganisch → Höld[erlin]? Aorgisch??? → "Tödlich??" cited in May, Goßens, and Lehmann, *Celan-Handbuch*, 309.
9. Derrida, *Sovereignties in Question*, 103.
10. Translation modified.
11. Derrida, 7.
12. Derrida, 9.
13. Di Cesare, *Utopia of Understanding*, 225.
14. Celan, *Von Schwelle zu Schwelle*, 59.
15. Hölderlin writes "In Lovely Blueness" that the human dwells poetically on the earth, "But the shadow/ Of the starry night is no more pure, if I may say so/ Than man, said to be the image of God. Is there measure on earth? There is/ None." In this poem, Hölderlin again grapples with the human's position in the world, particularly in relation to the divine. The gods are rich in virtue and the human seeks to imitate, but as finite, will never fully succeed. Yet, if the human has a purity of heart, she might measure herself against the divine. Thus, the response of "There is none" does mean that that there is no measure at all, but that the measure is not to be found on earth, from the side of the created, but from the divine, the creators. Recall from the

previous chapter that, for Hölderlin, what it is for a poet to be at home, to dwell, is to hold oneself open to what surpasses, to join together the finite and infinite through a creative imitation of the divine. Thus, the measuring of what is appropriate, of what is enough, is not that of calculation, but a comparison of the self to that which exceeds the self (Hölderlin, *Hymns and Fragments*, 235).

16. Carson, *Economy of the Unlost*, 41.
17. Carson, 51.
18. Carson, 106.
19. Carson, 117.
20. Carson, 118.
21. Plato, "Republic," 518d.
22. See also Jay, *Downcast Eyes*.
23. Celan, *Die Niemandsrose/ Sprachgitter*, 104.
24. Celan, 27.
25. Bambach, *Thinking the Poetic Measure of Justice*, 202.
26. Carson, *Economy of the Unlost*, 131.
27. The reference to "eyes talked into blindness" suggests Oedipus, who also features prominently in Hölderlin's work. As Charles Bambach explains, "This Oedipus reaches too far; his yearning for the truth is immeasurable, as will be his suffering. He has, as Hölderlin so poetically puts it, 'one eye too many' (III, 3–4). This compulsion to seek out the truth at any cost, beyond all limit and measure, will mark Oedipus as the figure who embodies the doubled, ambiguous legacy of all Enlightenment culture, its wonderful insight and terrible blindness. In his relentless pursuit of knowledge, Oedipus shows himself as the one who is both *ungeheuer* and *deinos*, the one who both inspires monstrous awe and is monstrously awful. No creature that walks upon the earth, beneath the lovely blueness of the sky, is more aw(e)ful than the human being." Bambach, 91–92.
28. Gadamer, "Die Gegenwärtigkeit Hölderlins," 181.
29. Di Cesare, *Heidegger and the Jews*, 225.
30. Tobias, "The Ground Gives Way," 583.
31. Tobias, 583.
32. Cited in Bambach, 211.
33. Böschenstein, "Hölderlin und Celan," 151.
34. We might also read this as an allusion to Moses, who, wandering with his flocks in the mountain, hears the voice of God and responds "Here I am." God tells Moses he will be the voice of the Jewish people and will lead them out of exile. Moses, however, claims that he is ineloquent and slow of speech, and resists agreeing to God's call (*Exodus* 4:11). God insists, and suggests Moses use his brother Aaron as a spokesperson. There is some debate about whether this passage means that Moses has a stutter or stammer or whether he is slow to speak because he is concerned with precision or whether he actually did not speak Hebrew because he was raised as an Egyptian, but each of these interpretations still evidence what seems to be Celan's chief concern here, namely the fate of an exiled people and the possibility of the failure of language.
35. Di Cesare, *Utopia of Understanding*, 206–7.

36. In his essay, "The Speechless Image," Gadamer addresses the status of contemporary art that no longer has representation of nature as its aim. When we compare contemporary art to the "resplendent eloquence" of classical art, we "have the impression of speechlessness" of the former. Yet, the speechlessness is not because contemporary art has nothing to say. Rather, it is that the artist "wants to say too much at once and is unable to find the words to express the pressing wealth of things he has on his mind" (RB 83). In these circumstances, we must seek new words. As searching, the modern artist is "less a creator than a discoverer" of these new possibilities (91).

37. Hamburger, *Poems of Paul Celan*, 215.

38. May, Goßens, and Lehmann, *Celan-Handbuch*, 94.

39. Derrida, *Sovereignties in Question*, 65.

40. Derrida, 88–89.

41. Derrida, 95.

42. Bruns, "The Remembrance of Language: An Introduction to Gadamer's Poetics," 44–45.

43. In an interview, Gadamer suggests the difference between hermeneutics and literary criticism is that the latter attempts to subsume a poem under a classification (e.g., this one love poem among all love poems, whereas the former is "the art of employing methods where they belong, not where they don't belong.") He cites Celan, and his own interpretation of Celan, as indicative of the hermeneutic approach: "Celan once put it beautifully: When a 'stone' is mentioned in a poem, it is, of course, important what can be meant by 'stones'; but what matters in the poem is *this* stone, the one the poem mentions. This is the secret to the capacity for judgment: that one makes something general concrete with respect to the given situation" (EPH 70).

44. Carson, *Economy of the Unlost*, 41. Gadamer also suggests that Hölderlin's poetry acquired a "tone of naming, i.e., the invocation of what is" (EPH 97). For Hölderlin, to name what is, is also to name what is not, particularly in naming the withdrawal of the divine. Even in this naming, there remains an "innermost and fervent stammering."

45. Heidegger, *What Is Called Thinking?* 146. "If thinking could dispose of that which ever and again gives food for thought, dispose it into its own nature, such thinking would be the highest thanks mortals can give. Such thinking would be the thankful disposal of what is most thought-provoking into its most integral seclusion, a seclusion where the most thought-provoking is invulnerably preserved in its problematic being. Not one of us here would presume to claim that he is even remotely capable of such thinking, or even a prelude to it. At the very most, we shall succeed in preparing for it."

46. Ziarek, "Semiosis of Listening."

47. Pöggeler treats this encounter at length in *Der Stein hinterm Aug: Studien zu Celans Gedichten*, 160–188.

48. Pöggeler, *Spur des Worts*, 259.

49. Cited in Bambach, 221.

50. May, Goßens, and Lehmann, *Celan-Handbuch*, 270–72.

51. For a fuller interpretation of this doubling, see Bambach, 222–26.

52. Adorno, *Prisms*, 32.
53. See Pöggeler, 23. Bambach, 253–65. Felstiner, *Paul Celan*, 277–79. Böschenstein, "Hölderlin und Celan." Manger, "Die Königszäsur: Zu Hölderlins Gegenwart in Celans Gedicht."
54. Di Cesare, 188.
55. Heidegger, *Anmerkungen* I–IV, 156. See also di Cesare, 208 and Trawny, "Heidegger and the Shoah," 175.
56. Trawny, 177.
57. Bambach, 225. As Charles Bambach similarly explains, "Heidegger never genuinely accepts the risk of real hospitality with Celan—that is, opening oneself or one's home to the other, the stranger, the foreign at the threshold of alterity. He never was able to break his studied silence on the topics so dear to Celan's heart. Instead, he retreated back into the conventions of hospitality that posed little risk at all."
58. Pöggeler, *Spur des Worts*, 161.
59. Di Cesare, *Utopia of Understanding*, 95–125.
60. Gadamer, "Are the Poets Falling Silent?" 78.
61. Pöggeler, 225.
62. Pöggeler, 226.
63. It is important to note that Celan drowned himself in the Seine River on April 20th, 1970.
64. Gadamer, 76.
65. Gadamer, 66.
66. Gadamer, 74.
67. Gadamer, "The Verse and the Whole," 90.
68. Gadamer, 90.
69. Gadamer, 91.
70. Gadamer, 91.

Chapter 3

Play, *Paidia,* and *Paideia*

Celan's poem "Speak You Also" appears in the collection *Threshold to Threshold* [*Von Schwelle zu Schwelle*], written between 1952 and 1954. The etymological origin of *Schwelle* refers to the beam placed at the base of a doorway or beneath a window as well as the beams used to hold water back from the shore.¹ The threshold, as that space between inner and outer, is both and neither. It is a Yes and No held together. It is a boundary only insofar as it can be crossed; it marks the possibility of opening, but also the possibility of trespass. In this way, the threshold is not a space between a prefigured inner and outer; it is instead what allows inner and outer to appear. The threshold delineates space at the same time as it makes that delineation ambiguous. Though from slightly different roots,² *Schwelle* also connotes *schwellen*, meaning a swelling or bulging. In this sense, the threshold marks an irreducible space, a space that expands beyond itself. Translated into English, *Schwelle* becomes limen, derived from the Latin *limes*. *Limes*, the root of words such as liminal and limit, also connotes a space in between as well as what surpasses that space.

We might, then, think of *Schwelle*, threshold, limen, as that space of encounter described in the previous chapter. We saw that Celan speaks of the place of encounter, afforded by the poem, as the site of presence and absence, of casting and gathering, as the familiar meets the wholly unfamiliar. The space of encounter is the turning of breath, *Atemwende*, that can be neither prefigured nor grounded, except in the very turning toward and gathering in of You and I. Furthermore, such a space is fundamentally ambiguous. It cannot be reduced to a particular pole and always exceeds what can be said. Yet, such ambiguity not only remains meaningful, but makes meaning possible in the first place. The threshold, as that space in between, is not static, but actively gathers both into its space, bears witness to previous encounters, and holds open the possibility of future ones. Here, the limit shows itself not as a barrier or final stopping place, but as an awareness of finitude and what lays beyond. Each threshold, then, is marked by a to and fro movement, like the crossing of the meridian. Because this space of encounter points both to itself and what is beyond, it affords the possibility of a utopia by providing the possibility of what could be otherwise. Utopia in this sense is yet to come, like Celan's rivers north of the future. Such a utopia is the site of encounter between I and You, present and future, presence and absence, that resists all totalization and reduction.

It is just this ambiguity of the to-and-fro movement that, according to Gadamer, characterizes play. In *Truth and Method*, he suggests that the commonality between the play of light, the play of waves, child's play, or even the play of words is that "what is intended is to-and-fro movement that is not tied to any goal that would bring it to an end" (TM 104). The aim in each case appears to be movement itself, rather than any external goal. He continues, "The movement backward and forward is obviously so central to the definition of play that it makes no difference who or what performs this movement" (104). The game or play is there only insofar as it engages in this movement across the meridian. Who or what performs is of no consequence because the player is absorbed into this structure of play. This is what Gadamer deems "the primacy of play over the consciousness of the player" (105). Thus, play is not the activity of an individual or something someone does, but is, rather, this very movement. This sense of play, though, may at first seem to be at odds with Celan's discussion of the to-and-fro movement arising from and giving rise to the site of encounter. If play does not attend to the particular, then how does it not become totalizing or overly general?

The answer to this question lies in Gadamer's wariness of the overemphasis of self-consciousness found in aesthetics. Gadamer introduces his discussion of play in both *Truth and Method* and "The Relevance of the Beautiful" as a "clue" to understanding the ontology of the work of art as well as our experience of art, particularly in contrast to the aesthetic consciousness of Kant and other eighteenth century thinkers. Although play is central to Kant's and Schiller's work on aesthetics, Gadamer wishes "to free this concept of the subjective meaning" that it has in their work and "that dominates the whole of modern aesthetics" (TM 102). Those approaches treat aesthetic experience as both disinterested and subjective, characterizing play as merely the mental activity of the creator or the spectator's frivolous encounter with the work. Gadamer's primary rebuke to modern aesthetics is that it abstracts so far away from everyday life that its account of the experience of art is rendered empty. The *sensus communis* of Shaftesbury that marked a genuine political, social, and moral community becomes a community actually populated by no one. Taste, which characterized a mode of knowing and contained an "ideal normative element"

(36), becomes a subjective attunement far abstracted from everyday life. For Gadamer, however, our engagement with art and play more generally cannot be disinterested. Instead, we are fundamentally transformed in our experiences of play. As he suggests in his autobiographical reflections, play overcomes the "prejudices of an idealism rooted in consciousness" because play can never be a mere object. Instead, "it exists in and for those who play it, even if one is only participating as a 'spectator'" (GR 23). Gadamer's account of play demonstrates the way in which the particular player must attune herself to the particular play that surpasses her. In other words, the player is neither wholly passively absorbed into the structure of play nor is play the result of either disinterested or calculated mastery. Thus, play is not the product of consciousness precisely because play cannot be prefigured. Rather, there is play only insofar is it played, and it cannot be played in any general or abstract way.

As Gadamer argues, the task of play is more to order and shape the movement, to actively attune oneself to what surpasses the self, rather than to solve a predetermined problem with a definite solution. In this way, play affords a threshold that allows the self to engage in the very possibility of doing otherwise in a way that exceeds our ability to fully cognize or master it, but that still remains meaningful. Because of its fundamentally ambiguous nature, that is, because play always allows for more to be said, play also is a site of resistance and transformation.

My aim in this chapter is to think through how play, as understood by Gadamer and Fink, serves as the bridge, or threshold, between poetry and education, but not in the way described either by Romantic aesthetics or by the majority of contemporary play theorists.[3] Whereas these approaches maintain an image of the human as rational animal and a subject among objects, emphasizing knowledge as rational mastery, following Gadamer and Fink, I argue for an account of play that dispels such dualisms and provides an account of the self as hermeneutic. What play demonstrates is that the cultivation of the self is always already with others and in the world. It is the orientation toward the other, the opening of a space for possible encounters, that allows the possibility of doing otherwise, and thus the possibility of freedom.

In the following, I turn to different accounts of play in the history of philosophy. In each of these accounts, we see a coupling of play and education that identifies the significance of play for development. For example, in Plato's *Republic* and *Laws*, we see that play (*paidia*) is central for a child's education (*paideia*) and that the good philosophical life is one that involves play. As discussed in the first chapter, Kant and Schiller identify play's role in the development of autonomy and freedom. Although these accounts correctly identify a liminal dimension of play that gives rise to development and understanding, they primarily regard play as an activity of youth or characterize it as serving for the development of skill. By emphasizing mastery, they thus primarily see play as the product of self-consciousness or fail to account for play's autotelic nature. Furthermore, they tend to see the telos of human play as the development of rational autonomy.

We find a wariness toward this rational mastery in Hölderlin's call for a new poetic education. His central concern is to locate the originary unity that gives rise to difference and that allows for the finite, tragic human to attune herself to others and to the eternal harmony of creation. That is, he seeks the threshold for engaging what exceeds us. A poetic, rather than aesthetic, education would be less concerned with the development of autonomous reason, which would rely on subject-object dualisms, and more concerned with giving form to oneself through the creative cultivation of a poetic stance in the world and toward the Absolute. His wariness toward play is that it seems to be an escape from such responsibility. Since he understands play to be frivolous, Hölderlin thinks it does not take seriously the immense weight and responsibility of human existence.

Like Hölderlin, Fink argues that Western metaphysics has forgotten the world and misunderstands being by equating being with essence and by equivocating between existent beings and being as such. By conflating being and beings, metaphysics also renders nature static. Fink calls for a nonmetaphysical mode of thinking that, conversely, inquires into how the world is the totality of both being and all beings that we find in the world bound by time, space, and finitude (WE 195). Similarly, Fink attempts to think the Absolute that gives rise to being in the first place and how we might orient ourselves to that primordial harmony without falling into the false divisions of metaphysics. He argues that such an approach requires a new understanding of the finite human's relation to nature and the absolute. Unlike Hölderlin, however, he argues that it is precisely through play that such an orientation is cultivated because the play of the human mirrors the play of the Absolute. Like Gadamer, Fink understands play as a fundamental characteristic of human existence through which we give form to and create ourselves.

Although I will argue against elements of some of these traditional theories of play, my aim is neither to reject them out of hand as relics of metaphysics nor to call for starting from scratch. Rather, we should examine the history of philosophy through this play of dialogue. Following Gadamer's hermeneutic approach, I will move to and fro in this conversation. For example, we can see how the philosophy of the Greeks led to the conceptual mode of thinking in metaphysics, but we would be wrong to read this tradition unidirectionally. In his introduction to *The Idea of the Good*, Gadamer explains,

> I ask that the reader take what follows as an attempt to read the classic Greek thinkers the other way round as it were—that is, not from the perspective of the assumed superiority of modernity, which believes itself beyond the ancient

philosophers because it possesses an infinitely refined logic, but instead with the conviction that philosophy is a human experience that remains the same and that characterizes the human being as such, and that there is no progress in it, but only participation. That these things still hold, even for a civilization like ours that is molded by science, sounds hard to believe, but to me it seems true nonetheless.[4]

For Gadamer, in a departure from Nietzsche and Heidegger, the issue of twisting free from or overcoming metaphysics is not the primary issue. Rather, his concern is more to see how we are situated in the continuous conversation of philosophy. To treat metaphysics as a reified system is to commit the same error that modern philosophical metaphysics does, namely rigidity and the arrogance of self-certainty. We exist, says Gadamer, as conversation and in dialogue. So, the aim of hermeneutics is to recognize the shared human condition of existing as beings in a world that addresses us. Our relation to philosophy is no different. Thus, "Philosophy is rather a continual self-overcoming of all of its concepts, as a conversation is a continual self-overcoming through the answer of the other" (LL 43). This self-overcoming is not that domination or mastery, but the opposite: as the conversation unfolds and expands, it cannot be self-same. New questions and answers develop as "the history of philosophy is a continual dialogue with itself" (LL 43). Like Penelope constantly undoing her weaving, Gadamer explains, philosophy constantly renews itself. In the following, I aim to demonstrate this conversation with and in the history of philosophy. Instead of giving the final word on that tradition, I seek to open up those places that, even in the rigidity of metaphysics, allow for liminal, playful spaces that resist such totalization. Furthermore, this approach demonstrates that tradition is neither static nor causal, but dynamic, reaching to memory and forward toward what is yet to come.

TOWARD A DEFINITION OF PLAY

Before turning to the different ways of taking up play in philosophy and education, we should first clarify what play is. This, however, is no simple task. As the play theorist Brian Sutton-Smith remarks, "Play is difficult to understand because it is ambiguous."[5] Play is at once lighthearted and serious, real and non-real, human and non-human, free and rule-bound, rational and irrational. The anthropologist Robert Fagen expresses frustration regarding the evasiveness of play, suggesting that it is the resistance to conceptualization that evades: "The most irritating feature of play is not the abyss, not perceptual incoherence as such but rather that play taunts us with its inaccessibility. We feel that something is behind it all, but we do not know, or have forgotten how to see it."[6] Whereas Fagen seems to suggest that there is actually something behind play that we have forgotten, I believe it would be better to understand play as groundless. We often forget this dimension of play by assuming some sort of ground or by trying to look behind things for one, but, as Gadamer and Fink argue, because play is spontaneous and not prescribed, it cannot be determined beforehand. Play grounds itself, provides its own space and time, through being played. Still, by its very groundlessness, play does indeed taunt us in its inaccessibility. Any attempt to pin play down, especially conceptually, frequently obscures whatever play is. Instead, we understand play by playing along with it.

Play, according to Fink, is a fundamental human phenomenon, in addition to work, love, struggle, and death. Play differs from each of these other phenomena, however, because it has its own self as its telos. Play is a spontaneous activity that has itself, rather than another future goal, at stake; it interrupts everyday life while at the same time maintaining everyday continuity. In "Oasis of Happiness," he explains that the playworld "always has a real setting, but is, however, never a real thing among real things" (PSW 25). Play can do this because it "escapes from the intrusiveness of the rational concept into the polysemy of its masks" (22). It is a surplus of meaning. Fink argues that play is not unreal. Rather, it is there and involves the very objects, experiences, and modes of engaging in the everyday world. Yet, it has its own time and space that are not simply mirror images or copies of the everyday world. For this reason, Fink argues that play is non-actual as appearance. Because play is spontaneous and groundless, it is only there as appearance.

As Gadamer argues, what characterizes play is its "as if" structure. Play is not an escape from reality, but a mode of engaging reality in a different way. Play differs from other activities particularly by its "as if" character. When we play, we play as if we are something. In so doing, we take seriously the play-space and the activity at hand. The space shapes play, but it does not strictly determine it. The opposite of play is not seriousness, but not taking part, not taking play seriously. Thus, our primary orientation in play is one of responsiveness and attention to what plays before us. Again, such attention is not disinterested, but transformative as we play through these other modes of being. Through play we are transformed as we engage in possibilities that we could not otherwise access.

Here a practical example might help. Let's consider the way an activity, such as a conversation, grounds itself. When I talk with my sister, for example, there are certain expectations we have. First, we both expect the other to say something meaningful, not in the sense of saying something deep or provocative, but simply that she would say something that I would understand and vice versa. This is the second expectation, then, namely that when we speak, we expect to be understood. This understanding, however, does not map itself onto a foundation of understanding. Neither is any sort of method applied. Rather, the understanding is anchored in language, tradition, and customs, but also arises through the very happening of the conversation. There are particular contours or boundaries that belong to the conversation that we navigate as we talk with one another. Furthermore, the conversation we have does not exist prior to our having it, but it also is not something magically conjured from nowhere. Even if I have imagined the conversation ahead of time or imagined the points I want to make, this is not the same as the conversation that I then do have with my sister. I have to be open to what she has to say and also where the conversation takes us. Thus, it is only through our conversing that anything like a conversation arises. We could talk meaningfully about the conversation at a later time, too, so there is something substantive that belongs to it as a conversation. We could not abstract it from its happening as a kind of conversation. In this way, the conversation grows out of and grounds itself. There is no other foundation for it to which we could appeal, yet we still could provide an account of the conversation, just as the conversation might also be able to provide an account for something else, such as the relationship my sister and I share. Indeed, although our very relationship is grounded by over thirty years' worth of conversations, such that those conversations provide a basis for our relationship, none of those conversations or our relationship itself could dictate precisely how our current conversation comes to be. Instead, the conversation grounds itself in a quite concrete way. It is a basis of meaning, not only in the brief exchange when she informs me of her flight time, for example, but also in that it furthers and gives meaning to our relationship. Gadamer takes conversation to be a kind of play. In this conversation, there is the to-and-fro exchange of question and answer. Play grounds itself as it unfolds; it cannot be predetermined. Through the play of conversation, my sister and I are both transformed.

    It is this possibility of doing otherwise and the "as if" structure of play that connect play to freedom, Fink argues. In all of life, every choice we make is a decision of freedom, yet at the same time it is through that free choice that we "form the entire way in which we are responsible for conducting our lives" (PSW 207). The moment of free choice, of transcendence, is simultaneously a moment of determination laden with the burden of responsibility. In play, however, because the activity is non-actual, our orientation to freedom is different. Because our goal is nothing but play itself, we can, in a "non-actual way" escape this burden of responsibility. We can transcend ourselves, make the "irrevocable decisions of [our] freedom revocable, leap free from [ourselves], and . . . begin anew and cast off the burden of [our] life history" (206–7). Indeed, in a surprising reversal, "Play liberates us from freedom" (207). At first, this account of play strikes us as the very escapism that

Hölderlin would find wanting. Yet, in play, we return to that originary freedom that makes decision possible at all. We "touch on a depth of world Being in us, touch on the playing ground in the Being of all existent things" (207). Because play liberates us in a non-actual way, we do not escape freedom; we are not actually liberated from ourselves. Thus, play is not without purpose, but rather it serves no other purpose than to play. In play, we experience the groundlessness of being and can, for the first time, symbolically express the indeterminate and unfathomable play of the world totality.

Fink argues that it is precisely the indeterminacy, the non-actuality, of play, that represents the indeterminacy and groundlessness of the world itself. In the next chapter, I develop more clearly what Fink understands by world. Here, though, I would like to make a few initial remarks about the connection between play and the world to emphasize how this account requires us to reject the view of play as a mere behavior, and thus gives us reason not to accept many of the ways play is understood in anthropology, developmental psychology, and the majority of philosophy. Fink writes in *Play as Symbol of the World* that the world comes to appearance in the non-actuality of play and that humans relate to the world through this play:

> The world comes to appear in the appearance of play: it shines back into itself in taking on an intraworldly relation, . . . taking on features of the prevailing whole. The proof of the shining back of the world into itself, into a particular intraworldly thing, into the human being who emulates the world "as if"—as if "all-powerful," as if "without responsibility," as if within all possibilities at the same time—this shining back, seen from the cosmos, is the same as what we have called, seen from the human being, the ecstase toward the world-whole. (208)

The world, as granting appearance, allows for humans, characterized by understanding, to relate themselves to the world. Although all beings are innerworldly, only the human being has a relationship to the world, and so only the human being is a cosmological being, *ens cosmologicum*: "not because he gives shape to the world, rather because he alone among all living creatures can hold himself out into the totality that surrounds, binds, joins, and maintains everything, gives everything space and leaves everything time" (WE 373). Metaphysics views the human as a centaur, half rational-human and half desiring-animal, who sheds her animality by developing reason, thus separating herself from nature as an autonomous subject. Fink instead describes the human as a *Weltwesen*, a world being, who creatively participates in the play of world and earth and is inseparable from nature. The world is not the result of the subject's concepts; rather, the subject is constituted by the world. Like Hölderlin, Fink argues that the human is always already a member of a community. To be human is already to open oneself in understanding toward the world and others. In identifying the human as *ens cosmologicum*, Fink preserves both the animality of the human and the particular way she comports herself to the Absolute.

Humans differ from nonhumans specifically in the ability to express this relationship to the Absolute symbolically, an expression which occurs most clearly in play.[7] Although play resists the strictures of logic, because it is governed by rules and is a mode of understanding and meaning, play is not illogical or irrational. Instead, play possesses its own logic and is ultimately a mode of understanding in which the play of the finite and infinite is realized: "In human play the whole of the world is reflected back into itself, letting features of in-finity emerge and shimmer in and on something innerworldly and finite" (PSW 205). Human play is "the symbolic activity of bringing the sense of the world and life to presence" (30). In this way, the human participates in the creation and destruction that belong to life.

As the constant movement and play between creating and destroying, concealing and unconcealing, the Absolute is the playspace of being and nothing. Furthermore, as groundless, it is without a why. It has no external telos. Play, the only basic phenomena that is also without purpose, thus allows this absolute groundlessness to shine back in play. Play is itself worldly: "Play comes to be a 'cosmic metaphor' for the total appearance and disappearance of existing things in the time-space of the world" (PSW 77). Play allows the world to appear by giving form to what was unformed. Through play, humans not only express, but also process their connection to what surpasses them by preserving the tension between being and nothing, finite and infinite. As Fink explains, "the playful ecstase of the human being toward the world and the proof of the shining back of the whole of the world into the intraworldly symbol are the same relation" (208). Human play is the symbolic expression of the play of the world totality. In other words, human play does not merely represent cosmic play, it symbolically expresses the groundlessness of both itself and the totality. In play, humans are open to the world as the world provides the openness for all that exists. As Fink argues, the world play has no player. There is no agent of the world play. Instead, the world play is the coming to appearance of all that exists. If human play parallels the world play and is a groundless coming to appearance, then the sense of agency or of a player controlling an activity does not belong. It is precisely for this reason, then, that play is not merely a behavior, because behavior, especially in an anthropological sense, fails to grasp the ontological dimensions of play in failing to understand the world and the non-actuality of play.

Returning to the sense of liminality expressed earlier, we see again that the ambiguity of play is not something to be surmounted, but rather should be preserved in its richness of meaning. Like Hölderlin's Absolute and Celan's poetry, play resists conceptualization, but still remains intelligible and recognizable. To engage in play, we must attune ourselves to what surpasses us. Yet, while play shares in the liminality of the Absolute, of poetry, of nature, or of finitude, for example, and there are playful dimensions in each of these elements, it would be a mistake to equate each of these to each other. Indeed, what play calls for is the preservation, rather than reduction, of difference. Similarly, play is, I will argue, the cultivation of the self; it is not a mere copying of the everyday world in which we find ourselves. As Mihai Spariosu and others note, while all ludic, playful things are liminal, not all liminal things, such as dreams and illness, are ludic.[8] What distinguishes a playful, liminal experience is not only that it preserves the ambiguity of the liminal experience, but that it also holds an ambiguous relationship to that ambiguity.

In the following, I examine how play has been understood in some areas of the history of philosophy. At first glance, these accounts seem to disavow play as merely frivolous or as a stepping stone on the way to reason. Yet, a reexamination of them show more how we might reconceive of play in relation to freedom as holding open the in-between, liminal, space of human existence. Still, because these accounts do not consider this ontological dimension of play and rely on the dualisms Fink and Gadamer seek to overcome, they do not go far enough to provide an account of the relationship between play and poetic education.

PLAY, PHILOSOPHY, AND REASON

In the Western philosophical tradition, play has been identified since antiquity as a significant locus of moral development. In play, knowledge and understanding are developed and practiced. We find the roots of such coupling of play, *paidia*, and education, *paideia*, in Plato, although his attitude toward this pairing is at times inconsistent.[9] Because Nietzsche, Fink, and, to a lesser degree, Gadamer, blame Plato and his legacy for the dualisms anchoring Western metaphysics, I suggest we begin with an examination of Plato's account of play to see how these consequences ripple out into later theories and whether there might be resources in Plato's own work to resist such dualisms.

In Book IV of the *Republic*, Socrates states that in order for children to grow up as law-abiding, they must begin with lawful games. Socrates explains, "But when children play the right games from the beginning and absorb lawfulness from music and poetry, it follows them in everything and fosters their growth, correcting anything in the city that may have gone wrong before—in other words, the very opposite of what happens when the games are lawless" (*Republic* 425a-b).[10] Similarly, in *Laws* I, the Athenian stranger argues that "the correct way to bring up and educate a child is to use his playtime to imbue his soul with the greatest possible liking for the occupation in which he will have to be absolutely perfect when he grows up" (643d). Here, play and games are quite serious. The virtues of lawful games engender properly rational and lawful citizens. Since the aim of education, from childhood on, is to foster virtue and the desire to become perfect citizens, play is made subordinate to these aims.

In order to foster virtuous education, the guardians of the city must be careful to protect against music and poetry that are innovative. Such innovations would introduce a kind of lawlessness into games, thus threatening the education of the youth. For example, in *Laws* VII, the Athenian stranger remarks that no one has yet grasped how much child's play affects the laws of the state. If children always play the same way, that is with the same games, rules, and conditions, the adult life will also be peaceful and will not require constant alteration (797b). Most children's games do not always follow the same rules, however, and are rather prone to innovation. He warns that legislators who view such innovation as part of harmless "games" fail to take seriously that children who introduce change into their games will be different from the generation before them and will thus demand a different sort of life with new institutions and laws (798c). In the *Republic*, too, the guardians must protect against improvisation and innovation. Any music and poetry that is permissible must reflect the "conventional notions of justice, goodness, and beauty" (801d). Thus, such activities as music, dance, and poetry, frequently associated with frivolity, turn out to be rather serious endeavors because of their pedagogical role.

On this model of ideal education for the ideal city, the *as if* does serious work. In order for children to learn to be farmers or builders or any other occupation, they must play at that occupation. They must act *as if* they are farmers, builders, or judges; they must be able to imitate the real farmers and builders. Play is always mimetic, but here Plato seems to equate *mimesis* with rational imitation. Whereas earlier ancient conceptions of play focused on the chaotic play of fate or the agonistic play of power, Plato conceives of play as rational and orderly. In other words, Plato replaces the agonistic, chaotic play of Becoming with the well-ordered rational play of Being.[11] As children engage in lawful activities, their growth as lawful citizens is also fostered. Furthermore, even the imitation of child's play is never simple mimicry, but an activity that allows children to know and understand that which they imitate. The Athenian Stranger argues that anyone who judges representations in painting, music, or other fields, "should be able to assess three points: he must know first *what* has been represented; second, how *correctly* it has been copied; and then, third, the *moral value* of this or that representation produced by language, tunes, and rhythms" (669a-b).[12] So, as children are trained in the proper games of imitation, they recognize the truth of both the imitation and what is imitated as well as its moral import. The play of the ideal city both teaches and requires the player to take this cognitive approach toward play.

It is this identification of imitation, truth, and virtue that prompts Socrates' criticism of the poets in Book X of the *Republic*. Socrates contends that he is giving a different, and superior, account of the good life than that given by the poets, especially Homer. According to Socrates, although poetic works remain derivative appearances, the poets make it seem as if they present the genuine truth. Thus, receivers of the works believe the artist to be a sort of genius, knowledgeable about all sorts of different subjects from biology to geometry to carpentry: "If he is a good painter and displays his painting of a carpenter at a distance, he can deceive children and foolish people into thinking that it is truly a carpenter" (598c). Ultimately, however, the only thing the artist knows is imitation, and even this is hardly knowledge in the more robust sense that Socrates espouses. Because the poet and artist are not oriented toward the truth in their imitations, their works reflect only a kind of knack, not craft.

The real danger in these sorts of poetry and art is that the spectators believe they are actually receiving the truth, when, in reality, they are being led to falsehood. Socrates' criticism falls on two levels. The first is that the good painter deceives children or foolish people; they believe him to be omniscient and trust his account. The second is that these people then become convinced that their own capacities, or lack thereof, should be called into question. They sense that they have been deceived, but because the artist is so convincing, they cannot determine what is true and what is false. If these simple people begin to doubt the knowledge they had before, then they have good reason to doubt the guidance and knowledge of the guardians and to turn away from what is actually good and true.

As Socrates suggests in the *Republic*, correct knowledge and trust in the guardians are fundamental to the success of the ideal city. Since "imitation really consorts with a part of us that is far from reason" (603a), it weakens the reason necessary for this good society. Socrates suggests challenging Homer directly: since Homer is capable of writing on every subject, then he must in fact know what the good society is. Furthermore, if he has this knowledge and shares it, then we would be able to determine which cities are better governed because of Homer's writings (599c). Socrates concludes, however, that Homer would not be able to name a single city that has benefited from his false accounts of virtue. Since poets are unable to promote true virtue, Socrates concludes that we should not allow the imitative poet into a well-governed city, "for he arouses, nourishes, and strengthens this part of the soul and so destroys the rational one, in just the way that someone destroys the better sort of citizens when he strengthens the vicious ones and surrenders the city to them" (605b). Thus, not only do imitative painters or poets trick the audience, but in this trickery, they also cultivate irrationality. They not only damage the rational part of the soul, but in fact *destroy* it. In so doing, they also foreclose the possibility for the good city since they have destroyed its good, rational citizens.

The lies of the poets cannot produce good, rational citizens since the poets do not promote justice. Instead, they make it seem like unjust people are happy and that injustice is profitable (*Republic* 392a-b). The poets also tell stories of the gods in the wrong way, claiming that the gods act poorly or create bad things (391e). For example, the poets give accounts of Hades that make people fear death due to its supposedly miserable nature (386b). While the poets' accounts may be charming because of their rhyme and meter, they cannot be compelling based on their supposed truth value or intellectual merit. The only poetry that would be allowed in the ideal city would be songs of praise that contribute to the good education of the citizens.

As we have seen, in *Republic* and *Laws*, to protect against the sort of imitation that leads away from the truth, if play is permitted, it must involve the right sort of imitation, that is, it must be a rational imitation of what is true rather than an imitation of an imitation. Play, as mimetic, must therefore be extremely serious. In *Laws*, the Athenian Stranger suggests that the true imitation will also be imitation of the gods because we are perhaps puppets of the gods. The gods may have created us to "serve as their plaything, or for some serious reason," but we do not know what those reasons are (644e). We are like marionettes whose strings are pulled about by another force. We do know, however, that "we have these emotions in us, which act like cords or strings and tug us about; they work in opposition, and tug against each other to make us perform actions that are opposed correspondingly; back and forth we go across the boundary line where vice and virtue meet" (644e). It is therefore not the gods who pull the strings, but our emotions. Yet, we are blessed with a golden and holy cord that allows us to keep the emotions in check through the power of calculation [*logismos*]. Calculation, he suggests, is gentle, and so requires us to cooperate with it so that the right element will prevail (645b). If we are playthings, then correct play requires calculation in accordance with reason and remaining on the right side of the boundary line between virtue and vice.

Following his discussion of the proper education of the youth in *Laws* VII, the Athenian Stranger returns to the idea of humans as playthings. Because humans are the toys of the gods, "Every man and woman should spend life in this way, playing [*paizonta*] the most beautiful games [*kallistas paidias*]" (803c). Whereas many contend that the purpose of serious activity, such as war, is leisure or peace, the Athenian Stranger argues that the most serious thing, play, protects the human against his enemies by winning the gods' favor through dancing and sacrifice. So, to be on the correct side of virtue, humans must both control their emotions and play the most beautiful games.

Fink finds Plato's deeming the human being as *paignion theou*, a puppet of the gods, to be an "odd designation" because the human, otherwise conceived as a "free, creative player" is here "humbled, pressed down into a marionette, degraded by the philosopher's 'evil eye' into a thing that is moved about" (PSW 233).[13] Fink's interpretation echoes that of Megillus in response to the Athenian Stranger's assessment of humans of playthings: "That, sir, is to give the human race a very low rating indeed" (804b). The Stranger responds, in a way also entertained by Fink, that this is not to suggest that humans are worthless or unserious, but that perhaps the gods, too, play in some way.[14] Later, the Athenian Stranger refers to "the divine checkers-player [*petteutēs*]"[15] who is responsible for improving the situation of souls with good character and relegating a deteriorating soul to an inferior situation (903e). Here we find the play of the divine game to be similarly serious and calculated in determining what is appropriate for each soul. Fink contends that the divine play in Plato is as moralized as the play of the poets permitted in the city and results in a "purification of the representation of God" (PSW 149).[16] This marks an essential move in the history of Western philosophy, according to Fink, namely that "The god of metaphysics thinks" (101). Because thought is the activity of the gods, and play is an imitation of the gods, play now becomes an imitation of thought. Again, we find that what was the play of fate is now subsumed under reason.

Fink argues that Plato conflates the mimetic nature of *technē* with the mimetic nature of play. According to the former, when craftspeople create, for example, a bed, they imitate a pattern. The created object mirrors the model. To act morally, we imitate or mirror the behavior of praiseworthy humans or ideals or the form of the good. According to the latter, when painters imitate craftspeople in their play, they also engage in mirroring, but whereas craftspeople actually produces shoes or tables or beds, the painters produce only imitations of imitation (PSW 107). As such, the product of play does not actually exist. The poet's creations are ontologically and epistemologically empty (111).

Fink argues that this conflation arises because Plato distorts our common understanding of mirroring. If we think about a tree reflected in water, for example, we recognize the difference between the tree, the water, and the tree reflected in the water. The reflection is not nothing. It is there; it is actual. Yet, the mirroring also opens the space for something non-actual to appear. The tree does not actually exist in the water. This mirroring is not cut off from reality, but rather stands in relation to reality in an irreal way. As standing in relation to reality, this mirror play is not a flight from the world, but rather takes the world seriously in a different way. This non-actuality is what Fink deems the playworld. The playworld is not nothing, but exists as irreal. As we saw above, for Fink, play is the medium of non-actuality that allows the world to come to appearance in a different way (PSW 208). The playworld is different from, not less than, other actual things. Thus, for Fink, we must "distinguish the production of products that still encompass an irreal dimension in their actual content from the fabrication of other artificial things" (114). Because Plato does not make this distinction, though, he robs play of its seriousness. Furthermore, because Plato relegates painting, and thus the image, to an inferior status below philosophy and calculation, Plato also initiates the subordination of the "sensuous image for pure non-sensuous thought" (99).

THE PLAY OF DIALOGUE AND DIALECTIC

Gadamer draws a similar conclusion. For him, the forms of play articulated by Socrates in the *Republic* and *Laws* afford no latitude and are always second to philosophy. Yet, says Gadamer, we would be mistaken in our interpretation of Plato if we thought that this rejection of the poets of the day necessarily follows from Plato's own ontological assumptions. Rather, we should understand Plato's decision as opposing the political and intellectual, specifically Sophist, culture out of the "conviction that philosophy alone has the capacity to save the state."[17] Plato's rejection of the poets and the ideal cities developed in the *Republic* and *Laws* should not be read as literal instructions for curriculum development. Plato aims instead at calling into question traditional moral ideas and pedagogies. In other words, Plato's conviction that philosophy saves the state is realized not in rules, but in questioning. Thus, Plato's discussion of *paideia* is opposed to the *paideia* of the day that advances musical or physical agility. Instead, Plato sees education as "the shaping of an inner harmony in the soul of a person, a harmony of the sharp and the mild in him, of the willful and the philosophical."[18] Like the marionette described in the *Laws*, humans must harmonize what is dissonant. Gadamer explains, though, that Plato's *paideia* is the "unification of the irreconcilable: the schism of the bestial and the peaceful in the human being."[19] Such unification is thus never wholly complete, but is necessary to prevent the human from turning into a tame animal or a wolf. Thus, the aim of the dialogues is not to give guidelines, but rather to hold up the mirror for humans to see themselves and engage in critical reflection. For Plato, then, the Socratic elenchus is the correct type of play and the one that ought to be engaged in philosophy.

The mirroring enabled by the raising of questions in the dialogue fundamentally differs from the mirroring of the painters and poets described in *Republic* X. Gadamer explains that when I imitate another's actions, like the child imitating the builder in play, I am learning to do it myself. But if I imitate and only imitate, like the poet manipulating a mirror to reflect things seemingly at random, then I am merely shaping my exterior to match something external. I try on someone else's identity rather than appropriating it as my own. Thus, such imitation of imitation is self-forgetting. Indeed, that is also why imitative poetry and painting are enjoyable; they allow for a flight from the self. Thus, says Gadamer, Plato's critique of the poets is not only that of their creating "false and dangerous contents of mimetic art" but also a *"critique of the moral consequences of 'aesthetic consciousness.'"*[20] If wisdom requires us to know ourselves, then what would be more antithetical than this sort of self-forgetting? Whereas poetic imitations lead to this self-forgetting, the song or poetry of praise prevents it. Because the song of praise arises out of shared language and common concern for the state, it returns us to our ideals. Even still, because these songs of praise are of the ideal state and not the current state of Athens, Plato's aim is not to prescribe poetry as such, as Fink seems to suggest, but rather to serve as the mirror that requires the reader to recognize herself in the text and to call into question traditional practices. Each step of the dialogues is an inducement to philosophize.

Whereas Fink focuses on the literal reading of Plato's texts, Gadamer's interpretation suggests that Plato's dialogues are themselves rather more playful than Plato's own account of play.[21] For example, at the moment in the *Republic* that Socrates describes the education of children and the use of play for training, he remarks, "I forgot that we were only playing, and so I spoke too vehemently . . . as if I were angry with those responsible for it." (536b-c). Here we see two very different senses of play. On the one hand, we have the play described in the *Republic* as a way to cultivate virtue through proper imitation. On the other hand, we have Socrates characterizing the dialogue as such as a kind of play that requires both taking it seriously but also recognizing it as play.

Gadamer suggests that this self-awareness of the dialogue is what should draw our attention. Plato focuses on philosophy to recover the shared reality and language from the Sophists. Plato's concern in these dialogues is this movement of philosophy. Gadamer explains in *Plato's Dialectical Ethics* that "Platonic philosophy is a dialectic not only because in conceiving and comprehending, it keeps itself on the way to the concept, but also because, as a philosophy that conceives and comprehends in that way, it knows man as a creature that is thus 'on the way' and 'between.'"[22] On Gadamer's reading, Plato demonstrates that the movement of philosophy is one that does not presuppose the definite concept or its own wisdom. As *philo*sophy, the movement of philosophy is one of desiring and striving for that wisdom.[23] Di Cesare highlights that, in order to understand this movement between question and answer, we should bear in mind that the Greek prefix *dia-* means "through," thus emphasizing the openness between the two. The dialectic "recognizes itself as a kind of *between* that grants the provisionality, indeterminacy, and incompleteness that emerge from it. By knowing itself as *finite*, it accepts *infinite* openness."[24] The dialogues, as opening this indeterminate space in between, offer us a possibility to engage in what we would not be able to otherwise. For example, in the *Republic*, the dialogue opens considerations of other forms of justice for the city, and that is taken seriously not because it is an imitation of something serious, but because we actively engage ourselves in it.

Gadamer writes that the dialogues are meant to serve as an antidote to the aesthetic consciousness espoused by the Sophists, "And the only valid way to represent that discussion becomes Plato's dialogue, that song of praise which affirms what is of concern to everyone and which throughout the 'play' which represents the educational state does not lose sight of the serious issue: the cultivation of the political human being and of justice in him."[25] The dialogues are not an escape from reality, but a way of returning to reality in a transformational way. The same is true of Plato's myths: he offers a work of fiction neither to dazzle and charm nor to master a specific teaching. Plato's dialectic is opposed to "the dazzling art of the forceful answer" provided by the Sophists.[26] Rather, the myth induces us to play along with it, allowing an encounter "in a play in which the soul recognizes itself."[27] Gadamer suggests further that this song of praise, the true poetry, offered by Plato is not a mere imitation of preexistent norms. Rather, "The poet turns *himself* into the tool of his art. He forms by speaking. But instead of things, what the poet forms is more often than not the human being himself as the latter expresses himself in his existence, as he experiences himself in action and suffering."[28] If the poet is merely the imitative poet, then there is nothing undergirding this formation. But, if the poet is speaking in the form of the dialogue, then the poet speaks both the self and other, offering the possibility of encounter.

Even in this encounter, as Socrates demonstrates, there remains something that resists a total laying bare. We do not understand the myth by stripping away the mythology, but by allowing ourselves to enter into the play offered before us. Because Plato's purpose is of utmost seriousness, he "gives his mimesis the levity of a jocular play."[29] By this, Gadamer again does not mean that the play is frivolous, but that the dialogue invites the movement of philosophical questioning in a way that also places itself in question.[30] In *The Idea of the Good in Platonic-Aristotelian Philosophy*, Gadamer argues that we should read the model city dialectically by interpreting the institutions as metaphors. Reading dialectically does not mean simply turning to opposites. Rather, "It means relating these Utopian demands in each instance to their opposite, in order to find, somewhere in between, what is really meant—that is, in order to recognize what the circumstances are, and how they could be made better."[31] Gadamer contends that we do not understand the dialogue by reading only the metaphors or the literal interpretation of the dialogue, but by learning to think utopically. In "Platos Denken in Utopien," Gadamer writes that the reader should aim less at gaining a naïve understanding and more at learning to think in the forms of such plays of reason [*Vernunftspielen*].[32] That is, we should learn to recognize the "in between" that offers both what is present and what is yet to come. In this way, the dialogue recognizes not only shared language and common understanding but also the risk of language that cannot be contained. Language, as illustrated in the Socratic dialogues, demonstrates the precarity of fixed definitions and a stable polis.

Plato, in attempting to recover the meaning of truth and philosophy against the Sophists, acts as the poet. He preserves the memory of shared language while pointing toward futures yet unknown. Plato himself gives form to the human being in his dialogues. In discussing Gadamer's interpretation of Plato and the poets, Dennis Schmidt writes, "The being of language, which is what poetic language is most adept at exposing and releasing, has this potential because, as part of the formative and phenomenal stuff of the 'in-between' on which the place and possibilities of praxis take place, *the being of language renders unthinkable the very notion of the polis as a stable place that might be the secure home of autonomous subjects.*"[33] What language—specifically poetic language—shows is the groundlessness of political life and human existence in general. By coupling together poetic speaking and listening with the play of the in-between, Plato, as understood by Gadamer and Schmidt, recognizes that this groundlessness resists mastery and yet still requires us to give form to such existence. Play and poetic speaking are both transformative and risky.[34] Although Plato presents us with utopias in the form of the ideal state, the dialogue itself suggests a different site of utopia as the possibility of encounter. Plato locates human fragility and liminality at the center of philosophical questioning.

Gadamer's analysis of Plato recovers important dimensions of play and dialogue against more literal interpretations of Plato's texts. On the latter, play remains understood either as a flight of fancy or as a way to develop skill.[35] Similarly, by suggesting that philosophy provides a harmonizing function, thinkers have presupposed the dualism of the human as a bifurcated rational animal. On these accounts, play is either irrational or subordinate to reason, thus losing either its seriousness or its autotelic dimension. As either wholly separate from or in the service of the everyday, play lacks the very liminality that allows for freedom. In the next section, I trace how this malediction of play appears in other philosophical accounts.

IMITATION AND RECOGNITION AT PLAY IN TRAGEDY AND VIRTUE

Whereas Plato explains that the good life is play, Aristotle states outright that the aim of the good life cannot be play. He recognizes that both play and *eudaimonia* are autotelic and chosen for their own sake (*Nicomachean Ethics* 1176b10).[36] Furthermore, both are associated with pleasure. Still, he argues, "Happiness . . . does not lie in amusement [*paidia*]" (1176b23). Because the good life is the one associated with the highest form of virtue, that is, with that best element of us, the best life is one of contemplation, not amusement. Furthermore, since amusement is a kind of relaxation, and relaxation is necessary for the sake of activity, play qua amusement cannot be the highest good. Similarly, in *Politics*, Aristotle suggests that leisure, which allows for intellectual activity and pursues no other end, is superior to occupation. Aristotle is quick to clarify that in leisure, "we ought not to be playing, for then play would be the end of life. But this is inconceivable" (1137b35). Play might be employed, like sleep, as medicine to allow us to relax, which will in turn allow us to work. Leisure, though, as engaging in contemplation, is for its own sake. The pleasure that arises from play is that of relaxation or a release from the toil of work, whereas the pleasure of leisure "is the best, and springs from the noblest sources" (1138b9). If Aristotle's aim is, like Plato's, to cultivate virtuous citizens, then he must warn them against mistaking play, which is ignoble, for leisure, which is noble.

Despite rejecting play as the highest good, Aristotle's motivations are similar to Plato's. Stephen Kidd argues, for example, that Aristotle draws Plato's concept of the gods as thinkers to greater consequence. Because the gods require no sleep, do not work, and have no appetites, they have no need of relaxation. What remains for the activity of the gods is contemplation. Aristotle writes in Book X of *Nicomachean Ethics* that "the activity of God, which surpasses all others in blessedness, must be contemplative; and of human activities, therefore, that which is most akin to this must be most of the nature of happiness" (1128b21-24). Thus, the aim of human activity is to imitate the gods, as it is for Plato, but because Aristotle associates play with physical, rather than intellectual, activity and pleasure, play is wholly separate from this activity of the gods.[37] Aristotle, like Plato, argues that the cultivation of virtue through proper education is paramount for a good society. Such education includes play in music and rhythm, but it must be oriented toward what is noble and "not merely in that common part of music in which every slave or child or even some animals find pleasure" (*Politics* 1341a15). In learning music and rhythm, the child should aim not at becoming a professional musician, but rather at becoming a judge, that is, the right kind of spectator who attends to what is noble rather than what is common.[38] Here again, we find that play is subordinate to reason.

Although Aristotle's account collapses play into frivolous recreation, I suggest that we can locate playful elements to rehabilitate.[39] In Aristotle's account of tragedy, for example, we find a thorough account of the spectator experiencing possibilities she could not otherwise to return to a transformed understanding of herself. We find a playful *as if* in the development of virtue, characterized by openness and understanding rather than mastery. These elements share more with the account of play advanced by Gadamer and Fink than with that of play as escape. In the following, I examine these elements to offer a corrective against this tendency to dismiss play as frivolity.

Aristotle seems to follow Plato, especially in the discussion of mimesis, in subordinating poetry to philosophy. Aristotle writes in the *Poetics* that the poet "is a poet by virtue of the imitative element in his work, and it is actions that he imitates" (1451b28-29). Thus, to be a poet is to be an imitator, but of what might happen rather than what has happened. This speculative dimension of poetry, he argues, aligns poetry more with philosophy than with history by similarly engaging in universals. If poetry is mimetic, then it imitates philosophy as the original.

Aristotle identifies two causes for the origin of poetry. First, the human's earliest learning occurs in imitation, which is an advantage not shared by lower animals. Second, such imitation brings delight because it enables us to see realistic representations and to learn from them (1448b5-15). From these natural inclinations, poetry developed. Here, then, we find a sense of poetry akin to play, namely that poetry allows us to engage in new ways of understanding that we would not otherwise. Whereas Plato describes the mimesis of poetry, though, as mere imitation or copying, Aristotle describes mimesis as allowing us to recognize and understand what shows itself before us. In other words, while Plato's poet creates by simply mirroring, Aristotle's poet creates by bringing something forth and offers something instructive.

Gadamer contends that this sense of recognition is central to Aristotle's account of tragic poetry. Against aesthetic consciousness, tragedy is defined on the basis of the spectator's engagement. Aristotle clarifies that tragedy, as poetry, is the imitation of actions, but also of "incidents arousing pity and fear" (*Poetics* 1452a2). Thus, the spectator of a tragedy does not engage in disinterestedness, but suffers these emotions. Moreover, this affective response is not passive, but actively engaged in this process of learning how things are on the basis of what things could be. Aristotle's theory of tragedy, Gadamer argues, "may serve to exemplify the structure of aesthetic being as a whole" (TM 125). Whereas the aesthetic consciousness espoused by Romantic aesthetics relies on an overly subjective judgment of taste that results in total abstraction from the particular experience of art, tragedy, as Gadamer sees it, emerges out of communal meaning and examples. This shared meaning allows us to recognize both the situation and ourselves in that particularity.

The experience of the tragic is not a brief intoxication that reawakens us to our true being. Rather, by recognizing the tragic plot unfolding before us and our own feelings of pity and fear, we recognize ourselves in that shared story. Whereas the play of recreation might be an escape or sleep to return us to our true being, the play of tragedy is always our own world that we come to belong to and recognize ourselves "more profoundly" in it (TM 129). Importantly, the tragic offers the recognition of cultural touchstones. For example, Aristotle claims that audiences can easily identify "the murder of Clytemnestra by Orestes and of Eriphyle by Alcmeon" (*Poetics* 1453b24). Gadamer explains that, "Recognition, as understood by Aristotle, presupposes the continuing existence of a binding tradition that is intelligible to all and in which we can encounter ourselves" (RB 100). Importantly, this bind does not strictly determine the response. Instead, Gadamer means that we are born in and through tradition; the tradition of shared meaning is what renders something intelligible and recognizable in the first place. We recognize our role in that tradition through witness of the tragedy, but we also encounter ourselves as human. In the movements of reversal and discovery in the tragic plot, we recognize the human condition as vulnerable and finite, as ignorant and loving (*Poetics* 1452b9). We learn about the human actions that give rise to and respond to tragedy.

I believe that it is here that we see those elements of play that are more than frivolity. The tragic poet, by imitating what could be, serves as poet by preserving the memory of tradition and by bringing forth a world in which we can bear witness to ourselves. In everyday life, we cannot experience our own death as such. Tragedy opens a space for us to hold life and death together in a way we could not otherwise. Witness to what is and what could be arises in this liminal space. Tragedy presents us with a world both our own and not, with a situation that invites our participation but rejects our mastery. The tragic play opens a site of resistance and transformation; it opens a site of freedom. Tragedy teaches us what it is to be human.

The relationship between recognition and transformation undergirds Aristotle's theory of virtue. Aristotle writes in the *Nicomachean Ethics*, "For the things we have to learn before we can do, we learn by doing, . . . so too we become just by doing just acts, temperate by doing temperate acts, brave by doing brave acts" (1103a26-1103b2). We become just and temperate by performing these acts "*as* just and temperate men do them" (1105b7) or "in the way in which the man of practical wisdom would determine it" (1107a1).

In order to become virtuous, we must be able to recognize both the courageous person and the appropriate response in a given situation. Thus, a person becomes virtuous not automatically, but over time through her development. She acts *as if* she were a temperate person, for example, by performing temperate acts. She acts *as if* she were courageous by doing courageous things. We do not develop merely through theoretical reflection or adopting skills, but through doing, acting as if something is the case.

The person on the way to virtue imitates the virtuous person, but such imitation is not a mere copying. Rather, the imitation is of what is meaningful in the virtuous action and interpreting it in a new context. Gadamer suggests in *Truth and Method* that when we encounter a work of art, we recognize what it is that the work represents or imitates. What is most profound about recognition is not that we see what we already know: "The joy of recognition is rather the joy of knowing *more* than is already familiar. In recognition what we know emerges, as if illuminated from all the contingent and variable circumstances that condition it is grasped in its essence" (TM 113). Although Gadamer here specifically addresses art, I believe this account of recognition holds for recognition in general. While recognition reaffirms what we know, it also exceeds what we know. We move beyond the familiar. The recognition of the virtuous action is also a self-recognition and self-understanding in showing both what is familiar and what emerges anew. This recognition does not leave us unchanged. Rather, it calls us toward transformation.

Acting as the courageous person is not the same, however, as Sartre's man of bad faith who believes he is a waiter by performing as a waiter, or de Beauvoir's description of nostalgia for childhood as bad faith, for bad faith involves a self-deception and a kind of playing *at* that I do not believe is present in Aristotle's account. The person of bad faith might be, then, like the rash man who is a pretender to courage (NE 1115b29-30), wishing to appear a certain way rather than committing to being a certain way. Acting *at* forecloses the transformation invoked by acting *as if*. The point here is that we do not develop virtue through mere theoretical reflection or the adoption of skills, but through doing, acting as if something is the case. Gadamer identifies Aristotle's account of practical reason as "a kind of *model of the problem of hermeneutics*" (TM 320-21). By this, he means that Aristotle provides an account of responding to a situation not through calculation, but through an attunement to what confronts us. Only by recognizing the ambiguity and particularity of the situation before us are we able to respond. There is something playful about this encounter between the self and what surpasses us as we navigate the liminal space of imitating the life of virtue. That is, through imitation that seeks neither to copy nor to imitate, we engage in new possibilities that confront us and allow ourselves to be transformed by them and to transform ourselves in return.

PLAYFUL FREEDOM

In Kant's formulation of the categorical imperative, we find an "as if" structure similar to Aristotle's. Kant follows the first formulation of the categorical imperative, "act only in accordance with that maxim through which you can at the same time will that it become a universal law" with "act *as if* the maxim of your action were to become by your will a universal law of nature."[40] That is to say, even if a maxim were not universal, we must act as if it were. It is important to note that in the second formulation, though, Kant does not say that we should use others and ourselves *as if* ends rather than means, but that they are indeed are such. Still, in the third formulation, we see that "every rational being must act *as if* he were by his maxims at all times a lawgiving member of the universal kingdom of ends" or as the formal principle says, "act *as if* your maxims were to serve at the same time as a universal law."[41] Thus we must act as if we belong to the kingdom of ends and as if others are also rational lawgivers in this kingdom. Again, the playful "as if" dimension permeates Kant's account. This "as if" is serious, though, even if it is playful (or, perhaps, because it is playful).[42] The "as if" enables us to formulate maxims and choose moral actions.

We also find play in how actions are chosen. Kant describes duties of virtue, that is, duties relating to one's ends, as that "for which external lawgiving is not possible"[43] and "based only on free self-constraint."[44] As Kant explains, "for if the law can prescribe only the maxim of actions, not actions themselves, this is a sign that it leaves a playroom [*Spielraum*] (*latitudo*) for free choice in following (complying with) the law."[45] Similarly, ". . . the duty has in it a latitude [*Spielraum*] for doing more or less, and no specific limits can be assigned to what should be done."[46] Here Kant quite clearly demonstrates that even within duty and the law, autonomy remains playful. Indeed, his account of autonomy would be unsuccessful if this play were not afforded, for the agent could not choose how to give herself the law and would thus be heteronomous. Although Gadamer accuses Kant of strong formalism and abstraction and finds Kant's insistence on the dual nature of humans quite problematic, we should not overlook the centrality of this *Spielraum* for free choice of actions.

Kant recognizes a groundlessness belonging to morality, precisely because the freedom and world of understanding that ground the intelligible world are inaccessible. As Kant explains, "it is impossible for us to explain, in other words, *how pure reason can be practical*" and "[it] is just the same if I tried to fathom how freedom itself as the causality of a will is possible. For then I leave the philosophic ground of explanation behind and I have no other."[47] What would provide this ground is the idea of a pure world of understanding, yet this is merely "a useful and permitted idea for the sake of a rational belief, even if all knowledge stops at its boundary."⁴⁸ This pure world is itself a kind of playspace, meaning that it is not fully real, but we act as if it were, as it lies beyond conceptuality and even comprehensibility.

As discussed in the first chapter, Kant imbues his theory of aesthetic judgment with play, particularly in connection to freedom. The enlivening spirit of the aesthetic experience allows us to engage ourselves both as finite and free. We awaken to possibilities we could not otherwise experience. Gadamer lauds Kant for asking philosophically about the experience of art and beauty in its own right and for celebrating the delight we find in the autonomy of art (RB 18). In his discussions of taste and genius, Kant recognizes that the free play of the imagination "allows us 'to go on to think much that cannot be said'" (21). Thus, the play of the faculties allows us to attune ourselves to what cannot be fully conceptualized. Gadamer suggests that Kant's overall aim in the Third Critique is to release art from subordination to conceptual knowledge while at the same time preserving art's relation to cognitive understanding (164). In other words, Kant strives to explain that, although aesthetic experience is nonconceptual, it is not opposed to conceptual understanding. Still, because Kant affords no cognitive content to aesthetic experiences, there is no possibility of recognition. Importantly, while Gadamer ascribes a cognitive element to play, he does not think of play as purely, or even primarily, cognitive. Rather, in play there is an act of understanding that often exceeds our ability to fully cognize it. By exceeding our capacity for conceptualization, this excess or superabundance is the nonconceptual element of play.

While Kant does grant this playspace of reason, he, like Plato and Aristotle, ultimately subordinates this play to reason. Where play is understood in its ability to give shape to and form to the self and the playspace, Kant shifts away from this formative attunement by turning aesthetic experience into a pure judgment of taste that is universally communicable. Although the judgment of taste is subjective, it simultaneously loses any particularity by appealing to the abstract *sensus communis*. Gadamer suggests that this idea of perfect taste is dubious. Indeed, "One does violence to the concept of taste if one does not accept its variability" (TM 51). For Gadamer, taste cannot—and should not—be a universal aesthetic principle. Because aesthetic experience is now understood as disinterested, thus separate from knowledge and morality, and abstracted from everyday life, art itself becomes a wholly separate sphere.

Following Kant, Schiller maintains art's autonomy from everyday practical life. Art does not provide cognitive content or access to truth. Our experience of art is nonconceptual. Still, Schiller argues that, although art is autonomous, it is not wholly separate from practical life. He identifies a bridge between the two precisely insofar as freedom appears in both aesthetics and morality.⁴⁹

Freedom, according to Schiller, arises from the harmonization of the formal and material drives by the play drive. Play harmonizes matter and form by holding them in an endlessly creative tension rather than resolving them into a rule. This free play is manifest in beauty. Schiller contends that beauty is grounded not in theoretical, but practical reason. Because freedom exceeds cognition, it cannot be represented by thought. Beauty, though, allows freedom to show forth in appearance. The freedom is precisely that of appearance showing forth as itself without being grounded in a reason external to it. In this way, a causal chain of necessity is interrupted.

In the *Kalliasbriefe*, Schiller maintains Kant's formalism, but remains concerned that Kant's version results in an empty formalism. For example, Schiller believes Kant's appeal to the arabesque as paradigmatic of beauty indeed "seems to miss the concept of beauty completely."[50] Although Schiller grants the autonomy of aesthetic experience, he does not also want to separate aesthetic consciousness from art itself. Missing from Kant's account is precisely the sensuous, thus Kant fails to account for the human condition as both rational and sensible. Schiller thus strives to retain a connection between form and sense. Kant argues that beauty pleases through a concept, thus through the understanding, but Schiller denies this.[51] He explains that the beautiful object pleases by its excess of form. That is, the object appears as self-determining and not restricted by its material. It appears to give form to itself, beholden to no rule or necessity external to it. Because the self-determination of beauty as freedom shows itself in appearance, the experience of beauty occurs in intuition and therefore cannot be separated from sense. As self-determining and excessive, the object appears free.

Drawing an analogy to the animal world, Schiller suggests that the more a creature seems to be free from its material, the more beautiful it is. A Clydesdale and a Spanish palfrey might be the same mass, but the latter is the more beautiful because it seems free from its mass when it gallops and bucks whereas the former merely plods along.[52] An art object is beautiful not because it imitates a particular object or representation. If that were the case, then the object would not appear as free but as held against an external criterion. Instead, the object is an appearance of freedom that challenges us to imitate it in its freedom. In the *Kalliasbriefe* he writes, "That is why the realm of taste is the realm of freedom—the beautiful world of the senses is the happiest symbol, as the moral ought to be, and every object of natural beauty outside me carries a guarantee of happiness which calls to me: be free like me."[53] Although the realm of art is wholly separate from practical life, the appearance of freedom in beauty beckons us to exercise our autonomy in a similar fashion.

Schiller argues that the experience of beauty inspires us to cultivate gentility and respect. The beautifully composed dance or painting calls us to "have consideration for the freedom of others" and to "show [our] freedom."[54] Freedom means neither domination nor passivity, but comportment and tact. From what appears *as if* free, we similarly form ourselves. As Schiller clarifies in a footnote to Letter XX, when something relates to the "totality of our various functions without being a definite object for any single one of them," then that thing shows its aesthetic character. For Schiller, then, the aesthetic always refers to this totality. Thus, an aesthetic education, "an education to taste and beauty . . . has as its aim the development of the whole complex of our sensual and spiritual powers in the greatest possible harmony" (AE 143). The freedom cultivated in aesthetic education is not free from all compulsion, but rather shows itself as constrained neither by nature nor logic. Aesthetic freedom occupies the space in between "the sensuous determination of the physical" and the "rational determination [of] the logical or moral" (AE 142). As this in between, beauty returns us to ourselves as whole by offering an indeterminacy through which we can choose what shape to give ourselves.[55] Although beauty is the space between and spanning matter and form, it does not simply fill in the gap between them because the distance between them is in fact infinite. Yet, through beauty, we are able to activate both sense and reason, which in their striving cancel one another out and hang in balance. This is not an empty balance, but a thorough freedom as each actually becomes what it is through the other.[56] He declares in Letter XXI that Beauty is our "second creatress," after Nature, for it offers "the possibility of becoming human beings" (AE 149). Beauty offers the freedom to become what we ought to be. Although Schiller does not identify the beautiful object as playful, I think there is such an element in beauty's self-grounding and excess. What beauty shows is precisely the possibility of doing otherwise, of giving shape to ourselves in new ways.

Like Plato, Schiller considers the possibility of a new republic guided by the principles of beauty, although Schiller grants appearance vis-à-vis freedom into this republic.[57] The aesthetic offers not only the possibility of humanity, but also of a human community. In both of these utopic states, citizens develop into good citizens neither through domination nor self-determination. Rather, goodness develops through the cultivation of an attunement to Beauty initiated through play.[58] Yet, Schiller's "aesthetic state" differs from Plato's Republic because Schiller embraces, rather than exiles, art and poetry. In a 1793 letter to Körner and again in Letter XXVII of the Aesthetic Letters, Schiller further clarifies that his aesthetic state is unlike Plato's Republic because, in the aesthetic state, all things are equal to one another because beauty regards all things as ends in themselves:

> Beauty, or rather taste, regards all things as ends in themselves. . . . Everyone is a free citizen and has the same rights as the most noble in the world of aesthetics, . . . which is quite different from the most perfect Platonic republic,

even the gown I wear on my body demands respect for its freedom from me, much like a humble servant who demands that I never let on that he is serving me. In exchange, it promises to use its freedom in such a way that it will not curtail my own freedom.[59]

To be free is to have no external influence or coercion. The poplar that bends in the wind is beautiful because what it is to be a poplar is to bend, whereas the birch is beautiful if it grows straight up. Clothing is beautiful when it is neither too tight nor too loose. Thus, the freedom of the human is as important as the freedom of the dressing gown, pot, or poplar. Schiller echoes this in Letter XXVII: "In the Aesthetic State everything—even the tool which serves—is a free citizen, having equal rights with the noblest" (AE 219). He adds an important qualification, though. This State of Aesthetic Semblance, if it exists at all, is quite rare. It exists "only in a few chosen circles, where conduct is governed, not by some soulless imitation of the manners and morals of others, but by the aesthetic nature we have made our own" (AE 219). Thus, unlike the ideal state in the *Republic* or *Laws*, this ideal state cannot come about through training or imitation. Instead, the aesthetic state exists as a need in every "finely attuned soul" and, in actuality, only for those select few who have made aesthetic nature their own.

Like Plato and Aristotle, Schiller seems to direct his work to the upper classes to specify how leisure time should be best spent. Part of Schiller's concern is due to the failed experiment of the French Revolution. Although the Enlightenment promised freedom and democracy through reason, it resulted in terror and tyranny. Schiller argues that the population was unprepared for Rousseau's social contract (AE 12-13). The triumphant call of reason failed to account for humans in their totality and abstracted too greatly from everyday life. The aesthetic state, which is yet to come, thus will not actually be free unless it allows for the appearance of freedom engendered by the harmony of drives. Schiller's aesthetic letters are thus meant to resist the totalizing forces of Enlightenment reason not by collapsing one drive into the other, but rather by preserving the creative tension between them.[60] Even if the aesthetic state cannot be fully achieved, moving toward it by inspiring the right sorts of attitudes could at least protect against the violence of reason.

Play preserves this tension between the drives, but Schiller clarifies that not any sort of play suffices; only aesthetic play achieves this harmony. For example, physical play also arises from superabundance and is made possible because of a lack of necessity. When the lion is not gnawed by hunger or provoked into battle, it "fills the desert with a roaring that speaks defiance and his exuberant energy enjoys its *self* in purposeless display" (AE 207). Such play is accompanied by freedom, but it is, according to Schiller, freedom from any external compulsion rather than freedom from necessity.

Aesthetic play requires a greater freedom, a "leap" away from any material concerns such that "what is in fact unnecessary soon becomes the best part of his delight" (AE 211). Rather than delighting with pleasing objects, one who plays aesthetically instead cultivates herself into something pleasing. What, in physical play, were the uncoordinated movements of vitality now become the coordinated steps of dance; the roar of the lion or shrieks of delight are now poems and songs. Here again we find the connection between freedom and the cultivation of an attunement to what is other. Jacques Rancière writes, "The aesthetic free play is, in the strongest sense of the term, a suspensive state, a state that suspends the logic of domination by actualizing a freedom that is the seed of a new humanity, because it is a freedom without opposite, or rather one that has *partialness* as its only opposite, the separation and the function of the humanities."[61] Rancière argues that a kind of rupture belongs to the beautiful. The aesthetic experience promises a third way that mediates between the formal and material drives. As the possibility of freedom for a new humanity, this play is neither frivolous nor escapist, but fundamentally serious. Aesthetic play resists domination and totalization by preserving what is other.

Although Hölderlin argues that Kant and his inheritors rely on false dualisms, here it seems that Schiller, rather than assuming a division in the first place, gestures toward an original unity that must be restored. If it is the case that beauty, as the limen between matter and form, passivity and activity, sense and reason, allows us to become what we are, then this unification is a return to what is already harmonized rather than the imposition of unity on dualisms. Aesthetic education seems here to be less an overcoming and more a restoration of the self. Schiller makes a similar claim in "On Naïve and Sentimental Poetry" that the Greeks did not experience the same sort of alienation as the moderns. Regarding the objects of nature, he writes, "They *are* what we *were*; they are what we *should become* once more. We were nature like them, and our culture should lead us along the path of reason and freedom back to nature" (NSP 180–81).[62] We strive to be like the Greeks who were one with nature and harmonized in their existence. To be naïve like the Greeks is not to be foolish, but, like a child, to overlook the artificial and focus on the simple nature of things. Now, however, we have freedom, and have "lost both happiness and completeness" (192). Yet, we cannot merely take on the ancient perspective. We must rather develop our own guides. Schiller clarifies that all poets are either naïve or sentimental. The former is one with nature; the latter has an urge for such unity. Schiller does not claim that the ancients are necessarily naïve and the moderns necessarily sentimental, but that those tendencies characterize the ages. If the modern longs for completion, it can only be through sentimental poetry. He writes, "This road taken by the modern poets is, moreover, the same road humans in general must travel, both as individuals and as a whole. Nature makes a human being one with himself, art separates and divides him; by means of the ideal he returns to the unity" (202). Again, only through attending to our current condition can we pursue this harmony. Thus, Schiller shows that our relation to tradition is dynamic. We cannot seek a return to harmony by simply reappropriating ancient culture. Instead, the modern poet points both to what was and what is yet to come. Schiller further clarifies that, although the naïve and sentimental poets differ in their relations to nature, both have the common task of giving full expression to human nature. Moreover, what is necessary is a union of both. Too much of an emphasis on the naïve power of freedom does violence to reason; too much an emphasis on moral ennoblement does violence to the sensible (244). Neither alone can fully express or contain "the ideal of beautiful humanity, an ideal that can only emerge from the intimate union of both" (249).

What Schiller's account of poetry demonstrates is that we become most fully human not through a domination of our nature, but through a preservation of difference. To become who we are, we must attune ourselves to what is other. Even then, there remains something inarticulable and indeterminate, yet meaningful. We give form to ourselves not through rational calculation, but through the play of the in between. I grant, following Gadamer, that while Schiller does correct Kant's account of disinterested aesthetic consciousness, he still relies on an overly strict distinction between art and practical life. Furthermore, his explicit discussions of play rely on an overly subjective approach that views play as the product of the spectator. Missing is attention to how the spectator herself is taken up in play and is engaged in dialogue with the work in its particularity. Still, because Schiller insists that this possibility for humanity cannot be separated from the community and must involve sensibility, his separation of art and the world is perhaps not as thoroughgoing as Gadamer argues (or even as much as Schiller himself desires). Schiller's interpretation of the freedom in the play of appearance suggests something akin to the non-actuality of play argued by Fink. Yet, whereas Fink maintains that the non-actuality and groundlessness of play expresses the groundlessness of the world totality and abyssal freedom, Schiller's Kantian tendencies seem to suggest that a noumenal, rational world remains behind those appearances.

In this chapter, I have attempted to outline accounts of play in philosophy. Although many of the figures discussed equate play with frivolity, a closer examination of their accounts, especially regarding art and beauty, demonstrates that play is indeed serious by offering the possibility of doing otherwise. The recognition such possibilities afford call for our transformation. As in Rilke's "Torso of an Archaic Apollo," we are addressed by the demand that we must change our lives. Attending more to how the appearance of freedom shows us both who we are and who we ought to be will allow us to see more clearly how a poetic education, rather than aesthetic education, moves beyond a subjective judgment of taste to a cultivation of self-formation. In the next chapter, I return to Gadamer and Fink to provide a more robust account of play as the site of encounter and possibility of otherwise. I argue that an alternative picture of the self must account for the particular abyssal ground and inherent otherness that belong to human existence. Historical attempts to ground education in universal laws and reason or freedom as human agency have failed to attend to that abyssal dimension. Moreover, such accounts have failed to attend to the liminal space of the self. One way in which we might conceive of how education, as groundless, remains meaningful while neither abstracted from rules nor merely relative to individual experiences is by turning our attention to the playspace of education.

NOTES

1. Dudenredaktion, *Das Herkunftswörterbuch*, 766.
2. Dudenredaktion, 766.
3. There is a wealth of literature on play, especially in the fields of anthropology, sociology, psychology, and animal studies. Because Fink and Gadamer, in particular, center their discussions of play in response to Kantian and post-Kantian philosophy, my aim is to follow these conversations rather than addressing play studies more broadly. Moreover, many contemporary play theorists view play, especially in regard to development, as a behavior or development of skill. Thus, they do not necessarily recognize play's autotelic nature or they do not consider human development as oriented toward the abyssal ground of existence.
4. Gadamer, *The Idea of the Good in Platonic-Aristotelian Philosophy*, 6.
5. Sutton-Smith, *The Ambiguity of Play*, 214.
6. Fagen, *Animal Play Behavior*, 493.
7. Although Fink contends that humans are uniquely capable of this symbolic relation, his claim should not be read as separating humans off from non-humans. It is not that humans play because they are not animals, but rather that humans play because of the kind of animal (i.e., the *ens cosmologicum*) they are.
8. Spariosu, *Modernism and Exile*, 26–27.
9. For other, more detailed discussions of Plato on play, see Ardley, "The Role of Play in the Philosophy of Plato," Gundert, "Zum Spiel bei Platon," Nagel, *Masking the Abject: A Genealogy of Play*, 29–46, Roochnik, "The 'Serious Play' of Book 7 of Plato's Laws," and Spariosu, *God of Many Names*, 141–93.
10. All references to Plato's work are from Plato, *Complete Works*.
11. As Spariosu argues, "Plato attempts to redefine *mimesis* as imitation or duplication against archaic miming, present in both *mousike* and ritual, thus separating mythopoetic language in general from its central cultural function within a prerational mentality." With the development of rational philosophy thought, Plato moves away

from understanding *mimesis* as miming and play as ritualistic response to the play of fate to understanding *mimesis* as imitation and play as supporting rational values and behaviors. Spariosu, *Dionysus Reborn*, 17.

12. Italics in translated text.

13. In his "Notes on 'Play and Philosophy,'" Fink writes that the designation of the human as plaything conceals an explosive ambiguity: Is it that the player participates in a higher freedom through play? Or is it that our freedom is actually embedded in "obscure sources" and especially "in the hands of the divinity—like a plaything"? (PSW 282).

14. Huizinga similarly contends that, "The Platonic identification of play and holiness does not defile the latter by calling it play, rather it exalts the concept of play to the highest regions of the spirit. We said at the beginning that play was anterior to culture; in a certain sense it is also superior to it or at least detached from it. In play we may move below the level of the serious, as the child does; but we can also move above it—in the realm of the beautiful and the sacred." Huizinga views Plato's account of play as correctly identifying play's ritualistic dimension. Play, like that of the divine, is a serious form of play, but outside the necessities of everyday life. Huizinga, *Homo Ludens*, 19.

15. The Stranger's reference to the checkers-player seems to reference Heraclitus's Fragment 52, "Time is a child playing draughts, the kingship is a child's." Heraclitus, "Fragment 52," in Hermann Diels and Walther Kranz, eds., *Die Fragmente der Vorsokratiker*, vol. 1 (Zurich 1985). This fragment, too, becomes essential for Fink's interpretation of the world as play. See especially *Play as Symbol of the World*, 51–52. Whereas Heraclitus, according to Fink, views the playful power of gods and humans as poietic, for Plato, such playful power is technic.

16. For a fuller discussion of the role of religion in Fink's account of play, see Alvis, "God's Playthings," 88–117.

17. Gadamer, "Plato and the Poets," 47.

18. Gadamer, 54.

19. Gadamer, 54.

20. Gadamer, 65.

21. Discussing the *Timaeus*, Gadamer writes, "Even Plato's contemporary readers certainly did not accept the idea that Plato really meant all this literally. In every word of the *Timaeus* one can detect Plato's joyful play with the stories he is telling . . . I think that overall one has to picture the *Timaeus* as a game of Plato" (GR 400–401).

22. Gadamer, *Plato's Dialectical Ethics*, 3.

23. "The indirect tradition of which informs us of the principles in Plato's doctrine is not evidence of some dogma which lies concealed behind Plato's written work and which could possibly undermine our understanding of Plato's dialectic. On the contrary, it articulates and confirms the limitedness of all human knowing and shows why the highest possibility of such knowing must be named not *sophia* but *philosophia*" Gadamer, *Dialogue and Dialectic*, 155.

24. Di Cesare, *Gadamer*, 130.

25. Gadamer, "Plato and the Poets," 67.

26. Gadamer, *The Idea of the Good in Platonic-Aristotelian Philosophy*, 99.

27. Gadamer, "Plato and the Poets," 68.
28. Gadamer, 60.
29. Gadamer, 70.
30. Gadamer, *The Idea of the Good in Platonic-Aristotelian Philosophy*, 96–97. Gadamer connects this seriousness or steadfastness with dialectic, which is not simply an art that can be learned: "The unerring way in which Socrates lived his life in Plato's portrayal of him" demonstrates that what "gives Plato's dialectic as a whole its underlying meaning is that he demands justification in *logos* from the persona of Socrates." For this reason—and not for reasons of aesthetics and taste—we must read the dialogues as imitations of real discussions that gather the partners into a play in which "they all have something at stake." On Gadamer's reading, Plato offers a playful dialectic that requires a particular stance toward the discussion. Thus, the aim is not theoretical mastery, but steadfast attunement to what plays out before us.
31. Gadamer, 71.
32. Gadamer, *Plato im Dialog*, 288.
33. Schmidt, *Lyrical and Ethical Subjects*, 30.
34. Schmidt, 31.
35. These are not the only ways in which play is conceived in the history of Western philosophy, though I believe them to be the most dominant tendencies. Brian Sutton-Smith argues that we might distinguish among seven different rhetorics of play, including play as progress, fate, power, identity, imaginary, self, and frivolous. For our purposes, I suggest the rhetorics of play as progress or as frivolous are most prevalent, though elements of the other rhetorics are certainly to be found in philosophy or as part of both progress and frivolity. Sutton-Smith, *The Ambiguity of Play*, 9–12.
36. All references to Aristotle are from Aristotle, *The Complete Works of Aristotle: The Revised Oxford Translation*.
37. Kidd, "Play in Aristotle," 364.
38. On this point, see Nightingale, "Liberal Education in Plato's Republic and Aristotle's Politics," 163.
39. Nagel, *Masking the Abject: A Genealogy of Play*, 56. Mechthild Nagel's discussion of Aristotle's "malediction of play" identifies play with *paidia* in the *Nicomachean Ethics* and with *mimesis* in the *Politics* and *Poetics*. She explains, "Three different kinds of hierarchical ranking of play can be identified: first, in the *Nicomachean Ethics*, play is ranked lowest and is squarely denounced as an activity unworthy of a virtuous person; secondly, in the *Politics*, play is considered a 'harmless' activity, which can be taken up for educational and recreational purposes by the youth and lower classes (the demos); and finally, in the *Poetics*, play gains a higher status . . . The play for amusement, enjoyed by the masses, is valuable if it is not tainted by 'bad' elements, i.e., Dionysian elements. Thus in tragedy we find a play that is valued for its own sake, but it is appropriately purified." While Nagel is correct that there are important differences in Aristotle's attitude toward play in the different texts and that when play does arise, it is seen primarily as rational play, I suggest that attending only to where Aristotle directly addresses play as *paidia* gives an incomplete picture of what he seems to be up to in the *Nicomachean Ethics*. I maintain that there is a fundamentally playful dimension to his work despite his malediction of perhaps not so much play, but amusement.

40. Kant, *Groundwork of the Metaphysics of Morals*, 4: 421. Italics added for emphasis.

41. Kant, 4: 438.

42. Spariosu, *Dionysus Reborn*, 36. Spariosu explains that Kant's *als ob* is informed by Plato: "If the thing-in-itself (*Ding an sich*) is unknowable, then cognition becomes possible only in the *as if* mode, and can manifest itself, at least the primary sensorial level, only as paly of appearances. Hence the necessity in the Kantian thought, just as in the Platonic one, of distinguishing between good and bad illusions, good and bad presentations, good and bad play . . . .That Kant is fully conscious of the Platonic source of his *as if* approach to knowledge is apparent in his references to the Platonic doctrine of eternal Ideals (which is the model for his own doctrine of transcendental ideas)."

43. Kant, *The Metaphysics of Morals*, 6:239.

44. Kant, 6:383.

45. Kant, 6:390.

46. Kant, 5:393.

47. Kant, *Groundwork of the Metaphysics of Morals*, 4:462.

48. Kant, 4:462.

49. For a lengthy discussion of Schiller's understanding of freedom, particularly in response to Kant, see Beiser, *Schiller as Philosopher: A Re-Examination*.

50. Schiller, "'Kallias, or Concerning Beauty: Letters to Gottfried Körner' (1793)," 146.

51. Schiller, 153.

52. Schiller, 164.

53. Schiller, 173.

54. Schiller, 173–74.

55. Beiser suggests that many interpreters draw parallels between Schiller and Sartre on this point insofar as both think we give form to ourselves. Yet, Beiser argues, there is an important difference between the two since Schiller maintains that this creativity is not totally free or indeterminate, but rather is limited as the choice of how to balance our competing drives. Beiser, *Schiller as Philosopher: A Re-Examination*, 234. See also Hamburger, "Schiller und Sartre."

56. In a footnote to Letter XIX, Schiller clarifies what this means: "I do not mean that freedom which necessarily appertains to man considered as intelligent being, . . . but only that freedom which is founded upon his mixed nature. By acting rationally at all man displays freedom of the first order; by acting rationally within the limits of matter, and materially under the laws of reason, he displays freedom of the second order" (AE 137).

57. For a fuller discussion of Schiller's response to Plato, see Pugh, *Dialectic of Love*.

58. See also Spariosu, *Dionysus Reborn*, 64.

59. Schiller, "'Kallias, or Concerning Beauty: Letters to Gottfried Körner' (1793)," 170.

60. Acosta, "The Violence of Reason," 76. María del Rosario Acosta explains that Schiller's insistence on the sensible as complement to reason is because sensibility, by exposing us to others and receiving them, resists the violence of totalizing reason.

She writes, "Aesthetics is precisely what allows us to expand our gaze. It seems to be the outlook that, instead of moving precipitously toward the exclusion of all that is strange and toward the negation of everything that resists our comprehension, would be capable of undertaking the experience of this strangeness, thereby making it the very point of departure for our experience of freedom."

61. Rancière, "Schiller and the Aesthetic Promise," 129.

62. We treasure, Schiller claims, the humble flower or humming of bees because of "the silent creativity of life in them, the fact that they act serenely on their own, being there according to their own laws; we cherish that inner necessity, that eternal oneness with themselves" (NSP 180). The objects of nature creatively unfold according to their form. Humans long to give form to themselves in a similar sort of way. Here again we hear the sense of *Bildungstrieb* that runs throughout Schiller's work. We are driven to give form to our lives through creative expression not to master our nature, but rather to cultivate our attunement to that very nature.

Chapter 4

Becoming Who We Are

A Conversation

In the *Gay Science*, Nietzsche presents us with a question and answer: "What does your conscience say? . . . 'You shall become who you are'" (GS 270). Here we find the question that Gadamer locates in Celan's poetry, "Who am I and who are You?" The self encounters itself as both this I and You in dialogue. The imperative to "become who you are" is also the imperative, "Do Not Split the No from the Yes." Becoming what one is gathers past, present, and future into an uncanny play. How can one become what one already is? And how can one be what one is not yet? What this suggests is that the self is not self-same. To become who one is means neither staying the same nor becoming simply anything. Rather, it means that the self is fundamentally liminal as this threshold between past, present, and future selves.

   Nietzsche's aphorism seems to be a play on Hölderlin's translation of one of Pindar's odes: "Become that which you have learned" [*Werden, welcher du bist erfahren*].[1] Becoming who we are thus requires self-knowledge.[2] Babette Babich notes that Nietzsche cited Hölderlin's poems at length only twice in his later works.[3] Both poems have this sense of becoming as a return to the self. From "The Rhine," Nietzsche cites, "For as you began, so will you remain" and from "Lebenslauf," "But not for nothing does / our arc return us whence we began."[4] Here, we find intimations of Celan's meridian and rivers north of the future. In casting ourselves out, we return to ourselves in a transformational way. We encounter ourselves in conversation. It is this sense of becoming who one is that is at stake in the account of education I advance in this chapter. As Gadamer explains in *Truth and Method*, *Bildung* "is not achieved in the manner of a technical construction, but grows out of an inner process of formation and cultivation, and therefore constantly remains in a state of continual *Bildung*" (TM 10). *Bildung* is a constant state of becoming through the unfolding of cultivation. What is cultivated becomes one's own.

As we saw in the discussions of Celan's poetry, what is one's ownmost is time, memory. Understanding one's own requires knowing the measure that is appropriate. Again, this measure is not an absolute measure, but an attunement to the self as finite and as liminal.

In the previous chapter, I examined the ways in which play features in the history of Western philosophy. Though play is frequently equated with frivolity or subordinated to reason, I argued that these discussions still shed light on important dimensions of play, namely the significance of the in-between, the movement between foreign and familiar, and the development of an attunement to that play. Still, these accounts do not go far enough because they still rely on an overly subjective view of play and an understanding of the human as a rational animal. What is missing is this orientation toward limits, particularly toward the limits of what can be said and the limits of the self as finite. I argue in this chapter that a more robust sense of play, which is not merely the behavior of a subject but rather an ontological stance in the world, also requires a more robust sense of language and space.

What distinguishes the accounts of education of Fink and Gadamer from those discussed in the previous chapter is that what is at stake in education is neither merely the attainment of knowledge, nor a form of self-mastery. Rather, what is at stake is self-cultivation that develops out of the person and is oriented toward the world and others. This requires, too, that we listen for what might have been excluded or missed or silenced, but this listening and investigation into difference still happens in the play of language and dialogue. Play and education, like poetry, are always on the way and always characterized by alterity. Play, poetry, and education, as liminal, mark the navigation of the in-between through an attunement toward the multiple elements that give rise to and also surpass our selves. I argue that poetic education, as playful, is liberatory because it fosters the development of each person in her own particularity and in relation to others. Moreover, it fundamentally resists totalization. Here, play is not at the service of education, but rather is itself the education. To be educated is to have a comportment of creative responsibility to others and the world. Poetic education is the becoming of who we are through the conversation that we are.

In the following, I turn first to Nietzsche's discussion of the play of the Apollonian and Dionysian and his "artist metaphysics" to discuss how the play of art provides insight into the play of becoming and the self. For Nietzsche, the self is a fiction, yet our task is not to disavow the self as fiction, but to creatively give style to it. Against the metaphysics of presence, Nietzsche demonstrates that there is always an excess or superabundance of meaning. Drawing on Nietzsche's account, especially regarding Heraclitus, Fink argues that the world is the world of play. As *ens cosmologicum*, world beings, we participate in that world play, yet in a way that is never fully cognizable. To become what we are, for Fink, is thus to attune ourselves to that world totality. Because the world totality is the totality of all, including being and nothing, our attunement toward such totality is abyssal and finite. Furthermore, as world players, we are interwoven into our environments. Thus, Fink provides insights into how the human develops this comportment to the world, not like a subject among objects, but as a playful being open through understanding to both the foreign and familiar. Like Fink, Gadamer believes that the human is characterized by her comportment toward what exceeds her and that this comportment is developed through the play of question and answer in dialogue with another. For Gadamer, our existence is becoming, but becoming through language.

As we have seen in the previous chapters, this dwelling in language means holding open the space for what remains to be said. In the dialogical exchange in play, we can call our practices into question while still remaining open to them and open to new possibilities and change. The comportment required by play does not mean that we abandon our practices or break radically with the everyday, but that we engage it in a different way.

FROM ARTIST TO COSMIC PLAY

Fink contends that play is the "central metaphysical concept in Nietzsche," a metaphysical intuition, illustrated by the play of the Apollonian and Dionysian drives.[5] In Nietzsche, Fink also locates traces of what Heidegger considers the ontological difference, that is, the difference between being and beings, in Nietzsche's inversion of Platonic ideals. Against the metaphysics of being that he locates in especially in Pythagoras and Plato, Nietzsche hearkens back to Heraclitus and the world of becoming.[6] Nietzsche argues for an ontology of becoming characterized by the Dionysian as the temporalization of time and the Apollonian as temporalized in time. The play of becoming is thus the cosmic coming to be and passing away of appearance.

In the *Birth of Tragedy*, Nietzsche suggests there are two artistic powers constantly in play in the primordial unity [*Ur-Eine*] of nature: the Apollonian, the "image-maker," and the Dionysian, the imageless music (BT 14). Whereas the Apollonian tends toward creation, the *principium individuationis*, and order, the Dionysian tends more toward intoxication [*Rausch*] and annihilation. The Apollonian shows itself in beautiful dreams and as an order illuminated and individuated. The Dionysian, conversely, shows itself in rapture and the darkness of excess and self-forgetting. The two drives exist in continuous conflict and play of oppositions in nature itself.[7] Thus, they are not the product of the artist. Rather, the artist is compelled by these drives to create art, and specifically in the case of Greek tragedy, reflects these drives through an imitation of that primordial unity. The ancient Greeks, Nietzsche writes, knew this tension acutely and so created the Olympians to explain this strife. The same impulse that gave rise to this creation is the that which also calls art into existence and both hold up "a transfiguring mirror" that allows the Greek to see what nature indeed is (BoT 24). Dennis Schmidt describes this as "self-conversation" in which art, as the play between the Apollonian and Dionysian, opens up a space where this conversation could be had. Art presents us with what we could not otherwise see, namely the conflicting drives of nature that cannot be resolved in logic.[8] Furthermore, the work of art, as a semblance of a semblance, delights us with the recognition that all reality is semblance (26). The tragic thus opens a space—a playspace—for an encounter with the self. As transfiguring, the mirror does not merely copy. Every encounter with the mirror of tragedy involves a strangeness where what is familiar becomes foreign.

It is precisely this loss of the foreign, as the loss of the Dionysian, that Nietzsche identifies with the collapse of ancient tragedy. Nietzsche accuses Euripides and Socrates of stripping away the Dionysian in pursuit of the rational because they believed that everything beautiful or good must be rational. With the loss of the Dionysian comes the loss of "that epic condition of losing oneself in semblance" or "the delight in semblance" (61). Nietzsche describes Socrates as a cyclops, who attempts to see all as it truly is, thus fully embodying the metaphysics of vision. Yet, Socrates must come to realize "how logic curls up around itself at these limits and finally bites its own tail" such that what Socrates finally sees is that tragic knowledge that "needs art for protection and as medicine" (75).

Although Nietzsche later distances himself from *The Birth of Tragedy*, he still maintains that the critical insight of this text was that of the Dionysian mode, that "highest affirmation born out of fullness, out of overfullness, an unreserved yea-saying even to suffering, even to guilt, even to everything questionable and strange about existence."[9] Rather than trying to master ambiguity through reason or to disavow suffering, the one who says yes to life playfully affirms this ambiguity. Such life affirmation is particularly embodied by the artist.

Nietzsche comes to associate this fullness and superabundance of meaning with the play of both the child and the artist. In *Philosophy in the Tragic Age of the Greeks*, he writes, "In this world only play, play as artists and children engage in it, exhibits coming-to-be and passing away, structuring and destroying, without any moral additive, in forever equal innocence. And as children and artists play, so plays the ever-living fire. It constructs and destroys, all in innocence. Such is the game that the aeon plays with itself."[10]

Here, the appeal to Heraclitus is unmistakable. Existence is the constant coming-to-be and passing-away that is gathered together in the eternal fire. In the development of his writing, Nietzsche draws play and power more closely together. He references Heraclitus's Fragment 52: "Time (aeon) is a child playing draughts, the kingship is a child's." To be childlike is, on the one hand, to be earnest in play, beholden to no pre-given meaning, and, on the other hand, to affirm the play of fate or chance as beyond one's control. Thus, although Nietzsche employs a rather agonistic view of play in the strife of the Apollonian and Dionysian, here play as power is joyful and affirmative, echoing his imperative of *amor fati*.

This joyful affirmation undergirds the *Gay Science*, where Nietzsche tells us that one thing is needful: "To 'give style' to one's character—a great and rare art! . . . For one thing is needful: that a human being should attain satisfaction with himself, whether it be by means of this or that poetry and art" (GS 290). Our greatest task is to give style to ourselves. Rather than striving to find an ultimate ground or justification for life, we must rather fashion ourselves. We must, at times, look on ourselves from an artistic perspective, that is, from the perspective of construction and destruction. We are serious creatures, but at times, we must be playful in that seriousness. In GS 107, titled "Our Ultimate Gratitude to Art," Nietzsche claims that art allows us to be satisfied with ourselves for we act as the artist in "rounding off something" or "finishing the poem" so that we do not carry eternal imperfection "across the river of becoming," but rather are able to "feel proud and childlike." Art, he writes, "furnishes with eyes and hands and above all the conscience to be able to turn ourselves into such a phenomenon." Because art allows us to see the creative act of becoming and opens up the possibility of otherwise, we ourselves recognize our own lives as neither fixed nor prescribed, but also part of this flux. We can deny that, or we can affirm it through this self-styling. Again, importantly, Nietzsche believes there is no "self" that is self-identical, but we can still cultivate this attitude. We do so, he says, through "all exuberant, floating, dancing, mocking, childish, and blissful art less we lose the freedom above things that our ideal demands of us."

He carries this idea through to *The Will to Power* 797, writing, "The phenomenon 'artist' is still the most transparent:—to see through it to the basic instincts of power, nature, etc.! Also those of religion and morality! 'Play,' the useless-as the ideal of him who is overfull of strength, as 'childlike.' The 'childlikeness' of God, *pais paizon*." Although Nietzsche refers to play here as useless, his commitment to the revaluation of values should give us pause in thinking that he thereby means that play is only useless. Here, I take Nietzsche to mean that in play, just as in the case of art, there remains something excessive that cannot be reduced to an external purpose. Rather, it is useless in its self-sufficiency and superabundance. This, too, is echoed in

Nietzsche's discussion in *Thus Spoke Zarathustra*. Zarathustra describes that the spirit passes from the camel to lion to child. The camel, with the "sacred No" obediently desires to be burdened, but then is transformed into the lion with the rejection of "Thou shalt!" with his "I will!" Finally, the lion, who could reject old values, but not create new ones, becomes the laughing child, who speaks the "sacred yes." The child, Zarathustra explains, "The child is innocence and forgetting, a new beginning, a game, a wheel rolling out of itself, a first movement, a sacred yes-saying."[11] The play of the child is the play of time, of constant coming into and passing away of being, and self movement. She sees her own finitude not as something to be overcome, but as part of that eternal play. The child joyfully affirms this self-styling and appearance as reality. Whereas the camel only accepts predetermined values, the child creatively plays with those values and shows them to be what they are, namely appearance. Here, appearance is not the alternative to a true reality. Rather, appearance is reality.

This joyful creative play and revaluation of values is the will to power. The *Übermensch* is the one who takes this will to power as task and recognizes his own play as part of the cosmic play. Nietzsche attributes a similar play of creation and destruction to the world itself. In the last aphorism of *The Will to Power*, Nietzsche asks, "Do you know what 'the world' is to me?" The answer, shown in the mirror, is that the world is "without beginning, without end . . . not an empty space . . . but rather as force throughout, as a play of forces and waves of forces, at the same time one and many." The world is not an empty container of existence, but the eternal and joyful play of forces. It is self-creating and self-destroying, both mysterious and illuminating. It has no goal outside of this play of power. Indeed, its power is precisely in this eternal play. The world, Nietzsche claims, is the will to power, and the human is also this will to power as participant in the play of the world.[12]

What Nietzsche's accounts of play show is an alternative conception of the human. To become who we are, we must recognize ourselves as players, as ones who must give style to ourselves. Because there are no ready-made essences or definitions, we interpret the manifold perspectives before us.[13] If it is the case that we are fundamentally interpreters, and I think that it is, then the larger point is that we fundamentally inhabit language and worlds of meaning. Although Nietzsche's emphasis is primarily on the individual, as wary as he is of the herd mentality, there remains a sense that humans exist in shared language and world.[14] Interpretation, play, and creativity are not simply behaviors, but ways of being in the world. To try to get to any absolute meaning or to overcome the self is to deny life. There is no such absolute ground. Nietzsche's criticism of the history of philosophy's insistence on being and substance shows that although there is no absolute meaning, we should not thereby fall into nihilism. Neither should this lead us into a glib relativism of anything goes. Rather, he demonstrates that there is always more that could be said, and that multiplicity should be preserved. Our greatest task in life is to affirm both particularity and plurality and to cultivate our attunement to our finitude.

EDUCATION AND *ENS COSMOLOGICUM*

Like Nietzsche, Fink is wary of what he takes to be the metaphysics of presence, which views the human as the rational animal tasked with determining these ultimate essences. Although he does not ascribe the will to power to the world, like Nietzsche, Fink contends that the world is the play between being and nothing, creation and destruction, finite. In human play, we mirror the play of the cosmos. In "Play as Symbol of the World," he writes, "In human play the whole of the world is reflected back into itself, letting features of infinity emerge and shimmer in and on something innerworldly and finite" (PSW 205). He writes similarly in "Oasis of Happiness" that human play is "the symbolic activity of bringing the sense of the world and life to presence" (30). In this way, the human participates in the creation and destruction that belong to life. Because Fink thinks that the play of humans, as *ens cosmologicum*, mirrors the play of the world, before turning to his account of human play and education, I will first flesh out more what he means by world play.

Weltspiel

Fink begins his lecture course, *Welt und Endlichkeit*, with the suggestion that philosophy must begin with the world because philosophizing begins as the "inversion of all familiarity with the world [*Weltvertrautheit*]" (WE 195). Although the world is the most familiar thing we encounter, we have very little understanding of what it is.[15] Metaphysics, he claims, has historically presupposed this familiarity without actually inquiring into the world itself. Like Gadamer, Fink does not think we can merely escape metaphysical thinking. We cannot get outside of tradition. We can, however, attune ourselves to our conditionedness in relation to tradition to recognize new possibilities. Fink calls us to think the world non-metaphysically, that is, to think the world more radically as the possibility of existence. That is, rather than relying on metaphysics' dualisms of subjective and objective, being and nothing, presence and absence, thinking the world must instead mean attuning ourselves to the world as the totality of all, including both being and nothing. Fink argues that such an approach requires a new understanding of the finite human's relation to nature and the Absolute.

Fink argues that the world, as totality, is what allows being and beings to come to appearance. Fink credits Kant's work as "the first exhibiting of the cosmological horizon of the idea of being."[16] Kant makes this cosmological turn in his account of space and time as a priori intuitions of the subject. These intuitions are the conditions of the possibility of appearance of objects for a subject in a way that mirrors the world totality's own condition. Since space and time are a priori intuitions of the subject and the conditions of possibility of appearances, all objects belong to this field of the subject similarly to how all objects belong to the world as totality.[17]

Fink remains concerned, though, that Kant does not go far enough. In describing the world in subjective terms, Kant renders the world a principle of reason that does not exist anywhere in itself. Fink maintains conversely that the world is neither simply produced by a subject nor a mere manifestation of the subject's reason. As we saw in the previous chapter, Fink believes that the world gives being space and allows it time (PSW 140). In *Welt und Endlichkeit*, Fink explains, "The world is not a mere container in which things are gathered, . . . it is rather essentially also that which grants every being appearance, the rise into light and its finite tarrying" (307). Here, Fink rejects the subject-object distinction. The world does not stand over against subjects or hold them like a container. In "Play as Symbol of the World," Fink writes, "The world is near and far in a different way than a being can ever be near and far. All nearness and farness of beings is made possible by the spatiality and temporality of the world" (PSW 132). Because the world gives space and allows time, the world grants things their innerworldly appearance. Similarly, he explains that the world is neither the aggregate of things that exist nor a horizon of understanding; "In fact, it is neither *an objective nor a subjective totality*: the world is the clearing of *being* (WE 374). The world is the origin, the open totality, that grants beings their appearance in the first place.

Although the world, as the "totality of appearances," is not set over against world beings, the world does still remain distinct from what appears in the world (WE 117). Fink deems this the cosmological difference. Whereas Heidegger uses the ontological difference to distinguish between Being and beings, Fink's cosmological difference distinguishes between the world and beings in the world. This difference is twofold. First, the world is the totality of appearances, including humans as inter-worldly beings, but as totality, it differs from world beings and resists any attempt to fully cognize it. The world, as what grants appearance to all things, is not itself a thing. Second, despite the fundamental difference between the world and world beings, the world remains intimate and familiar for humans.

The world grants appearance, and thus grounds existence, yet, according to Fink, the world is itself groundless. The world is fundamentally marked by nothingness. Fink asserts that there is an Absolute that unifies both the world as the world that grants appearance and the human beings that constitute themselves in the world. Like Hölderlin, Fink draws on Heraclitus's interpretation of the cosmos as the beautiful joining of *ta panta*, the all, and *hen*, the one or the Absolute.[18] He supplements this with Nietzsche's description of the constant creation and destruction, joining and separating of the cosmos.[19] The Absolute, as the groundless totality that gives rise to all being, is the play between being and nothing, presence and absence. The world, too, is groundless insofar as it has no origin but itself, yet through this groundlessness, it provides a ground for innerworldly (*binnenweltlich*) things and a site for unconcealment.[20] The world is the condition for the possibility of experience.

Like the world, the earth is neither a thing nor material. Whereas the world allows things to be brought to light, the earth conversely resists any attempt to lay things bare. The earth is the dark, finite, and erotic dimension of humanity that philosophers abandoned when they came to understand the human as a rational animal. While the world unconceals, the earth conceals. This concealedness is more than the absence of intelligibility or clarity. It is a power that simultaneously makes present and withdraws. As both foreign and familiar, the earth is the originary site of alterity. We do not encounter the earth as earth. It itself is never factically given or perceivable:

> It is not here and not there, and also not everywhere in the sense of "in all places"; it is much more that which gives all place to places of things at all first in total. . . . It cannot be pointed to as an object, cannot be brought to the imagination as a thing or element. And yet it is not nothing. It is more being [*seiender*] than things and elements. . . . We always know, even if darkly, about the earth, but we never find it in the direction of objects; we can never imagine it. (SM 280)

Fink identifies the earth with *physis*, with nature, as that which gives rise to beings, but cannot be mastered, especially by science. There remains a fundamentally abyssal element to the earth that resists conceptualization. Thus, the earth resists the totalizing impulses of the metaphysics of presence. The earth reminds us that there is something beyond us, toward which we can attune ourselves, but never fully understand. The earth, as fundamentally other, opens the space for encounter. Thus, says Fink, our relation toward the earth should be one of gratitude and cultivation of an orientation toward our own finitude. This orientation requires us to recognize our own vulnerability and to see ourselves at risk and at stake.

Although we cannot know either world or earth in their entirety, we, as *Weltwesen*, can express our relation to the world symbolically through play.

Through the groundlessness of play, we can symbolically express the play of the world totality. Again, as Fink explains in *Welt und Endlichkeit* that, "The human is the world-being—not because he gives shape to the world, rather because he alone among all living creatures can hold himself out into the totality that surrounds, binds, joins, and maintains everything, gives everything space and leaves everything time" (375). This symbolic play thus resists any sort of subjectivization of this relationship. The world is not the result of projections or concepts of the subject; rather, the subject is constituted by the world.

Despite his emphasis on the finitude and situatedness of world-being, by focusing almost exclusively on the insurmountability and inaccessibility of the world and the cosmological nature of human existence, Fink arguably pays too little attention to the particular place of human existence. This is seen most readily in the fact that he discusses the space-giving nature of the world without also attending to the specific places that allow for the happening of world through them.[21] For example, in discussing the symbolic participation in play, the emphasis lies more on the expression of the totality of the play rather than on the particularity of the playspace or the player. Rather than specific participation, the emphasis on totality instead implies anonymity and substitutability in that participation. Yet, if we recall the earth as the site of alterity, then such substitutability is impossible. There always remains something that resists full totalization.

The Education of *Ens Cosmologicum*

These concerns about an over-emphasis on the inaccessibility of the earth or of the world totality are tempered more when we look more at Fink's account of education. Here, we find a more extensive treatment of co-existence and particular human history in relation to education. In the 1951/1952 lecture course, published as *Natur, Freiheit, Welt*, Fink traces the history of pedagogy and its modern forms to suggest how we should conceive of education for *ens cosmologicum*. Fink sees pedagogy, and more importantly upbringing,[22] as inextricably connected to nature, the world, and freedom. Pedagogy, as the science of education, has to do with what humanity is and how it should be. Since humans are, according to Fink, world-beings (i.e., *ens cosmologicum*), pedagogy must also give an account of being in the world as well as a being's relationship to itself. Fink's concern is that contemporary accounts of pedagogy have lost sight of what the human actually is. By insisting on becoming a science of children or education rather than seeing itself as a philosophical practice, pedagogy divorces itself from what should be its very content. Because pedagogy is always a recommendation for a way of life, it cannot rely on preexisting values. Rather, says, Fink, pedagogy cooperates with the ideal *Bildung*; it accompanies the projection of meaning in human life (NFW 54). In this lecture, Fink makes no attempt to develop a specific pedagogical program or educational guidelines, but rather to return pedagogy to its philosophical roots in a more radical way by investigating the groundlessness of education for *Weltwesen*.

When practiced as a science, pedagogy is technique, a mode of oppressive action that "reifies, constrains under certain specifications" and that "amputates human existence" of the very questions of meaning that religion and philosophy address (NFW 27). The science of education and upbringing attempts to assert its independence and self-sufficiency as a science, but in so doing, it removes the possibility of accounting for those things that provide any meaning. In this way, Fink sees contemporary pedagogy as fundamentally nihilistic.

Furthermore, contemporary pedagogy hinges on a distinction between the theoretical and the practical. True pedagogy, that is, pedagogy that understands itself as a practice and as philosophy, cannot be a science: "Pedagogy is greater than every science, not in the apparent sense of an identifiable hierarchy; it is greater because it is a mode of the movement of human freedom" (NFW 40). Science, which can deal only in particulars and decisions, has no space for this movement of freedom. Pedagogy, on the other hand, must concern itself with the understanding of the world if it is to avoid nihilism. In this sense, then, upbringing and philosophy stand in a mutual relationship. Not only can we have a philosophical upbringing, but we are also brought up, educated, through philosophizing, as Plato suggests in the coupling of philosophy and *paideia*. Fink insists that not only must pedagogy be rooted in philosophy, but also that philosophy must itself be rooted in the world.

If pedagogy is to be returned to philosophy, then we must be wary of reappropriating the language of metaphysics without investigating its concepts. As discussed above, Fink rejects the notion of the human as a half-animal, half-rational centaur, or a subject among objects. Rather than describing the human as one of these dualisms, however, he proposes that the human is a kind of *Mittere*, an in-between or mediator. The non-human animal, he explains, requires no education or upbringing. Although non-humans care for their young and mature, the animal is already what it is.[23] The gods are similarly complete and so require no education. Humans, though, having been given the task of forming themselves, are yet incomplete, and require education to become who they are (NFW 27). Between animals and the divine, the human is both and neither. Thus, education cannot result in a reduction to either pole. Rather, "the intermediariness of the human, in which he 'connects with' everything that is, his openness for the light of ideas and at the same time for his inner intimacy with the self-concealing nature, that 'loves to hide itself,' must be grasped as the decisive trait" (59). Like Kant, Fink holds that we need education to become who we are, but for Fink, the human is fundamentally liminal. Thus, to educate the human, for her to become who she is, is to give shape to this liminality, not to overcome it.

As Fink develops his lecture, he draws a closer link between the human and the world. The human exists as a relation [*Verhältnis*] and "is a strange being, he lives in the totality of beings, is essentially worldly. That means not only that he, like all things within the world, appears, but rather most of all, that the structure of human existence is formed, effected, and defined by this world relation [*Weltbezug*]" (NFW 94). Not only do humans relate to the world as what grants their appearance in the first place and which provides their nature, but they also relate to the world as abyssal. The human recognizes that she steps out into the world. In order to recognize this, she must also recognize herself. Thus, the human also has a self-relation. Still, Fink does not claim that the human exists primarily as Descartes' cogito or as a kind self-consciousness.[24] Such conceptions of the self rely on the very dualisms Fink seeks to replace. Instead, the human has a relation to herself in standing open to the world totality, that is, in recognizing what surpasses her. Fink writes in *Existenz and Coexistenz*, "The human, the creature who understands being, addresses all other things in the way that and what they are; as making a claim on the being of a being [*Ansprecher des Seins des Seienden*], he lives *in* language, which is also to say *in conversation*. The human is meaningfully [*sprechend*] joined to fellow humans" (EC 126). In standing open to the world, the human both addresses and is addressed by the world. She takes an interpretative stance as she inhabits the world. Furthermore, she remembers the "*Urgrund*," the *physis* out of which everything grows, that appears between heaven and earth. Remembering this *Urgrund* means also remembering one's finitude and that one's own body comes from and returns to the earth. Yet, of our own death we know nothing. Fink identifies this as the clue that all of human existence is a movement between "*Heimat und Fremde*," between familiar and foreign. The human is, as Fink draws from Heidegger, with others, in the world, and toward her own death.

This world openness is also the sphere of freedom. Freedom is not the ability to do any or everything I desire, but rather is the sphere that allows for projection toward my possibilities, including the possibility of death (NFW 168).[25] In relating to myself as finite, I determine the measure appropriate to me. There is no inherent measure or value, Fink explains. He writes in *Grundfragen der Systematischen Pädagogik* that "The world openness of human existence makes freedom and self-formation possible, and thereby a humanity stamped, determined from out of a measure."[26] There is no absolute measure, but we still seek such a measure. In this way, the measure is more of a question than an answer. It does not exist as a thing among things, but rather as an address or a claim. As Annette Hilt explains, "In its groundlessness, the world is yet the ground of beings and thereby the originary demand on the human to give herself a measure; this claim is her measure."[27] Similarly, in *Natur, Freiheit, Welt*, Fink writes that freedom is the freedom to be what we fundamentally are, that is, *Weltwesen*. Thus, as with Hölderlin and Nietzsche, our task is to give form to ourselves through a recognition of our finitude.

Play and Self-Formation in Conversation

Bildung and *Erziehung*, formation and education, are ways of determining this measure, of giving style. Fink writes in "Zur Bildungstheorie der technischen Bildung" that

> Education is the human's venture to attain a world-orientation from his own power and with the limited means of his finite spirit, to arrive at truths from his own insight, even if only provisionally, to develop a sense of meaning of life coming out of human struggle, no doubt ambiguous and fragmentary, but yet is our property. In the process of education, the human truth of human existence [*menschilchen Daseins*] occurs, the *self-interpretation* of human existence [*humanen Existenz*] comes about.[28]

Thus, *Bildung* is a giving form to oneself as a self-interpretation. In doing so, however, we embark not in a narcissistic or navel gazing project. Rather, to cultivate this attunement, we cannot help but start from our own finite perspective and insights, but we project ourselves, we wager, into the world totality. We seek answers about human existence overall, not just about ourselves. For Fink, all existence is co-existence. We are born into language, into practices, into particular cultures and historical epochs.

Although mythology and religion also seek answers to the human condition, the answers they provide are taken to be eternal and unchanging. *Bildung*, conversely is always *unterwegs*. It is always the creation of meaning in the context of a particular culture and within a "temporary, abiding intersubjective '*Bildungswelt*.'"[29] Thus, against the objection that Fink ignores concrete life, here he emphasizes that we cannot consider education and formation separate from that such concrete life. He continues,

> Education is therefore not only an embodiment of the content of knowledge, but rather a form of existence of lively truth, a human way of life, through which the human, perhaps all too human, truth is stamped. The openness for the being and his fundamental domains and the corresponding finite assurances of a form [*Bild*] of the world in being human make up the movement of education.[30]

Thus, education is fundamentally temporal. While rooted in a particular context, it also projects itself forward. *Bildung* responds to the form of address by the world totality by remaining open toward what remains to be said. *Bildung* is becoming in two senses. It refers to the becoming of the individual in her self-formation, but also to the historical, cultural process of *Bildung* more generally. To become who we are, then, means not only an awareness of our own individual past, presents, and futures, but also having those in our wider contexts. To become who we are is again to be mindful of dates.

Fink explicitly connects education with speech by suggesting that education is the shared conversation between old and young about life and the world. When we speak of reality, we speak of all that is, of what corresponds [*entspricht*]. Education is an education into reality. He writes, "Education is insertion into what is real in and as *dialegesthai*, is an inserting in the flexibility of listening to the *logos*, which penetrates the world in a structured, connecting way" (NFW 182). By this, he means neither that the world has a predetermined order, nor that logic is a pure theoretical exercise. Rather, the world is shot through with meaning by being shot through with language. We belong to [*gehören*] the world as listeners and participants in this conversation.

Although there is no absolute measure, in giving form to ourselves, we must have some ideal to follow. As Nietzsche indicates, value is neither absolute nor arbitrary. Fink draws on this idea to suggest that the ideal toward which human education and cultivation strives is the very play of the cosmos. As Nietzsche illustrates in the fables of Zarathustra, the will to power does not seek force or violence, but rather finds itself in the playing child, *pais paizon*. The will to power appears as "the cosmic movement that penetrates all beings" in the constant play of construction and destruction (NFW 197). The human arrives at great health when she lives as the counterpart to the world by playing along with the cosmos.

All play is a copy of actuality, but in a transfiguring way. We see this, says Fink, most clearly in tragedy. Drawing on Nietzsche' account of the Apollonian and Dionysian, he explains, "In the tragedy, human existence holds itself in relation to the totality of its worldly dwelling. There it experiences, with a shudder, that it—like no kind of finite thing—is put into play in the playspace of its freedom . . . In the creativity of pure play, the human experiences himself as the co-player in the play of the world" (NFW 193). Apollo, like the world, grants light and individuation and plays in tension with Dionysus, like the earth, who dissolves and destroys.[31] In holding herself out into the play of forces, the human thus relates to the world as ideal. Through this play, we come to see who we are and who we are becoming in a new way.

As discussed above, Fink takes the human to be liminal. She is neither merely animal nor merely divine. Rather, she remains in tension between these: "The human appears not simply as an in-between thing as other things, between heaven and earth: he inhabits the abyssal dimension of the deep and the bright realm of light,—he is attached to Mother Earth and Father Ether: he stands in the tension of worldliness" (NFW 194). If education is allowing the human to become who she is, then she must be able to preserve, rather than surmount, this tension. Through play, we inhabit the in-between not as escape, but as return to who we are. We play between creation and destruction, joining and separating, letting be and annihilation.

Fink concludes *Natur, Freiheit, Welt*, "*Erziehen* means here and now: to collectively and always anew ground our belonging to the world in the conversation, that is full of the need and counsel of life,—to bring ourselves into the tension of the double relation" (195). The worldliness of our lives is the actual "field of education." Through this playspace of freedom, we are able to cast ourselves out in response to the question of "Who am I? And who are you?" Play enables us to inhabit this tension in a meaningful way.

ART, CONVERSATION, AND TRANSFORMATION

In the essay, "Die Vielfalt der Sprachen und das Verstehen der Welt," Gadamer suggests that the world is for the human who appears in and amid the world.[32] Like Fink, Gadamer believes that this does not mean that the world is merely a subjective projection or that it stands over against humans. Rather, the world is "for us a limitless space, in which we are in the middle and seek our decisive orientation."[33] The world presents us with the greatest task, namely, to seek an answer to this riddle of our existence. Yet, Gadamer claims, this is a moral—not logical—problem of determining what sorts of lives we want to lead. We respond to this task not through domination over the world, but through dialogue with other world beings. Thus, alongside our world horizons we find our speech horizons, which Gadamer emphasizes are plural. Similarly, in *Truth and Method*, Gadamer writes that "Language is the record of finitude not because the structure of human language is multifarious, but because every language is constantly being formed and developed the more it expresses its experience of the world" (453). There is no one language that can fully grasp the world, and indeed, that is not the role of language in general. It is not a tool. Rather, language is the way in which we exist in the world. To have language, he explains, is to have a world.[34] We are born into the world, into a plurality of languages and meanings. Such a world sets us a task, which is resolved not by planning or strategy, but through awareness of the free space of human being with one another, and also through what is unfamiliar.[35] This, he remarks, is what speech actually is and which hermeneutics serves, namely to develop the opportunity to convey what another means and to receive what the other says in response.

Gadamer concludes his essay by raising the question of *Bildung*. If the task presented to us by the world and others cannot be resolved merely by technical science, academic qualifications, or information networks, then our education also must be more than those things. Drawing on Hegel, Gadamer claims that *Bildung* is the capacity to view things from another's standpoint and to understand the other from her own point of view.[36] *Bildung*, then, is learning to respond to the address issued from another. Importantly, as we will see, Gadamer does not think we can merely take on another's perspective wholesale or remove ourselves from own vantage point in understanding another. Rather, through the to-and-fro play of dialogue, we can come to a shared, continuing understanding. Like Fink, Gadamer believes that education is the constant grounding anew—in conversation—of our belonging to the world. It is a way of trying to make ourselves at home in the world, although such a process is always underway and never fully finished. *Bildung*, like play and like language, is in motion.

As discussed in the previous chapters, Kant and Schiller point us in the right direction by foregrounding the role of the *sensus communis* and tradition in education and by turning to play as a significant part of our engagement with art and the world more broadly. Yet, as I have argued, the difficulty is that these accounts tend toward hypothetical rather than actual relationships. What I seek to develop instead is an account of education, play, and poetry that begins in alterity, that holds open the space between familiar and foreign in particular ways. Gadamer views conversation as the playful movement between self and other that cannot be predetermined. Conversation is not limited to dialogue between two humans, however, but can be found in other experiences, especially in our encounters with art. In each form of conversation, a claim is made on us by what appears before us. We might choose not to respond, or might respond in better or worse ways, but in each case, something particular calls us from outside of ourselves. We cannot abstract away from that particular other or view the world merely as a projection of our subjective inclinations. Rather, we are already at play in this shared space. If education is becoming who we are, and we are, as Gadamer claims, conversation, then this dialogical, transformative play also belongs to education.

The Play of Art

Before turning to Gadamer's account of conversation and education, I would first like to flesh out his account of the play of art in order to show how such play is an education. Importantly, Gadamer understands play as something we undergo rather than something we produce. Furthermore, the work of art is not simply a static object that we can think about for a while or use for another purpose (RB 126). It lays claim on us. The work of art addresses us and provides us with a task, which is, at the very least, simply to take seriously what presents itself to us, to listen to what speaks to us. Just as play and players are mutually constitutive, so are art and the spectator. Because of this claim on us, our play with the work cannot be disinterested or a subjective projection; nor is this participation fixed or calculable.

Gadamer clarifies that this engagement is the player being absorbed into the play. Thus, in the experience of art, play occurs as the relationship between the work and the viewer, the player. The work "is not an object that stands over against a subject for itself. Instead the work of art has its true being in the fact that it becomes an experience that changes the person who experiences it" (TM 103). Just as the work is presented to us, so we present ourselves to the work. In ordering and shaping these tasks, we also order and shape ourselves and maintain a certain comportment that transforms us since "all playing is a being-played" (107). Here, Gadamer distances himself even more from Kant by declaring that play has primacy over the players, such that play is not contingent on the players' mental activities. This does not mean, however, that the player is dissolved in the play, but rather that the play is for no other purpose and the player is such only insofar as she plays. Whereas we may be inclined to think of the spectator as merely passive and watching, she actually performs an essential role in play because the work "is something that only manifests and displays itself when it is constituted in the viewer" (RB 126). In other words, for the work to be a work, it must not only exist for someone as presentation, that is, as a call to play, but it also requires the viewer engages with it.

Because artistic presentation exists for someone, because it is *there*, the play becomes art through the "transformation into structure" [*Verwandlung ins Gebilde*] (TM 110). Gadamer explains, "Thus transformation into structure means that what existed previously exists no longer. But also that what now exists, what represents itself in the play of art, is the lasting and the true" (111). When the work is there for someone, it becomes recognizable as an intended whole. Here structure should not be understood in a stiff or fixed sense, but in the more organic sense of shape or form. The play of art attains its own form in this play and transformation. Thus, the play cannot be merely the subjective play of the viewer or of the artist. Rather, there now exists a work that can also be recognized by others. Whereas alteration suggests that something remains at the core the same as it was, like a substance with different accidents, transformation means that something has changed into something totally different.

That what existed exists no longer does not suggest a break with reality, but rather suggests re-creation. Different aspects are highlighted or diminished such that seeing it in this new way, we rediscover reality. The work now has its own world and its own "measure" (111). Thus, the work does not present us with a world through which we could escape our own or an experience that could be entirely appropriated. Instead, the play of art shows its own world and brings to light what was otherwise "hidden and withdrawn" (112). The transformation is not only transformation into structure, but transformation into the true. By this, Gadamer does not mean that the work of art now has an essence that corresponds to reality, but that it unconceals something that we could not otherwise see and that can also be experienced by others.

This possibility for transformation is central to Gadamer's challenge to accounts of aesthetic consciousness. He further clarifies this challenge by distinguishing between experience as *Erlebnis* and experience as *Erfahrung*. While both are experiences, the former emphasizes an interruption of everyday life, whereas the latter suggests an ongoing event. Drawing on Dilthey, Gadamer suggests that *Erlebnis* refers to a kind of psychological experience of what is truly given in an intense, meaningful way (TM 57). In aesthetic experience, the work of art tears us out of our immediate contexts while simultaneously relating us back to the whole of our existence (60–61). We experience both something unlike anything else and of the infinite whole of life.[37] While this account of *Erlebnis* suggests a movement back and forth between the particular individual and the infinite, because the experience requires such a ripping or leaping away, Gadamer contends that the break relies on abstracting away from the very context that gives rise to the work of art. This results in an "untenable hermeneutic nihilism" (74). Gadamer's concern is that without continuity with the world, the experience of art is meaningless.

In experience as *Erfahrung*, conversely, that meaning found in everyday life is preserved. Hearing the sense of *fahren* connoting a venturing or moving, we find that *Erfahrung* is ongoing and formative.[38] The experience of art is not cut off from the everyday, but is "mediated by historical consciousness" (TM 84) and an experience of recognition. Viewing a work of art does not involve a simple immediate apprehension, but requires seeing-as and understanding-as, such that this engagement precludes an absolute abstraction between the meaningful work and the meaningful world. Instead, such as in the example of absolute music, "only when we understand it, when it is 'clear' to us, does it exist as an artistic creation for us" (79). What is also essential here is that we *recognize* the work as a work, and something to be interpreted. Even the most alienating or foreign work, such as a piece by John Cage or a readymade by Duchamp, still seems to bear a degree of familiarity for us in that we even recognize it as a work. To understand a work of art means it cannot be divorced from the world. The work may challenge our very notion of art, but that challenge could not be presented to us if we did not in some way recognize the piece as art.

Furthermore, because this recognition is a recognition of what is represented there, what is *dargestellt*, our interpretations are not arbitrary, but belong to the work. In experiencing art, we encounter an "unfinished event" and are "part of this event" (85). Thus, the work becomes most fully what it is through our mediation in the play between work and spectator. The work opens up a particular play-space, such that it represents something in its coming-to-presentation and this relationship cannot be differentiated.[39] Furthermore, the work maintains its own reality because what it presents is always presented in a specific way that could not be presented without the work. In presenting the world, it also presents itself, which gives rise to "an increase in being" (TM 135).[40] This is precisely what the transformation into structure allows, namely the *"event of being that occurs in presentation*, and that belongs essentially to play as play" (115). Through the play of art's transformation into structure, we are similarly transformed and not merely altered. Yet, there remains continuity not only between the work and the world, but also between the self and the work since the understanding of the work entails self-understanding (TM 83). There cannot be, then, an experience of the work that is not also an experience of the self and the preservation of hermeneutic continuity.

What allows for this continuity is the relationship between imitation and recognition. As Gadamer notes, in play and imitation the child is "affirming what he knows and affirming his own being in the process" (TM 113). Even the child who imitates her mother at work is not simply aping but expressing what she knows. It is the application of what is familiar in new situations. Although imitation is like a mirror, what is mirrored is not simply the form of something, but the truth of something. The work of art as imitation and representation draws us to recognize that which we already know, to rediscover what we have forgotten, and to recreate ourselves in the transformation. Memory is not simply a capacity, but it, too, is something that must be formed. Gadamer references Nietzsche's description of active forgetting. Forgetting is not a lack or an absence, but clearing space for what is most essential to come to the fore: "Only by forgetting does the mind have the possibility of total renewal, the capacity to see everything with fresh eyes, so that what is long familiar fuses with the new into a many leveled unity" (TM 14).[41] Memory and recognition, then, are not mental plays of the faculties, but ways of being in the world.

As we have been discussing, the work of art is not static, but dynamic. It has its own time. Gadamer distinguishes between simultaneity and contemporaneity in our experience of art. Whereas simultaneity suggests that works from different epochs can be held in the same consciousness all with the same claim to validity, contemporaneity instead brings together two different moments such that the work presents itself to us in its full presence and has a claim to something lasting. Simultaneity cannot account for the different truth claims presented by the works. In experiencing time as contemporaneity, we find again that the actual presence of the work cannot be separated from its presentation. Each re-presentation or repetition "is as original as the work itself" (TM 37). Because the work is an event, its presentation cannot be separated from it, so even though each performance will be different from the first, mastering or separating out these historical moments would not restore the original. Nor is that to be desired. Instead, we recognize something in the work in such a way that bears on the present in a way that we recognize as continuous.[42] This is not to say, though, that every experience of a work is seamless or without conflict.

In playing with the work, we are held out into the open of the in-between that preserves this tension between self and other. We catch sight of ourselves in new and different ways, and it is this that allows the experience of art to be so singularly transformative. In his essay, "The Play of Art," Gadamer remarks that "'Art' begins precisely there, where we are able to do otherwise" (RB 125). As this possibility to do otherwise, art is a moment of freedom. At the end of this essay, Gadamer references Nietzsche, arguing that when we fail to recognize the "ontological dignity of play," we fail to recognize the interdependence between life and art and find only alienation. Instead, we must recognize that "our forms of play are forms of our freedom" (RB 130). For Gadamer, then, the freedom of play has important consequences for our daily lives. That is, if we stand before the work and participate in it, we, in some sense, have no choice but to allow ourselves to be transformed. We cannot be disinterested.

Gadamer's account thus challenges the aesthetic consciousness described by Kant and Schiller in two ways. First, Gadamer makes clear that the play of art here cannot be reduced to the subjective experience of the player. Indeed, the work takes priority over the spectator. Although Kant's appeal to disinterestedness is in order to achieve pure universal judgments of taste, in so doing, he cuts art off from reality, rendering the work fiction and void of content. Art, understood in this way, is only appearance. As such, the work and artist both lose their places in the world (76). Gadamer explains that the play of art is not a dream world for self-forgetting. The play of art is not mere appearance; it is there and lays claim on us.

Second, because the work is the transformation into the true, because it shows what was otherwise hidden and that we can now recognize, the play of art necessarily involves cognitive import. Gadamer writes, "the play of art is a mirror that through the centuries constantly arises anew, and in which we catch sight of ourselves in a way that is often unexpected or unfamiliar: what we are, what we might be, and what we are about" (RB 130). In the account of poetic education I have been advancing, I argue that such education is rooted in an orientation of the self rather than the refinement of taste. What is essential is the cultivation of an active relating to limits, whether to others, to the inarticulable, or to our own finitude that reaches both across the past and toward the future.

The way we engage the work is dialogical; the work fundamentally resists the monologue. How is it, though, that we could have such a conversation with the work? We remain open to, oriented to, the work. What we find, then, in the play of art is much like the movement Celan describes in his Meridian speech. The artwork is the site of encounter and that requires us to bear witness to what stands before us. We do so by casting ourselves out toward the work as well as receiving it. Moreover, to bear witness to the work is to be mindful of its dates and its time. In Gadamer's language, we tarry with it: "To tarry is not to lose time. Being in the mode of tarrying is like an intensive back-and-forth conversation that is not cut off but lasts until it is ended" (211). In this tarrying, "one is completely 'absorbed in conversation,' and this means one 'is completely there in it'" (211). To be completely there or absorbed in the conversation does not mean that we are lost in it, but that we are not disinterested. It also does not mean that we fully understand the work; there is always something left to be said.

Self-Cultivation and *Bildung*

Through conversation, art teaches us something about ourselves as well as how to cultivate an engagement with things other than ourselves. Education as *Bildung* is cultivation in the sense of self-transformation. As we have seen throughout, conversation is the basis of *Bildung*. Gadamer concludes an essay in *Hermeneutische Entwürfe* with the thought that "It is clear, that one sees more sagaciously when one takes the word [*das Wort*] as answer [*Antwort*] und that one trains the ear, as like all of our other senses, to hearken and to listen. Hermeneutics is the theory that one must learn how to listen."[43] In the following, I explain more specifically the nature of listening and how play, especially in our experiences of art and poetry, helps us cultivate this listening.

In *Truth and Method*, Gadamer suggests we re-examine the nature of *Bildung*, pivotal for classic German education, to understand how we should think of truth in the human sciences and what sort of experience it implies. Like Fink, Gadamer identifies a particular nihilism belonging to education modeled on the natural sciences. He explains that science attempts to achieve certainty by organizing its knowledge of the world and rejecting any knowledge or methodology that does not achieve this certainty. Such a universalization of method or achievement of absolute certainty is untenable. First, it is nihilistic because it rejects any sort of received or encountered meaning and instead seeks a fictional meaning-in-itself or view from nowhere. Second, as Nicholas Davey explains, methodological invincibility is dehumanizing for it fails to confront what it is to be human.[44] By this Davey means that methodological invincibility rejects not only the fallibility that belongs to being human, but also the very capacities for relationality, meaning, and tradition that give rise to understanding. He writes that Gadamer responds to this dehumanization in his discussion of *Bildung*. Gadamer "invokes the term *Bildung* for a strategic purpose: to demonstrate that alongside scientific and technical knowledge there exists another body of knowledge that is not the result of proof and demonstration but is laid down by tradition, received wisdom, and practical experience."[45] *Bildung* thus points to the other half of the truth that is missing from the account given by modern thinking. It reminds us that "the molding of our consciousness really does not take place through the methods of modern science" (GR 273) but through participation in social life and practice.

Rather than mastery, *Bildung* relies on understanding, which is broader than scientific knowledge and develops through formation and cultivation. This formation happens organically and not according to a set process or method. Moreover, this formation always happens with others and is always embedded in tradition. Although *Bildung* is self-formation and transformation, conversation still provides the basis for this formation. Gadamer, quoting Herder, remarks that *Bildung* is "the rising up to humanity through culture" (TM 10). *Bildung* is thus always a movement between the individual and the community. Although at first glance it seems like this sense of humanity rising up through culture is then a rejection of our animal nature or separates humans off from the earth as origin, Gadamer does not mean to make such a claim. Rather, *Bildung* refers to the task of the human to give shape to herself. As Gadamer explains in *Truth and Method*, "It is not accidental that in this respect the word *Bildung* resembles the Greek *physis*. Like nature, *Bildung* has no goals outside itself" (TM 10). Like Fink, Gadamer suggests that education is not a rejection of the animal through the perfection of the human, but rather the cultivation of the self out of the self. Thus, Gadamer resists the idea that through education we become human through an overcoming of the animal; he instead suggests that we become more ourselves. Furthermore, Gadamer especially highlights that because there is no external goal, *Bildung* is instead a constant state of formation. The movement of *Bildung*, where the individual finds herself in a culture without being absorbed into it, requires that she must learn how to relate to it and make it her own. In this way, the movement of *Bildung* mirrors the movement of play as the possibility of self-appropriation and openness, and it is thus also a movement of freedom.

Gadamer draws on Hegel's account of *Bildung* as the development and formation of the self through the rising to the universal. This movement is a task for the human that "requires sacrificing particularity for the sake of the human" (TM 11). Gadamer further interprets Hegel as stating that recognizing one's own and becoming at home in what is foreign "is in the basic movement of sprit, whose being consists only in returning to itself from what is other" (13). As we have seen throughout, Gadamer rejects the idea that we can discover universal standards or abstract away from particularity in order to find what is true. Furthermore, as he argues regarding Schiller and Dilthey, we cannot merely move out of ourselves and then return to ourselves in alteration. Indeed, Gadamer suggests that Hegel's account falls short precisely because it leads to the "dissolution of all concrete being" (13).[46] So, we should bear in mind when we read this account that Gadamer does not mean that formation requires appealing to such a universality, but that to become educated, we must recognize that there are experiences and perspectives outside of our own that help to expand our horizons.[47]

Gadamer continues, "It is not enough to observe more closely, to study a tradition more thoroughly, if there is not already a receptivity to the 'otherness' of the work of art or of the past. That is what, following Hegel, we emphasized as the general characteristic of *Bildung*: keeping oneself open to what is other—to other, more universal points of view" (15). Here again we find the sense that permeates all of Gadamer's arguments, namely the goal of education, and I would argue even further, the goal of life, is that of keeping oneself open to what surpasses us. As in the experience of art, our experience of the other yields transformation. Having experienced it, I cannot stay the same.

As Gadamer argues, hermeneutics is this very mode of keeping ourselves open to what is other, including the past. But, such openness is not passive. It is an active mode of understanding. As discussed above, we are born into worlds of meaning. We are born into particular practices, languages of meaning, geographical boundaries, and identities. Our existence is embedded in tradition. There is no getting outside of these contexts, nor do they strictly determine our identities. Still, they inform how we approach the world. As Gadamer demonstrates in his discussion of the hermeneutic circle, in order to understand anything, I first must anticipate its meaning. I project a "foremeaning" that tries to make sense of what is before me, or, in Gadamer's words, what I am prepared for it to tell me something (TM 271). Like in the case of the work of art, what is before me shows itself; it cannot be the result of my subjective projections. Thus, I am open to the address of the other. As what stands before me speaks, I develop and modify my understanding. Although there is no strictly neutral position, we begin with an awareness of our biases, of our pre-judgments, so that what is before us "can present itself in all its otherness" (272). Our anticipated meanings are always subject to revision and reinterpretation though this play of dialogue, of question and answer.

Davey explains that the fundamental way we encounter others is through conversation, but this conversation is not just persons alternatively stating facts into the distance. Conversation is instead a matter of holding open a tension as two things come together, such that "difficulty, distance, risk, and vulnerability are of the essence."[48] What is essential to education, to the realization that we are not self-contained, is the space that is opened up with and through our recognition of others. This recognition is not merely the awareness that others exist or the recognition we experience, for example, when recognizing the monument that stands before us is the same we have seen in history texts, but is instead a recognition that is also a preservation. This is to say that the recognition of alterity preserves and holds the other in her otherness, not like a specimen to be examined, but in a way that enables a spanning of this distance and difference. This difference with the other might also be disruptive for our own sense of self, since it frequently challenges our self-understanding and points to the question that we remain for ourselves. This reminds us again that we are not finished projects, but participants in meaning and transformation.

In "Education Is Self-Education" Gadamer provides a personal example to make this point:

> I had to [swaddle my daughter] myself on one occasion and in my wife's view—certainly she was right—what I had contrived was quite frankly a kind of straitjacket. But consider this, the child beamed and then fell asleep. So it is with communication, about which we still have no inkling, but which still accompanies this process of feeling at home, which I cannot emphasize strongly enough as the key idea of any kind of education (*Erziehung*) or cultivation (*Bildung*).[49]

In Gadamer's story, both he and his daughter first feel unease and then at home. She finds herself flailing about, anxious in a new situation, and yet as she becomes wrapped tightly, both literally by the blanket and metaphorically by the surrounding world, she settles down. Like being swaddled, there is no escaping that surrounding world, yet this restriction is calming rather than suffocating. Gadamer seems to have no idea how to swaddle a baby, but soon finds himself at home as well. He continues,

> It follows from this that, in one way or another, the young human being makes himself at home (*einhaust*) in a world. This is a word (*einhausen*) that the great philosopher Hegel has used. He could venture, through his own reflective usage, to coin new terms, for example: from *"hausen,"* (to dwell) to *"einhausen"* (to in-dwell). Making oneself at home in the world (*Sich-Einhausen*) reveals itself also in this courage for creating new vocabulary of which I already spoke.[50]

We belong to the world and with others through language, but never in a totalizing, definitional way. Rather, to communicate is to develop into a relation with what is other through the speculative element of language, that is, through never coming to a final word or end of the conversation. *Bildung* enables us to preserve what is other so that we neither master nor ignore it.

Gadamer suggests that Enlightenment impulses to achieve neutrality in pursuit of objectivity reveal a "prejudice against prejudice itself" and so fail to account for this being in the world (TM 272). For Gadamer, this means the Enlightenment thinkers failed to consider their own biases and mistakenly stripped reason from all its concrete forms. This actually leads to the false idea that we could free ourselves from tradition while still preserving meaning. Gadamer grants that we should not be beholden to tradition, but this relies on a mistaken understanding of tradition as well. Describing the anticipation of meaning in interpretation and understanding, Gadamer argues that the shared meaning that allows for such anticipation is always being formed. Tradition is the precondition for understanding, but we also "produce it ourselves inasmuch as we understand, participate in the evolution of tradition, and hence further determine it ourselves" (293). The sense of binding here does not mean that tradition opposes our freedom, but that there is no place outside of tradition. We remain free in our participation and determination that changes that tradition. Thus, whereas the natural sciences, informed by the tradition of Enlightenment, seek to decontextualize information in order to achieve certainty, Gadamer contends that understanding is wider than this since understanding involves knowledge, but also self-understanding. Similarly, he writes, "*Understanding is to be thought of less as a subjective act than as participating in an event of tradition*, a process of transmission in which past and present are constantly mediated" (291). Although understanding is thus firmly connected to its past, it remains firmly open to its present and future. Furthermore, our language, ideas, culture, and experiences all are rooted in tradition and cannot be abstracted. However, this does not mean that tradition is totalizing or that we cannot critically evaluate our practices. We may always reevaluate and change our practices, but just as one can only change the rules of play within the play-space, so can these changes only develop from within tradition.

Tradition and culture are not static, monolithic entities, but processes of transmission, *Überlieferung*, and, as Gadamer states, historically effected consciousness (*Wirkungsgeschichte*). Because tradition is dynamic and we are born into tradition, our understanding is effected by history. Yet, because we are in the midst of it, there is no view that would tell us exactly what that history is or how it should be understood. Instead, we find ourselves with the task of never fully illuminating that situation. As Gadamer writes, "To be historically means that knowledge of oneself can never be complete" (TM 301). In other words, because I occupy a particular situation, my ability to understand that situation is both made possible and limited by that situation.

Gadamer refers to this situation as a horizon: "The horizon is the range of vision that includes everything that can be seen from a particular vantage point" (TM 301). What this means, is that in order to know my horizon, I have to remain within it. There is no getting outside. But, I am not strictly confined to it. Indeed, says Gadamer, "The horizon is, rather, something into which we move and that moves with us" (303). The horizon of the past continues to grow and expand. To understand the horizon of another, I must transpose myself with the other. Importantly, this does not mean that I leave my own identity and adopt another. A horizon or another's identity is not like a coat I can try for a while to see how I feel in it. Nor does it mean that I subordinate another to my own standards. Rather, transposing involves rising beyond my and the other's particularity (304). Here again we find the language of rising to universality that we found in Gadamer's discussion of *Bildung*. What Gadamer means here, though, again is not that there is a universal that we could find by abstracting away from particularity. Indeed, the very point is that we cannot get outside of a horizon. Rather, it is that there is something beyond the particular individual and that is shared in common, namely the world of meaning, the *Sprachwelt*: "Thus, the world is the common ground, trodden by none and recognized by all, uniting all who talk to one another" (443). As we saw before, Gadamer believes that this speech world is not monologic, but plural. Thus, this experience of the universal is a recognition of this ongoing event of language. We find a similar experience in the transformation into structure of the work of art that allows us to recognize it. There is something beyond our own immediate experience that lays claim on us.

Gadamer deems this transposition the fusion of horizons. In the process of understanding, "as the historical horizon is projected, it is simultaneously superseded" (TM 306). My horizon is expanded because it now encounters something other than myself. In interpreting what confronts me, I bring myself to bear as it also presents itself. Like the anticipation of meaning of a work of art, my horizon cannot merely assimilate what stands before me. Rather, the projection is also exceeded by and transfigured by what it encounters. Gadamer explains that while my horizon is decisive, it is such not as a personal standpoint, "but more as an opinion and a possibility that one brings into play and puts at risk" (TM 390). Thus, the interpretation is enlarged and leaves both sides transformed. I put my own understanding into risk and play by being open to the possibility that the other may be right, requiring me to modify my belief in response. Such a fusion is not momentary, but ongoing through the "interplay of the movement of the tradition and the movement of the interpreter" (293).

What allows for this fusion of horizons is language. The fusion of horizons is a conversation, a site of encounter between self and other, that presupposes a common language or, as Gadamer notes, "creates a common language" (370). It could be the case that a full understanding is never reached, and indeed a perfect understanding is impossible, but insofar as any kind of conversation is possible, there is a shared space that holds open the play of question and answer. The other world I encounter is not an object of scientific inquiry. Moreover, I could not encounter another world if I did not also bring my own with me, for then the other world could make no claim on me. Thus, the fusion of horizons is possible because of conversation, but this conversation is not totalizing.

In education, we develop out of ourselves and are transformed. Our understanding increases and is ever more meaningful, but there is no final interpretation or understanding to which we can appeal. As such, there remains something beyond us, something fundamentally other. The parallels between *Bildung* and play crystallize especially here. Sean Gallagher, for example, suggests that play is always oriented toward the world, wherein "The possibility of losing oneself or transcending oneself in play is attractive or alluring only because of the possibility of finding oneself again . . . Play is productive for the self rather than destructive."[51] In this way, the movement of *Bildung* is indeed the movement of play as the possibility of self-appropriation and openness, and thus also a movement of freedom. The play of conversation first requires that I am willing to listen, to be addressed by the other, and through the transformation I undergo, I learn even more what it is to listen. Andrzej Wierciński explains further that the transformation that occurs in education comes about "by understanding our presuppositions and by opening ourselves radically toward the new. Understanding our presuppositions means that we question them and thus critically address what we already know."[52] Our form of listening as attunement to what surpasses us is thus not passive, but dynamically engaged in this play of question and answer.

One of the primary objections to Gadamer's hermeneutics is that an insistence on the fusion of horizons and the priority of tradition precludes the possibility of difference. Indeed, one of Hölderlin's primary concerns is that tradition stifles the creativity and formation necessary for becoming who we are. Habermas famously charges Gadamer with merging hermeneutics and tradition into a single point, thus sacrificing the potential critical dimension of hermeneutics to the authority of tradition.[53] His concern is that we are too willing to grant authority to tradition without attending to the role of power and the many ways tradition has been employed by oppressive enterprises. John Caputo recognizes against Habermas that Gadamer provides us with "mobile, flexible tradition."[54] The problem, though, is that Gadamer's account of tradition is overly conciliatory. He attempts to smooth over differences and fails to treat tradition with an eye of suspicion. Caputo writes, "[Gadamer] never asks to what extent the play of tradition is a power play and its unity forced by the powers that be."[55] Similarly, Robert Bernasconi, drawing on Derrida, worries that because Gadamer's understanding of the other always already presupposes a possible agreement, Gadamer cannot account for radical alterity or a sense of misunderstanding that is more than accidental. For Bernasconi, there must be a possibility for the oppressed to insist that the oppressor cannot understand her and still remain who he is, but it seems that Gadamer cannot provide this as a possibility.[56] Some feminist interpreters of Gadamer also question how to take up this language of "we" and tradition when their own voices have been systemically marginalized by that tradition. Marie Fleming argues also, for example, that not everyone belongs to tradition in the same sort of way. So, Gadamer's insistence that "we" belong to tradition not only elides those important differences, but also "aggressively discourages us from critically examining" what it means to belong to tradition.[57] Furthermore, she argues, it seems that one's relation to the other is merely instrumental. I cannot understand myself except with an other, but because the aim of conversation is unity, the other's actual voice is flattened and appropriated into my understanding.

As I have been arguing throughout, conversation never comes to a close. If I take the other seriously, then I cannot appropriate her into my understanding. Rather than instrumental to my own self-understanding, the other calls out, "Do you hear me?" Hermeneutics remains open to this question and asks itself the same. Thus, in the emphasis on tradition, hermeneutics does not appeal to a monolithic authority, but rather a series of practices that must remain open to their own questionability. Still, these thinkers are right to challenge the hermeneutic approach. Simply because one is committed to a certain philosophical position does not mean that one is thereby absolved of any oppressive attitudes. As I will argue, however, I believe hermeneutics has the resources to protect against such attitudes or to root them out if they do arise.

It is this sense of conversation that is at play in tradition. James Risser notes that tradition might be read in three different ways. First, tradition refers to "a style of interconnecting historical succession" as the handing over of tradition. The fusion of horizons belongs to this sense of tradition as we consider how the past bears on the past we are now creating. The second sense is that of the practices that give meaning to tradition or what it means to be in a tradition. This sense is fundamentally linguistic as preceding our own speaking and providing a world for understanding. The third sense is that of tradition as the "*voices of the other* who makes a claim on us." This is the sense that Gadamer means when he speaks of tradition as authority, meaning that we hold these voices of the past to speak something of the truth. In our interpretation of them, we recognize the strengths of their claims. Importantly, claims Risser, when Gadamer speaks of preserving tradition, we must be very careful to attend to which sense he means. Preservation is not to prevent tradition from experiencing any change. Indeed, it is the opposite! Preserving in the sense of *bewahren*, of letting the truth of the claim reveal itself, thus means instead to recognize the strength of the claim. Preservation, he argues, "has to do primarily with holding open" such that we could hear the extinguished voices of the past.[58] Indeed, this sense of preservation shows that rather than accepting the dominant tradition wholesale, we must actually listen for those voices that might resist that tradition.

Because hermeneutic experience is never finished, there remains a constant play of distance and difference, of familiar and unfamiliar. For Gadamer, we always have more we could say or conceptualize, and yet this dimension remains meaningful. Monica Vilhauer makes a similar point in speaking about Gadamer's sense of intelligible difference. To recognize something as different requires that it is intelligible as different. If the very meaning of otherness is something that cannot be made intelligible, then the other's alterity is reduced to a formal, contentless difference.[59] Seeing hermeneutics in its playfulness allows us, she argues, to gain better insight into the play and preservation of difference. She writes, "The very notion of play requires move and countermove, question and answer . . . We don't learn anything unless there is something *other* confronting us and challenging our expectations and prejudices."[60] To enter into play, we must remain open to what is other. This requires, too, that we listen for what might have been excluded or missed or silenced, but this listening and investigation into difference still happens in the play of language and dialogue.

One might argue that while Gadamer's analysis of play does allow for the otherness of the other, this play still remains not radical enough. It does not have the same rupturing quality as Nietzsche's or Derrida's, for example. Gadamer's play certainly does seem more collaborative than agonistic. In order to emphasize more the role of difference, I argue we look to Fink. Like Gadamer, Fink believes that our fundamental mode of being in the world is one of understanding and interpretation. Yet, he remains wary of an overemphasis on the unconcealment and light at the cost of the negative, radical moments of difference. Fink states that humans are characterized by their ability to participate in the play of the world and the earth. The earth is what makes being possible, but it is abyssal. In concealing itself at every turn, it resists any penetration. There is something essentially turbulent and disruptive about the earth. In participating in the play of the earth, human beings thus must orient themselves toward this abyssal origin and also allow the earth to remain itself in its incomprehensibility. It requires that we attune ourselves to what surpasses us, to what is incalculable. In his earth analysis,

Fink allows us to see better what this relationship between education and nature would be. For Fink, comportment toward the earth is ultimately an orientation toward finitude. As such, it requires us to recognize our own vulnerability and to see ourselves at risk and at stake. Fink allows us to think play more radically without abandoning the commitments of philosophical hermeneutics. There is a more agonistic element present, especially when he appeals to Nietzsche, but I do not take it that either means all forms of play are necessarily agonistic. Moreover, because Fink, and Nietzsche to a degree, insists that what is held open is the play of difference, rather than conquest, concerns about an overly agonistic model might be mitigated. Furthermore, Fink's earth analysis returns again to one of Hölderlin's central beliefs that the human is inseparable from nature. We find here a radical alternative to the subject as conceived by metaphysics, namely the *ens cosmologicum* who develops not out of, but through her animality and conditionedness.

As this *ens cosmologicum*, we are conversation. Reaching an understanding is never automatic or possible through domination. Instead, it requires "that both partners are ready for it and are trying to recognize the full value of what is alien and opposed to them" (TM 388). Even if an understanding is reached, it is not a final understanding. Gadamer explains, "the conversation that we are is one that never ends. No word is the last word, just as there is no first word. Every word is itself always an answer and gives rise always to a new question."[61] Understanding is always in motion, a play of to and fro, or, as Davey explains, "always restless, unquiet understanding."[62] Despite the prospect of an infinite conversation, we are finite. We will never be able to say fully what could be said. While living in language is familiar, because it is restless and because of the excess of meaning, language, conversation, and tradition, living in language resists calcification or stagnation.

For Gadamer and Fink, education is made possible through the movement of question and answer. Education is rooted in conversation, and each instance of understanding, or movement toward understanding, is educative. Wierciński makes a similar point, suggesting that,

> As we participate in the hermeneutic conversation, we can say that we participate in the event of education. Our lived understanding discloses the essential characteristics of human life in its temporality and finitude and thus reshapes our self-understanding by revealing the mystery of life in its entirety. The quality of the conversation depends far less on what we participants know about the subject matter. What is decisive is the understanding of who we are and want to become. [63]

In being addressed, we recognize something that is beyond us, that there is something that resists any self-sameness. To respond to this address requires, however subtle, a shift in perspective. Each address prompts us to ask, "Who am I and who are you?" Because each conversation is an event of understanding and each event of understanding an event of meaning, education—as the expanding of meaning and a responsibility to one's place—is a becoming of the conversation that we are.

NOTES

1. Hölderlin, *Sämtliche Werke. 5.*, 74.
2. Bambach, *Thinking the Poetic Measure of Justice*, 52. Explaining Hölderlin's attempt to find a measure for measureless tragedy, to hold together the contradictions of the finite human in relation to the infinite, Charles Bambach writes, "For the Germans to become wholly themselves, to gain insight into their own nature, they would need to experience their inwardness from the distant realm of the archaic Greeks. Pindar's gnome about self-becoming, understood within its Greek context, involved an awareness of the double meaning of Apollo's Delphic oracle: self-knowledge required an understanding of limits against limitless excess." As discussed in the first chapter of this volume, Hölderlin believes that the Germans have not yet achieved this self-knowledge.
3. Babich, *Words in Blood, Like Flowers*, 78.
4. Here we find echoes of Heraclitus's Fragment 51: "they do not understand how, while differing from (or: being at variance), [it] is in agreement with itself. [There is] a back-turning connection, like [that] of a bow or lyre." Robinson, *Heraclitus*, 37.
5. Cited in Bruzina, *Edmund Husserl and Eugen Fink: Beginnings and Ends in Phenomenology 1928-1938*, 532. Fink develops these ideas further in Fink, *Nietzsche's Philosophy*.
6. Fink contends that Nietzsche's arguments against Plato and Pythagoras rely on "caricatures," although Fink does grant that this turn toward play resists the reification of being found in much of the history of metaphysics. Unlike Heidegger, though, Fink does not identify Nietzsche as the "last metaphysician." Fink, "Nietzsche's Metaphysics of Play (1946)."
7. In "The Dionysiac Worldview," written in 1870, Nietzsche also clarifies that "Thus, whereas in dream the individual human being plays with the real, the art of the image-maker (in the wider sense) is a *playing with dream* . . . As long as the statue hovers as an image of fantasy before the eyes of the artist, he is still playing with the real: when he translates this image into marble, he is playing with dream." Thus, there are two senses of play with the Apollonian: the dream as the play with the real and play with the dream. He similarly identifies two senses of play in the Dionysiac: "If intoxication is nature playing with human beings, the Dionysiac artist's creation is a playing with intoxication." In observing these bidirectional forms of play, Nietzsche seems to be going beyond the *Spieltrieb* articulated by Schiller. Rather than play as the product or behavior of the subject, here we have a fuller sense of the human as being played, as addressed by the play of the *Ur-Eine*. Nietzsche, "The Dionysiac Worldview" in *The Birth of Tragedy*, 119–21.

160   Chapter 4

8. Schmidt, *On Germans and Other Greeks: Tragedy and Ethical Life*, 202.
9. Nietzsche, "Ecce Homo" in *The Anti-Christ, Ecce Homo, Twilight of the Idols: And Other Writings*, 109.
10. Nietzsche, "Philosophy in the Tragic Age of the Greeks," 111.
11. Nietzsche, *Thus Spoke Zarathustra*, 17.
12. Fink argues that most of Nietzsche's own philosophy and response to the history of philosophy is contained in this aphorism. Fink writes, "Its cosmological categories are identical with those of Parmenides of the Eon of being or of the primordial one. The world has no beginning and no end and yet it has a fixed form. In Parmenidean terms: the Eon is *ateleston* and *telesmenon*. Furthermore, Nietzsche's 'cosmos' is understood as a Leviathan of power. This directs the entire cosmos towards the path of an ontological interpretation of being as an Ergon which Aristotle questions in the discussion of *dynamis* and *energeia*, Leibniz in the concept of the monad and Hegel in the fundamental category of power. Power is conceived as play reviving a tradition from Heraclitus to Hegel. And although one can only understand Nietzsche's philosophical language if one hears the resonance of the two-thousand-year-old western tradition in it, he nevertheless deviates from the path of this tradition. . . . Nietzsche explicates his two fundamental thoughts of his positive philosophy, namely the will to power and the eternal return . . . Both opposing aspects have their unity and center in Dionysus. Although the aphorism refers to the will to power as the 'key to all puzzles' and thus emphasizes this aspect especially, the conceptual thrust of the entire thought shows the contrast of the will to power to the infinity of the eternal return." Fink, *Nietzsche's Philosophy*, 161–62.
13. In GS 374, Nietzsche asks whether we should not think that "all existence is not essentially actively engaged in interpretation. Rather has the world become 'infinite' for us all over again, inasmuch as we cannot reject the possibility that it may include infinite interpretations."
14. This is not an uncontroversial statement. Many interpreters of Nietzsche contest how to understand his account of language. On the one hand, Nietzsche argues in *Beyond Good and Evil* that we must protect against the seduction of words. Similarly, in "On Truth and Lies in a Nonmoral Sense," he expresses a wariness of philosophical language that fails to recognize that it is merely convention and does not reflect the actual essences of things. On the other hand, there is no way to revalue values outside of language. If language is constructed, then how could it be shared? I take Nietzsche to mean that we should protect against reified concepts in their life-denial. If we accept that language, like the world and life, is always in flux, then we can still have a shared space of meaning while acknowledging that our task of interpretation, which is not so much discovering true meaning as creating meaning, is never complete. See also Schrift, *Nietzsche and the Question of Interpretation*, 193.
15. The following discussion of Fink's understanding of the world is a modification of that in my article (Homan, "The Play of Being and Nothing").
16. Cited in Bruzina, "Translator's Introduction," liii.
17. Kant, *Critique of Pure Reason*, AK 24/B 38–39. See also Homan, 38.
18. Heidegger and Fink, *Heraclitus Seminar, 1966/67*, 65.
19. Fink, "Nietzsche's Metaphysics of Play (1946)."
20. *Binnenweltlich* connotes both the sense of *bei*, to be in or belong to the realm of something, and *innen*, to be within, thus suggesting the idea of belonging to the

world or being together with the world. This is similar to Heidegger's discussion in *Being and Time* that "being in" the world means that we are not in the world like beans in a jar, but that we belong to the world. Heidegger, *Being and Time*, 51.

21. Bertolini, "The Forces of the Cosmos Before Genesis and Before Life: Some Remarks on Eugen Fink's Philosophy of the World," 46. Simona Bertolini argues that Fink's later works lack the same attention to constructive phenomenology that would provide a better account of how communities concretely develop these practices.

22. The German here is *Erziehung*, which has a variety of different connotations including education, upbringing, parenting, and breeding. I am choosing to translate it as upbringing to distinguish it from both *Bildung* and *Pädagogik*, which entail a more formal sense of education, and to emphasize both the natural and social dimension that Fink associates with the word. *Bildung*, as Gadamer understands it, is not especially different from Fink's account of *Erziehung*, although Gadamer does not emphasize the natural dimension, that is, relation between *Erziehung* and *physis* as much.

23. Hegel, *Lectures on the Philosophy of World History*, 151. Hegel makes a similar point about the role of *Bildung* and human development as opposed to that of animals: "By means of discipline, education, and culture they become for the first time what they ought to be, rational beings. Humans have only the potential of being human when they are born. Animals are born nearly complete; their growth is basically a strengthening, and in instinct they have straight away everything they need. We must not regard it as a special benefit of nature for animals that their formation is soon complete, for the strengthening is only a matter of degree. Because humans are spiritual beings, they must acquire everything for themselves must make themselves into what they ought to be and what otherwise would remain a mere potentiality; they must cast off the natural. Thus spirit is humanity's own achievement." Fink differs insofar as he rejects the notion that humans develop into rational animals, that they must cast off the natural, and that there would be some predetermine essence we strive toward.

24. Fink claims, "We do not exist in *shared knowledge* [*Mitwisserschaft*] and express witness of human being only then when we first achieve a reduction of our self-consciousness and its relations, rather prior to that much more originarily in concrete, social ways of life with fellow humans, thus in the space of the social being with others" (EC 41).

25. Fink here refers to Heidegger's assertion in *Being and Time* that "Only being free *for* death gives Dasein its absolute goal and pushes existence into its finitude. The finitude of existence thus seized upon tears one back out of endless multiplicity of possibilities offering themselves nearest by—those of comfort, shirking, and taking things easy—and brings Dasein to the simplicity of its *fate*. This is how we designate the primordial occurrence of Dasein that lies in authentic resoluteness in which it *hands itself down* to itself, free for death, in a possibility that it inherited and yet has chosen" (BT 351).

26. Fink, *Grundfragen der systematischen Pädagogik*, 88.

27. Hilt, "Bilder des Nichts—Eugen Finks Frage nach dem Bild vom Menschen," 304.

28. Fink, "Zur Bildungstheorie der technischen Bildung," 17.

29. Fink, 19.

30. Fink, 17.

31. For more on Fink's interpretation of Nietzsche, see Babich, "Nietzsche's "Artists' Metaphysics" and Fink's Ontological 'World-Play.'"

32. Gadamer, "Die Vielfalt der Sprachen und das Verstehen der Welt," 344. He draws on the etymology of *Welt* to suggest that in the Middle High German, we find "*Weralt*," which thus shows the centrality of "*wer*," that is, "who" or "the human," to our conception of the world.

33. Gadamer, 345.

34. Here Gadamer distinguishes between world and environment. Animals have an environment, but they do not have a world because animals do not have language. Thus, for Gadamer, the world is necessarily a world of meaning, and there is no meaning without language. Importantly, though, he does not think language is the same as speech. Rather, language is the capacity to mean something. Although Fink also thinks our being in the world is in language, his view of the world as totality includes perhaps more than what Gadamer means. Still, Gadamer does not suggest that the world of meaning just is the world of language. There are elements of the world that surpass us and therefore cannot be merely the result of human articulation.

35. Gadamer, "Die Vielfalt der Sprachen und das Verstehen der Welt," 348.

36. Gadamer, 349.

37. Gadamer may be especially critical of Dilthey here, but he traces the problem to the reliance of *Erlebnis* on a certain givenness in its insistence on immediacy. It becomes, then, a matter of data and phenomena. *Erlebnisse* are things to be had, to be amassed, which then can be investigated like a scientific object. The structures that provide these experiences with meaning are simply accepted as they are. Gadamer admits that Dilthey, for example, does want to maintain continuity between these experiences and the whole of one's life, but that Dilthey's account seems to offer a false dilemma between positivist and pantheistic attitudes. The individual experiences something, a work of art for example, and this experience flows with all of her other experiences, but then she isolates this experience and investigates it, which tears her from this very continuity. Even though Dilthey does understand his project as a response to cold rationalism and he does try to reconnect experience to the totality of life, he does not fully succeed.

38. Risser, *Hermeneutics and the Voice of the Other*, 85. As James Risser explains, "Thus, unlike *Erlebnis* where the venturing out is a return to the order of life, an order in which one is now enriched, *Erfahrung* essentially entails a transformation of that life. Equally important, Gadamer's desire to link understanding to experiences as *Erfahrung* is tied to the way in which this experience is itself learning, is itself knowing."

39. Gadamer explains that reproduction is not a mere repetition, but an event of being: "The specific mode of the work of art's presence is the coming-to-presentation of being" (TM 152).

40. Gadamer writes, "The audience only completes [*vollzieht*] what the play as such is" (TM 107). To complete something is *vollziehen*, that is, to draw something to completion or fully. To understand, comprehend, and even reproduce or relate to

something is a matter of *nachvollziehen*. Thus, in every act of self-presentation and completion, there is the space for understanding and relation.

41. Nielsen, "On Poietic Remembering and Forgetting: Hermeneutic Recollection and Diotima's Historico-Hermeneutic Leanings," 130. Cynthia Nielsen explains, "In the activity of forgetting, we actively clear a space for new possibilities by reconfiguring the past for the present." She compares this to the activity of the jazz musician whose ability to improvise is rooted in her years of practicing scales such that, during the performance, her improvisation both forgets and remembers those scales in order to gather them anew in different ways.

42. This is especially clear in Gadamer's discussion of the festival that changes every year while at the same time remaining the same. Its essence is something different for "it has its being only in becoming and return" and only insofar as it is celebrated (TM 121). Here again we find the connection between anamnesis and mimesis. In the festival, the spectator forgets the demands of the everyday and in a sense loses herself to the celebration. The awareness of the events that have taken place between the celebrations, such as births or deaths and her own growth, is heightened. The distance she experiences and the world that is presented provide the very moment for her to recognize herself. For a thorough explanation of the relationship between art, play, and festival, see Gadamer's "The Relevance of the Beautiful" as well as Grondin, "Play, Festival, and Ritual."

43. Gadamer, *Hermeneutische Entwürfe*, 191.

44. Davey, *Unquiet Understanding*, 22.

45. Davey, 40.

46. For a more thorough discussion of Gadamer and Hegel on *Bildung*, see Odenstedt, *Gadamer on Tradition—Historical Context and the Limits of Reflection*, 153–220.

47. Grondin, "Gadamer's Experience and Theory of Education," 11. Jean Grondin explains, "This universality is by no means a universality of the concept or understanding. This is not the case of a particular being deduced from a universal; nothing is proved conclusively. The universal viewpoints to which the cultivated man keeps himself open are not an applicable yardstick, but are present to him only as the viewpoints of possible others. Thus the cultivated consciousness has in fact more the character of a sense."

48. Davey, 242.

49. Gadamer, "Education Is Self-Education," 531.

50. Gadamer, 532.

51. Gallagher, *Hermeneutics and Education*, 50.

52. Wierciński, "Hermeneutic Education to Understanding: Self-Education and the Willingness to Risk Failure," 116.

53. Habermas, "A Review of Gadamer's Truth and Method," 236.

54. Caputo, *Radical Hermeneutics*, 108.

55. Caputo, 112.

56. Bernasconi, "'You Don't Know What I'm Talking About': Alterity and the Hermeneutic Ideal," 192.

57. Fleming, "Gadamer's Conversation: Does the Other Have a Say?" 119.

58. Risser, *Hermeneutics and the Voice of the Other*, 72–73.
59. Vilhauer, *Gadamer's Ethics of Play*, 93.
60. Vilhauer, 92.
61. Michelfelder and Palmer, *Dialogue and Deconstruction*, 95.
62. Davey, 100.
63. Wierciński, 121.

Conclusion
The Play of the In-Between

In this concluding section, I want to take more seriously some of the objections raised in the previous chapter, namely that hermeneutics cannot fully account for difference. The concern remains that the account of poetic education I have given, stemming from a German academic culture and with emphasis on classic works of art and poetry, remains at bottom fundamentally elitist or conservative. Indeed, the tradition of *Bildung* has quite often gone part and parcel with traditional bourgeois values of culture and education. John Caputo suggests, for example, that Gadamer remains too Hegelian and too concerned with defending some version of a tradition or culture to ask the fundamental questions.[1] There is a worry, too, that such appeals to great Germans or the valorization of Greek art and thought reinscribe structures of oppression and marginalization. I agree that these are real and pressing concerns. However, some of this concern is reduced if we draw a distinction between two different senses of *Bildung*. If we take *Bildung* to be a process of enculturation that is dependent on something like the cultivation of taste, then it seems that these criticisms hold, for the cultivation of taste has often been associated with elitism. Moreover, such a cultivation of taste precludes those without access to or the material conditions for the experiences of great works of art (the definition of which is itself considerably fraught). Furthermore, if we take *Bildung* to be the development of a rational, autonomous, self-determining individual, then the problem still remains.

If we instead understand *Bildung* as a mode of being in the world that cultivates remaining open to what is other and becoming not only speaker but also listener, then we need not necessarily reinscribe the elitist principles or hierarchies of taste and culture. In the Afterword to *Truth and Method*, Gadamer explains that art is most fully art not when it is the tool of a sociopolitical will, but rather when it documents a social reality. He clarifies further that his use of classical concepts like "mimesis" and "representation" is not to "defend classical ideas but to transcend the bourgeois conception of the aesthetic as cultural religion" (TM 580–81). For Gadamer, then, art that is merely used as an instrument, including for moralizing or political gain, is no longer art. It is true that Gadamer very seldom references art that does not belong to the Western tradition and so it would be reasonable to suggest that he does in some ways perpetuate classical norms. Importantly, however, Gadamer sees these examples not as pinnacles of cultural achievement, but as loci of particular significant transformative experiences within a particular tradition. What is fundamental to *Bildung*, precisely in its various cultural manifestations, is the spontaneity and openness to what is other. To have this sort of open stance in the world is made possible by being in a particular and culture, for otherwise there would be no possibility for meaning.

Gadamer writes that "Hermeneutic work is based on a polarity of familiarity and strangeness . . . It is in the play between the traditionary text's strangeness and familiarity to us, between being a historically intended, distanced object and belonging to a tradition. *The true locus of hermeneutics is in this in-between*" (TM 295). Gadamer specifically addresses textual interpretation here, but because his account of hermeneutics is rooted in language, it applies to human existence in general as being in language. In the following, I aim to draw these ideas regarding the in-between, the liminality, of hermeneutics together more with a few examples of how such liminal spaces, and specifically play spaces, can foster resistance, transformation, and liberation.

IN-BETWEEN IDENTITIES

Gloria Anzaldúa argues that we need a new conception of the self that accounts for contradicting identities and tolerates ambiguity. She explains that when she places the identities of "Chicana, tejana, working-class, dyke-feminist poet, writer-theorist" in front of her name, she does so "for reasons different than those of the dominant culture. Their reasons are to marginalize, confine, and contain. My labeling of myself is so that the Chicana and lesbian and all the other persons in me don't get erased, omitted, or killed."[2] If an identity does not tolerate ambiguity, it effectively does not tolerate her. Naming is a "survival tactic." Rather than dissolving the ambiguity, she seeks a new account of the self that affords an understanding of these multiplicities. In *Borderlands: La Frontera = The New Mestiza*, she suggests this new consciousness would be *mestiza*, a consciousness of the borderland. *Mestiza* traditionally refers to a woman who is of both Spanish and indigenous descent. Growing up on the *tejas*-Mexico border, Anzaldúa was immersed in Mexican, indigenous, and white Anglo culture all at once. Although constantly pulled from both directions and feeling not at home in this in-between, her sense of self cannot be reduced to either side for one necessarily hearkens the other. Because her identity occupies this in-between, borderland space, Anzaldúa perceives herself as foreign and familiar. This new *mestiza* identity sees multiplicity and ambiguity not as a threat to identity, but as forming the very possibility of a self. The *mestiza* consciousness, through "continual creative motion" aims to "break down the subject-object duality that keeps her a prisoner" and instead reinterprets history, strengthens her tolerance for ambiguity, and is willing to "make herself vulnerable to foreign ways of seeing and thinking."[3] By embracing ambiguity and cultivating an orientation toward what is other, this new, creative *mestiza* consciousness is able to free itself from the confines of subject-object dualism.

In later works, Anzaldúa suggests that this initial understanding of *mestiza* identity became too oppositional, thus in some ways reinscribing the dualism she seeks to resist.[4] She turns to the idea of *nepantla*, which she describes as "a psychological, liminal space between the way things had been and an unknown future. *Nepantla* is the space in-between, the locus and sign of transition."[5] Those who occupy the in-between spaces are *nepantleras*, the "boundary-crossers, thresholders" who "from a listening, receptive, spiritual stance, rise to their own visions and shift into acting them out hacienda mundo Nuevo (introducing change)."[6] Although Anzaldúa describes *nepantla* as a psychological space, it is not merely the projection of a subject. Rather, this liminal space derives specifically from the material conditions of being at the border, from the barbed wire that one must constantly navigate. She frequently refers to the Rio Grande/*Río Bravo del Norte* to explain what it means to live in the Rio Grande Valley while also employing the river as a metaphor for identity:

> Identity is a river—a process. Contained within the river is its identity, and it needs to flow, to change to stay a river—if it stopped it would be a contained body of water such as a lake or a pond. The changes in the river are external (changes in environment—river bed, weather, animal life) and internal (within the waters). A river's contents flow within its boundaries. Changes in identity likewise are external (how others perceive one and how one perceives others and the world) and internal (how one perceives oneself, self-image). People in different regions name the parts of the river/person which they see.[7]

Thus, although she speaks of developing a new consciousness, this is not merely an intellectual activity or the product of judgment. Rather, the consciousness develops through a corporeal, embodied stance toward oneself and others in the site of encounter of the borderland. At the same time, this space cannot be reduced to a strictly physical space. Instead, it retains the very ambiguity of presence and absence, inner and outer, self and other. Because of its liminality, the space affords resistance.[8]

María Lugones and Mihai Spariosu similarly identify a connection between liminality and liberation, particularly in terms of exile and utopia. Importantly, both introduce play into their discussions. Writing about resistance to hegemonic, leveling structures, Lugones explains that what liberates is a preservation of the self as multiplicitous and irreducible to a static unity. What preserves such multiplicity is, she claims, the limen, which she describes as "the place in between realities, a gap 'between and betwixt' universes of sense that construe social life and persons differently, an interstice from where one can most clearly stand critically toward different structures."[9] Because of this gap between realities, oppressed people can engage in possibilities and realities not present in an otherwise oppressive structure because they are able to recognize something of themselves that exceeds what the oppressive structure allows. Thus, the limen "is the place where one becomes most fully aware of one's multiplicity."[10]

Mihai Spariosu similarly emphasizes the creative possibilities of liminality. Focusing specifically on exile, he argues that whereas political forces often employ exile as a way to neutralize resistance, the opposite result often occurs. He explains that, for the exile, the "ambivalent, in-between position gives him a vast amount of freedom or 'free play'" that can be leveraged in new ways. This "ludic-liminal experience . . . becomes also a form of utopia" because it "can then be used to effect changes on both the expelling and the receiving political systems or cultures."[11] Thus, like Lugones and Anzaldúa, Spariosu identifies this liminal space, frequently the result of oppression, as a site of resistance and creativity.[12] Despite totalizing forces, the self cannot be reduced to a singular identity because it contains within it its own alterity. The in-between preserves ambiguity and alterity. Furthermore, although these accounts at first seem agonistic insofar as they develop out of the dualities of oppressor and oppressed, normative and marginalized, at home and not at home, as Anzaldúa illustrates, oppositional attitudes only further reify the dualisms, thus forgoing the possibility of liberation. Instead, each of these thinkers proposes viewing the in-between not as something to be overcome or won, but rather as an important site of ambiguity that grounds formation in the first place. Thus, a more irenic attitude is cultivated in response to the other through the play that does not seek to surmount the other, but preserve her.[13]

In the essay, "Playfulness, 'World-Traveling,' and Loving Perception," Lugones argues that this site of the in-between is creative, and, moreover, fundamentally playful. Here she identifies play as antithetical to agon. Rather than battling or conquering an opponent, she explains, "Playfulness is, in part, an openness to being a fool, which is a combination of not worrying about competence, not being self-important, not taking norms as sacred and finding ambiguity and double edges a source of wisdom and delight."[14] Play is what affords this liminal, creative attitude that, rather than taking norms as reified, instead attunes the self toward ambiguity and multiplicity, toward "self-construction and re-construction."[15]

Lugones introduces this understanding of playfulness to explain how people travel across worlds. Because people are multiplicitous, they inhabit different worlds, and can move between and navigate these different worlds. Yet, this movement is not neutral. Women of color, she explains, are often required to travel to different worlds because their identities are marginalized. Such travel is creative, rich, and meaningful because it draws on a plurality of identities, but frequently the worlds traveled to are hostile white/Anglo worlds. Lugones distinguishes between arrogant perception and loving perception. The former refuses to identify with the other and feels a sense of superiority. The latter is willing to identify with the other and feels a sense of solidarity. To travel to the world of another is an act of loving perception that seeks to understand the other as she understands herself. To refuse to travel or to look down upon other travelers is an act of arrogant perception. Lugones came to realize that in some worlds, she was playful, but in others, she was not. Worlds of loving perception engender play; worlds of arrogant perception foreclose it.

Through play and loving perception, we can travel to others' worlds to understand their multiplicity and we can travel to new, non-oppressive worlds that reflect our multiplicity. Importantly, though, Lugones argues that these worlds are not utopic, in the sense of an abstract ideal, because they must be inhabited by "some flesh and blood people."[16] Thus, the worlds, the liminal spaces, opened by play are not abstract idealizations. The worlds are constructions that reflect ways of being in the world, such as being Latina in the United States or identifying as queer. Although these worlds, as worlds of meaning, are created, they are still becoming. They are not final or fixed. To travel between worlds requires a shift in the self; there is no absolute "I" who could undergo these moves. Rather, the self is multiplicitous as belonging to the creating of worlds. To be in a world playfully means

> We are not self-important, we are not fixed in particular constructions of ourselves, which is part of saying that we are open to self-construction. We may not have rules, and when we do have them, there are no rules that are to us sacred. We are not worried about competence. We are not wedded to a particular way of doing things. While playful, we have not abandoned ourselves to, nor are we stuck in, any particular 'world. We are there creatively. We are not passive.[17]

This sort of play, Lugones argues, is not the agonistic play of the masculine Anglo tradition that emphasizes competence.[18] Rather, it is loving. It seeks to identify with the other and to tarry with the other in creative ways in an openness to the other as well as to surprise, to being a fool, and to self-(re)creation. Moreover, it is not a flight from the self, but a transformation. Play offers the possibility to engage ourselves in ways we would not otherwise be able.

I read this sense of world-traveling as akin to the fusion of horizons described by Gadamer. To understand the other is to try to see the world as she does, but I cannot simply leave my own world or horizon behind to take on her identity. Furthermore, our worlds or horizons are not incommensurable, but shared, even if not in identical ways. To identify means to preserve, to let the other speak. This movement is a form of resistance because it foregrounds liminality as central. It refuses to fall into oppressive dualisms, but instead enables "multiplicitous persons who are faithful witnesses of themselves [to] also testify to, and uncover the multiplicity of, their oppressors and the techniques of oppression afforded by ignoring that multiplicity."[19]

Reading Anzaldúa through the lens of Nietzsche, C. Heike Schotten explains that Anzaldúa's creation of identity as this play of in-between resembles Nietzsche's playful revaluation of values. The task for revolutionaries is not to react to the past, but to engage it creatively, "to construct the new *from the material of the old*. Only then can the new become a way of life, and not merely a reactionary moment in an unproductive standoff between oppressor and oppressed."[20] Schotten further connects Lugones' explanation of play with the laughter of Zarathustra and the desire to "live joyfully within the terms of contradiction without being torn apart by them."[21] Here Schotten's pairing of Anzaldúa and Lugones with Nietzsche illustrates how, I argue, we engage in tradition. We cannot get out of tradition, but neither does it determine us. Looking to Nietzsche enables us to see what it is to give creative style to ourselves. He reminds us of the importance of creative forgetting that is possible only because one is already within values. Looking to Anzaldúa and Lugones requires us to confront the sexist and anti-Semitic tendencies in Nietzsche, and in much of the history of philosophy, that rely on racist presuppositions and gender dualisms and also fail to attend to particular embodiment. Again, though, this does not mean subsuming traditionally marginalized voices under the tradition by adding them to the canon. Rather, this engagement requires us to preserve alterity. This shows, too, that tradition itself is liminal. While tradition and language may be perceived like the *Sprachgitter* that confines, they are not fixed. Instead, they are also liberating as sites for new forms of engagement, understanding, and creation.

There is, though, a danger to this world-travel. As Lugones points out, it is very often the case that people who are historically and traditionally marginalized are required to travel to hostile worlds while those in privileged positions remain at ease in their own worlds. George Yancy, in "The Social Ontology of African-American Language" specifically addresses how

"Standard" American English presents itself as both neutral and proper without recognizing its historic roots as white Anglo speech. Thus, those whose language of nurture is "Standard" American English (SAE) are privileged, whereas those whose language of nurture is something else, such as African American Language (AAL), are required to take up SAE if they are to be taken seriously in institutions, such as the academic discipline of philosophy in the United States. This privileging of one language over another as the standard refuses to recognize the rich, nuanced, important ways of understanding in that language.[22] As Gadamer has argued, we cannot understand ourselves outside of language. Even if we can speak another language, it will not live up to how we understand ourselves in what Gadamer calls the mother tongue and what here Yancy calls the language of nurture. Language is not a tool, but our way of inhabiting, of flourishing, in a world. Part of Yancy's project is to address why he should be required, in Lugones' words, to travel to a hostile world instead of being able to write in a way that exceeds what could ever be expressed in SAE and one that allow for flourishing. Yancy writes, since African American Language is

> a rich cultural and philosophical site of expression, I believe that it is the job of knowledgeable and responsible Black philosophers—at least for those who are willing to admit that they speak both the Language of Wider Communication (or LWC) and the powerful vernacular shaped by African retentions and African American linguistic nuances—to invite [white philosophers] to enter African American semiotic spaces of discursive difference and overlap.[23]

In the rest of the article, Yancy does just this by moving back and forth between both describing and writing in SAE and AAL to demonstrate those very nuances and depths of meaning. For example, he writes,

> We always pushin. Whether its remaking and reconfiguring some superimposed language, creating musical instruments from some old found object, doctoring up a traditional instrument, because you know we gotta hear that twang and chromatic sound, or pushin the bounds of what it means to be human and democratic, we up on it, way out in front. Blusing. Bopping. Moving. Rapping. Hip Hopping. Historicizing. Morphing. Always in the process of red-shifting, even when we be down. And, yes, LANGUAGING. We are still in process. What next? Can't be sho. But I'll C U when WE get there.[24]

To insist that AAL is a language, and not a mere dialect or variation of SAE, is to affirm that AAL is an identity and "legitimate mode of identity construction," thus directly resistant to white supremacy.[25] By inviting SAE speakers to travel to his world, Yancy is making a claim on them to be open to transforming their understanding. What Yancy further demonstrates is that there is a way to move between the worlds in a way that does not melt away difference, but rather preserves it. He shows that language is creative and continues as an event, as "Blusing. Bopping ... Hop Hopping. Historicizing ... Languaging." That language, too, is cast out toward futures still unknown. In the previous chapter, we saw that Gadamer claims that making oneself at home reveals itself in the courage for creating new vocabularies. Here, we find the courage of creativity in also seeing being at home as not fixed in place, but also on the way. These creative moves, which belong to language as such, prevent and challenge attempts at totalization.

Similarly, in *Teaching to Transgress*, bell hooks reflects on Adrienne Rich's poem, "The Burning of Paper Instead of Children." Rich writes, "This is the oppressor's language yet I need it to talk to you." What do we do when the very language we have to articulate ourselves is the same that forces our silence? hooks reflects that Standard English is not the language of exile, but domination. The oppressors use the language, "shape it to become a territory that limits and defines, how they make it a weapon that can shame, humiliate, colonize."[26] Whereas language might be treated as a tool or mechanism of control, hooks points out that that language is still a site of dwelling. It is inhabited. And it is precisely in this way that language can become a site of resistance. By creating new meanings, syntaxes, and melodies, the enslaved black Africans transformed English. By rupturing the meanings, "so that white folks could often not understand black speech," they created a language that could speak anew. She writes, "The power of this speech is not simply that it enables resistance to white supremacy, but that it also forges a space for alternative cultural productive and alternative epistemologies—different ways of thinking and knowing that were crucial to creating a counter-hegemonic worldview."[27] As hooks explains, AAL and black vernacular are often counterhegemonic because they are not immediately understood by white folks. hooks acknowledges, like Yancy, that the language of higher education in the United States is not that of her own black vernacular. Yet, that is not reason to accept SAE as the only proper language. There remain avenues of resistance that can be carved out even more not by rejecting, but by reshaping tradition. She also highlights that spaces of silence, "the patient act of listening to another tongue" subvert the capitalist impulse to totalize everything and the cultural imperialist insistence on speaking SAE if one wants to be taken seriously. Thus, it seems that what hooks calls for is a preservation of that liminality that continues to speak in new ways and resists the reductionism of false dualisms. Moreover, while she calls for recognizing the importance of silence and listening, this does not preclude the demand to be heard and be recognized. The imperative question of "Do you hear me?" demands others open themselves to this address.

Shannon Sullivan, writing in response to Yancy, worries that, despite the generous invitation of hospitality he offers, travel by a privileged group to another's world risks undermining the creation of that resistance. Even well-intentioned people engaged in anti-racist work might still bring in cultural imperialism or white supremacism. Letting white people in on the code, Sullivan suggests, could end up feeding into the very imperialism trying to be avoided due to a presumed right, based on legacies of colonialism, that white people often feel they have to whatever they encounter.[28] Yet, she argues, this is not reason enough not to accept the invitation. There is also no certain answer as to whether and how the invitation should be accepted. Rather, the decision requires critical reflection about one's knowledge and aims in entering into that discussion and a consideration of how one's experiences are brought to bear. Moreover, it requires a willingness to let oneself be transformed by the conversation. This strikes me as very much like Gadamer's claim that the fusion of horizons requires a constant reflection of one's own horizon and an attunement to the other in her particularity. There is no guarantee that this will achieve understanding, but through this listening, both to ourselves and the other, we hold open the space for such a transformation into understanding. If we take seriously that we must perceive out of love, and not out of arrogance, then the other cannot be used simply for my own understanding. She cannot be assimilated or flattened.

THE PLAYSPACE OF HERMENEUTICS

Linda Martín Alcoff is sympathetic to many of the concerns feminist philosophers have regarding hermeneutics. She contends that hermeneutics, as conceived by Gadamer, fails to include the body and overemphasizes death without considering birth. Yet, what hermeneutics helps us to understand is how there are shared horizons of meaning within an ongoing tradition. If we are worried about cultural imperialism and colonialist attitudes, for example, we cannot pretend that our work is to discover the "authentic" nature of those colonized from a neutral perspective. Furthermore, every identity is not singular, but plural. Thus, moving away from what she deems a monotopic hermeneutics toward a plurotopic one allows us to see that "it is not simply that the other makes up the self, but that multiple others are constitutive aspects of our interpretive horizon, offering alternative and in some cases competing background assumptions and perceptual practices, fracturing the meanings of visible appearance and complicating embodied knowledge."[29] What Alcoff suggests is that to have a self is to inhabit a horizon, but different aspects of my identity come into play at different times and in different ways and are in play with others. The self is not self-identical, but multiplicitous in these interpretive dimensions. This does not mean that there is no self, but that the self is underway.

Alcoff also reads hermeneutics as an important resource for feminism, particularly in its emphasis on openness to alterity and understanding rather than knowledge. One of the most important contributions, though, is that hermeneutics draws on some "decidedly feminine characteristics in regard to one culturally specific but familiar version of traditional femininity, involving openness, passivity, a tendency to dialogue rather than command, and a heightened awareness of the interdependence and relationality of all properties."[30] These characteristics have been more traditionally associated with women, though Alcoff is clear that she does not believe them to be innate features or exclusive to a particular sex. For Alcoff, this is important because it means that recognizing the contributions of women need not appeal to typically masculine models. Rather, Gadamer's model also pushes us to reconsider the characteristics we associate with who counts as someone who is an expert or who, because of these characteristics, may have been epistemically discredited. Thus, hermeneutics challenges the very tradition to which it belongs. Through this challenge of hermeneutics to investigate its own presuppositions, we continue to be challenged as well to become better listeners.

The space created and preserved in our relation to others is complicated, and at times difficult and disruptive. The playspaces described by Kant and Schiller, however, seem rather two-dimensional and lacking much friction. In contrast, I think we must think of this space as textured. The expansions of meaning fostered by liminal playspaces do not happen without friction or without some attention to the environment. Indeed, the contours of these spaces demand our responsibility. Here an example might help. As Gadamer explains, our encounter with art is one of recognition, which requires serious attention to the space opened before us and demands our responsibility. One might think of the *Stolpersteine* placed by artist Gunter Demnig in many European cities.[31] The brass blocks, marked with "*Hier wohnte . . .*" followed by the name, age, and dates of the deportation and murder of a victim of the Shoah, serve as modes of preserving the names, and thus existence, of those victims. The blocks cause passersby to stumble, physically and intellectually, to recall what happened in that space. The blocks demand some sort of responsibility. The pedestrian might recall the horrors of the Shoah and be troubled by rising anti-immigrant sentiment or anti-Semitism in the city. The cyclist might navigate her bike around the patch of brass, knowing the blocks are slippery in the rain. The blocks can be ignored or go unnoticed, but these, too, are responses elicited by the stones. There remains something that resists a covering over and yet, by the very sparseness of information on the stone, also resists treating the memory of that person as a specimen or mere fact of history. We are prompted to imagine where this person lived, what her relation to the others was, what profession she had. They remind us of our responsibilities, of history and context, and that the space of our responsibility is, at times quite literally, textured and fraught. At the same time, the blocks remind us that we will never fully know the person whose voice they represent. Risser explains that we come to understand not by being thinking subjects, but through engaging the other who addresses us. He writes, "This other that is a speaking person in every dialogical encounter is also the other in the address of language, the other that speaks when 'language becomes voice.' It is this voice that awakens one to vigilance, to being questioned in the conversation that we are."[32] We would be similarly mistaken to think that the voice is there merely to teach us something.[33] As we have seen anti-Semitism growing again in Germany, we also know that the blocks alone are not enough to stave off this rising tide. Yet, I want to argue that the blocks continue to articulate the "I'm still here." They demand our vigilance. We must not stop listening.

As open to what surpasses, as open to the other, poetry is an orientation toward freedom. Freedom is not a thing among things or the ability to move frictionless in pursuit of our desires, but the possibility of relation to the other. Freedom is the possibility of encounter. Bruns points out that Celan sees poetry as oriented toward freedom, for "freedom is the outside, the region of the other . . . the movement of poetry is toward this region, or toward 'the "otherness" which it can reach and be free.'"[34] First, poetry is understood here as a movement, Bruns explains, not as on a quest, but a move of releasement, of *Gelassenheit*. Poetry is the movement of openness toward what is other. Thus poetry is essentially a releasement into responsibility. Second, this responsibility is a mode of freedom. As holding open the possibility for what is other, it is free. This poetic freedom is without ground, without why.

Poetic education, itself a movement of freedom, is likewise oriented toward the other, toward the limit. This orientation is characterized by tact. Gadamer draws our attention in *Truth and Method* to Helmholtz's appeal to tact in understanding the human sciences. Tact is a sensitivity to and knowledge of how to act in particular situations. To be tactful is to pass over something, not "to avert one's gaze from it, but to keep an eye on it in such a way that rather than knock into it, one slips by it" (TM 15). Tact is more than a feeling; it is "a mode of knowing and a mode of being" (15). Thus tact is an appropriate orientation toward a situation. To be tactful is not to handle a person or to avoid anything disruptive by employing different social niceties, but to hold open that space of alterity, to slip by it rather than knock into it (15). Davey explains, furthermore, "The courteous formalities of greeting, of allowing the other to be other and to be comfortable in that otherness, establishes not a cold distance but a space that enables intimate exchange."[35] Thus to treat a person tactfully is to recognize her as vulnerable and to preserve that alterity, but this requires genuine engagement with her. To treat a person with tact is to leave her intact. Furthermore, the language of tact returns us to this understanding as embodied. Tact, from *tactus*, always bears with it this notion of touching and feeling. This is even more so the case in German, where *Takt* refers both to the sort of tact discussed here as well as beat or pulse in the musical sense. To keep the beat requires hearing, feeling, that beat and responding accordingly.[36]

Keeping the beat and responding to the other are forms of play. As we have seen, play is always dialogic; even as bystanders we are fundamentally participants. It is a matter of question and answer, of to and fro movement. Furthermore, play always provides the space for us to come to know ourselves better and to take things seriously in a way we couldn't otherwise. There are spaces left for us to fill and complete. Play, too, marks the space where we can entertain possibility. What seems determined can be seen in a fresh light. Furthermore, play is always transformative. In the dialogical exchange in play, we can call our practices into question while still remaining open to them and open to new possibilities and change. There is, of course, always risk and vulnerability involved, but we must stand resolute even in our playfulness. The comportment required by play does not mean that we abandon our practices or break radically with the everyday, but that we engage it in a different way. This enables knowledge and truth to present itself in a way that we would not have otherwise.

Ultimately poetic education is learning to hear, to listen, and thus to belong. It is learning to respond to what is other in a meaningful way. It is important, too, that we hear the embodied language that belongs to this orientation. We touch the limits, we hold open the space for others, this freedom is "bursting," as Jean-Luc Nancy describes it.[37] Language itself is corporeal, the poet sings and dances, and education is giving shape. Poetic education is allowing for the meridian of the space of encounter.

In this play of the in-between, the play of poetic education, we come to have knowledge of ourselves, too, not through distanced reflection, but through conversation. Gadamer suggests, for example, that when Socrates engages in dialogue, "something dawns on him about himself and about his living with only pretended knowledge" (GR 30). Dialogue, as both friendship and challenge, calls us to wisdom. Poetic conversation orients us to the self that is both foreign and familiar. As we saw in the epistolary style of *Hyperion*, I cannot know myself except through dialogue, and here I would add, love, with another. In "Remembrance," Hölderlin writes, "Love fixes/ the eyes": the beloved is held in our gaze, not in a scientific way, but is remembered and enables us to see in new ways. Lugones reminds us that loving perception allows solidarity in trying to understand the other as she understands herself.

The conversation has not drawn to a close. No conversation ever fully draws to a close. Conversation, as a mode of friendship or act of love, is not simply an exchange, but a challenge.[38] It demands responsibility. While friendship and play provide access to knowledge we might not otherwise have, they also preserve that which cannot be contained. What this also suggests is that friendship and conversation do not split No from Yes. There always remains something both beyond our comprehension and meaningful to which we can relate. This is, I would suggest, a form of love. Love comes to us unbidden. Love can be neither surmounted nor calculated. Love attunes us. We hope for a coming word in the heart.

NOTES

1. Caputo, *Radical Hermeneutics*.
2. Anzaldúa, *The Gloria Anzaldúa Reader*, 164.
3. Anzaldúa, *Borderlands / La Frontera*, 82.
4. Anzaldúa, *The Gloria Anzaldúa Reader*, 302.
5. Anzaldúa, 310.
6. Cited in Ortega, *In-Between*, 19.
7. Anzaldúa, *The Gloria Anzaldúa Reader*, 166.
8. Ortega, *In-Between*, 34. Mariana Ortega makes the important point that "liminality is not a sufficient condition for liberation." That is, without action in response to this liminality, the in-between remains only possibly liberatory.
9. Lugones, *Pilgrimages/Peregrinajes*, 59.
10. Lugones, 61.
11. Spariosu, *Modernism and Exile*, 30.
12. Though neither cites the other, both Lugones and Spariosu draw their accounts of liminality and play from Victor Turner. Turner particularly focuses on the role of liminality in transition rites wherein the subject occupies an in-between space and moves between realities in a transformative experience as well as the ways in which cultures develop "anti-structures" that allow for the "liberation of human capabilities of cognition, affect, volition, creativity, etc. from the normative constraints incumbent upon occupying a sequence of social statuses, enacting a multiplicity of social roles, and being acutely conscious of membership in some corporate group such as a family, lineage, clan, tribe, nation, etc., or of affiliation with some pervasive social category such as a class, caste, sex, or age-division." This liberation, which Turner identifies as ludic and liminal, is not wholly separate from everyday life because it uses the very same categories, but in a reconfigured way. See Turner, *From Ritual to Theatre*, 44. See also Turner, *Dramas, Fields, and Metaphors*.
13. Spariosu seeks to develop a ludic-irenic account as an alternative to more agonistic approaches to play. Such an approach would be rooted in peace, rather than conquest. He writes, "For any irenic mentality, the other is not an object to be striven for, overcome, or joined in a temporary partnership, but is the originary cosponsor and correspondent of a mutually enriching world. No irenic mentality will experience

difference as conflict but, rather, as an openness and an opportunity toward a responsive understanding of other world." Spariosu, *The Wreath of Wild Olive*, 119.

14. Lugones, 96.
15. Lugones, 85.
16. Lugones, 87.
17. Lugones, 96.
18. Lugones writes, "An agonistic sense of playfulness is one in which competence is central ... Though I will not provide the arguments for this interpretation of Gadamer and Huizinga here, I understood that both of them have an agonistic sense of play" (94). Lugones attributes this agonistic view to Gadamer, suggesting that he emphasizes battle and conquest. She also argues that role-playing is the paradigmatic form of play for Gadamer. Such role-playing, which is a projection of the self, then relies on a fixed conception of self, which she argues against. Based on the account of Gadamer I have developed here, I do not think that Lugones' view matches what Gadamer actually argues. Gadamer begins his discussion of play by drawing on Huizinga, who does emphasize role-play, but Gadamer's position cannot be collapsed into Huizinga's. As we have seen, Gadamer does not think that conquest or winning is the aim of play. Indeed, he argues against this. Moreover, while Gadamer's view of the self may not be as fluid as the one Lugones advances, Gadamer does not believe in a fixed conception of the self. That Lugones does not provide reasons for her interpretation of Gadamer is at odds with Gadamer's own hermeneutics, which emphasizes that we give reasons for our interpretations and revise our interpretations in light of what the text states. Still, I take Lugones' point that we must be wary of accounts that implicitly seem to rely on (ant)agonism.
19. Lugones, 62.
20. Schotten, "Nietzsche, Anzaldúa, and Playful 'World'-Travel," 314.
21. Schotten, 318.
22. Anzaldúa also addresses the issue of SAE, particularly in academic contexts, at length in "Haciendo caras. una entrada," in *The Gloria Anzaldúa Reader*, 124–139.
23. Yancy, "Geneva Smitherman: The Social Ontology of African-American Language, the Power of Nommo, and the Dynamics of Resistance and Identity Through Language," 275.
24. Yancy, 298.
25. Yancy, 295.
26. hooks, *Teaching to Transgress*, 168.
27. hooks, 170–71.
28. Sullivan, "White World-Traveling," 302.
29. Alcoff, *Visible Identities*, 125.
30. Alcoff, "Gadamer's Feminist Epistemology," 233.
31. Demnig, "Stolpersteine."
32. Risser, *Hermeneutics and the Voice of the Other*, 208.
33. Horn, "Auschwitz Is Not a Metaphor."
34. Bruns, "The Remembrance of Language: An Introduction to Gadamer's Poetics," 39.
35. Davey, *Unquiet Understanding*, 244.

36. Vallega, *Sense and Finitude*, 99. Alejandro Vallega reflects at length on Gadamer's reading of Celan, focusing particularly on the summoning of words. He emphasizes that words, especially in Celan's poetry, are tactile. Thus, the poet's searching for them is also a matter of tact: "The poet does not seek word-less marks, and here is the powerful insight in Celan's recovery of words. The kneading of names is a matter beyond words, logic, syntax, images and visual representation. Words are a sensuous matter, the summoning of words is a matter of tact."

37. Nancy, *The Experience of Freedom*, 57–58.

38. Gadamer also suggests that it is no coincidence that the height of hermeneutics, as in Schleiermacher, occurs during the Romantic age that was "outstanding in its glowing cultivation of friendship" (GR 50).

Bibliography

Acosta, María del Rosario. "The Violence of Reason." In *Aesthetic Reason and Imaginative Freedom: Friedrich Schiller and Philosophy*, edited by María del Rosario Acosta López and Jeffrey L. Powell, 59–82. Albany: State University of New York Press, 2018.
Adorno, Theodor W. *Prisms*. Boston: MIT Press, 1983.
Alcoff, Linda Martín. "Gadamer's Feminist Epistemology." In *Feminist Interpretations of Hans-Georg Gadamer*, edited by Lorraine Code. University Park: Pennsylvania State University Press, 2003.
———. *Visible Identities: Race, Gender, and the Self*. New York: Oxford University Press, 2005.
Alvis, Jason W. "God's Playthings: Eugen Fink's Phenomenology of Religion in Play as Symbol of the World." *Research in Phenomenology* 49, no. 1 (March 4, 2019): 88–117.
Anzaldúa, Gloria. *Borderlands / La Frontera: The New Mestiza*. Edited by Norma Cantú and Aída Hurtado. 4th edition. San Francisco: Aunt Lute Books, 2012.
———. *The Gloria Anzaldúa Reader*. Edited by AnaLouise Keating. Durham: Duke University Press Books, 2009.
Ardley, Gavin. "The Role of Play in the Philosophy of Plato." *Philosophy* 42, no. 161 (1967): 226–44.
Aristotle. *The Complete Works of Aristotle: The Revised Oxford Translation*. Edited by Jonathan Barnes. Princeton, NJ: Princeton University Press, 1984.
Babich, Babette E. "Nietzsche's 'Artists' Metaphysics' and Fink's Ontological 'World-Play.'" *International Studies in Philosophy* 37, no. 3 (2005): 163–80.
———. *Words in Blood, Like Flowers: Philosophy and Poetry, Music and Eros in Hölderlin, Nietzsche, and Heidegger*. Albany: State University of New York Press, 2006.
Bambach, Charles. *Thinking the Poetic Measure of Justice: Hölderlin-Heidegger-Celan*. Albany: State University of New York Press, 2014.
Beiser, Frederick C. *German Idealism*. Harvard: Harvard University Press, 2009.

———. *Schiller as Philosopher: A Re-Examination*. Oxford: Oxford University Press, 2008.
Bernasconi, Robert. "Kant and Blumenbach's Polyps: A Neglected Chapter in the History of the Concept of Race." *The German Invention of Race*, December 1, 2006, 73–90.
———. "Kant as an Unfamiliar Source of Racism." In *Philosophers on Race*, edited by Julie K. Ward and Tommy L. Lott, 145–66. Hoboken, NJ: John Wiley & Sons, Ltd, 2007.
———. "Kant's Third Thoughts on Race." In *Reading Kant's Geography*, edited by Stuart Elden and Eduardo Mendieta, 291–318. State University of New York Press, 2011.
———. "Will the Real Kant Please Stand Up—The Challenge of Enlightenment Racism to the Study of the History of Philosophy." *Radical Philosophy* 117 (2003): 13–22.
———. "'You Don't Know What I'm Talking About': Alterity and the Hermeneutic Ideal." In *The Specter of Relativism*, edited by Lawrence Schmidt, Vol. 178–94. Evanston: Northwestern University Press, 1995.
Bertolini, Simona. "The Forces of the Cosmos Before Genesis and Before Life: Some Remarks on Eugen Fink's Philosophy of the World." In *Phenomenology of Space and Time: The Forces of the Cosmos and the Ontopoietic Genesis of Life: Book One*, edited by Anna-Teresa Tymieniecka, 37–46. Cham: Springer International Publishing, 2014.
Blumenbach Johann Friedrich. *Über den Bildungstrieb*. Göttingen: Johann Christian Dieterich, 1789.
Böschenstein, Bernhard. "Hölderlin und Celan." *Hölderlin Jahrbuch* 23 (1982-1983): 147–155.
Bruns, Gerald L. "The Remembrance of Language: An Introduction to Gadamer's Poetics." In *"Who Am I and Who Are You?" And Other Essays*, edited by Richard Heinemann and Bruce Krajewski, 1–52. Albany: State University of New York Press, 1997.
Bruzina, Ronald. *Edmund Husserl and Eugen Fink: Beginnings and Ends in Phenomenology 1928-1938*. New Haven, CT: Yale University Press, 2004.
———. "Translator's Introduction." In *Sixth Cartesian Meditation*, by Eugen Fink, vii–xcii. Translated by Ronald Bruzina. Bloomington: Indiana University Press, 1995.
Caputo, John. *Radical Hermeneutics: Repetition, Deconstruction, and the Hermeneutic Project*. Bloomington: Indiana University Press, 1988.
Carson, Anne. *Economy of the Unlost:* Princeton, NJ: Princeton University Press, 2002.
Celan, Paul. *Collected Prose*. Translated by Rosemarie Waldrop. Manchester: Carcanet Press Limited, 2003.
———. *Die Gedichte*. Edited by Barbara Wiedemann. Frankfurt am Main: Suhrkamp, 2005.
———. *Die Niemandsrose / Sprachgitter: Gedichte*. Frankfurt am Main: S. Fischer Verlag, 1980.

———. *Poems of Paul Celan*. Translated by Michael Hamburger. Persea Books, 2002.
———. *Von Schwelle zu Schwelle*. Munich: Deutsche Verlags-Anstalt, Verlagsgruppe Random House GmbH, 1955.
Cocalis, Susan L. "The Transformation of 'Bildung' from an Image to an Ideal." *Monatshefte* 70, no. 4 (1978): 399–414.
Davey, Nicholas. *Unquiet Understanding: Gadamer's Philosophical Hermeneutics*. Albany: State University of New York Press, 2006.
Demnig, Gunter. "Stolpersteine," October 13, 2012. http://www.stolpersteine.eu/.
Derrida, Jacques. *Sovereignties in Question: The Poetics of Paul Celan*. Edited by Thomas Dutoit and Outi Pasanen. 1st edition. New York: Fordham University Press, 2005.
Di Cesare, Donatella. *Gadamer: A Philosophical Portrait*. Translated by Niall Keane. Bloomington: Indiana University Press, 2013.
———. *Heidegger and the Jews: The Black Notebooks*. Medford, MA: Polity, 2018.
———. "Heidegger's Metaphysical Anti-Semitism." In *Reading Heidegger's Black Notebooks 1931–1941*, edited by Ingo Farin and Jeff Malpas, 181–94. Cambridge, MA: The MIT Press, 2016.
———. *Utopia of Understanding: Between Babel and Auschwitz*. Translated by Niall Keane. Albany: State University of New York Press, 2013.
Diels, Hermann, and Walther Kranz, eds. *Die Fragmente der Vorsokratiker*. Hildesheim: Weidmann, 1985.
Dilthey, Wilhelm. *Poetry and Experience*. Edited by Rudolf A. Makkreel and Frithjof Rodi. Princeton, NJ: Princeton University Press, 1985.
Dudenredaktion. *Das Herkunftswörterbuch: Etymologie der deutschen Sprache*. Bibliographisches Institut GmbH, 2015.
Eze, Emmanuel Chukwudi. "The Color of Reason: The Idea of 'Race' in Kant's Anthropology." In *Postcolonial African Philosophy: A Critical Reader*, edited by Emmanuel Chukwudi Eze, 103–40. Hoboken, NJ: Blackwell, 1997.
Fagen, Robert M. *Animal Play Behavior*. Oxford: Oxford University Press, 1981.
Felstiner, John. *Paul Celan: Poet, Survivor, Jew*. New Haven, CT: Yale University Press, 2001.
Fink, Eugen. *Existenz und Coexistenz: Grundprobleme der menschilchen Gemeinschaft*. Würzburg: Königshausen & Neumann, 1987.
———. *Grundfragen der systematischen Pädagogik*. Freiburg im Breisgau: Rombach, 1978.
———. *Grundphänomene des menschlichen Daseins*. Edited by Egon Schütz and Franz-Anton Schwarz. Freiburg im Breisgau: Karl Alber, 1979.
———. *Natur, Freiheit, Welt: Philosophie der Erziehung*. Edited by Franz-Anton Schwarz. Würzburg: Königshausen & Neumann, 1992.
———. "Nietzsche's Metaphysics of Play." Translated by Catherine Homan and Zachary Hamm. *Philosophy Today* 63, no. 1 (2019): 21–33. https://doi.org/10.5840/philtoday201967254
———. *Nietzsche's Philosophy*. Translated by Goetz Richter. New York: Bloomsbury Academic, 2003.

———. *Play as Symbol of the World: And Other Writings*. Translated by Ian Alexander Moore and Christopher Turner. Bloomington: Indiana University Press, 2016.
———. *Sein und Mensch. Vom Wesen der ontologischen Erfahrung*. Freiburg im Breisgau: Karl Alber, 1977.
———. "Welt und Endlichkeit." In *Sein und Endlichkeit: Vom Wesen der menschlichen Freiheit*, edited by Riccardo Lazzari. Freiburg im Breisgau: Karl Alber, 2015.
———. "Zur Bildungstheorie der technischen Bildung." In *Bildung im technischen Zeitalter: Sein, Mensch und Welt nach Eugen Fink*, edited by Annette Hilt and Cathrin Nielsen, 13–33. Freiburg im Breisgau: Karl Alber, 2005.
Fleming, Marie. "Gadamer's Conversation: Does the Other Have a Say?" In *Feminist Interpretations of Hans-Georg Gadamer*, edited by Lorraine Code, 109–32. University Park: Pennsylvania State University Press, 2003.
Franco, M. "The Influences of Neighbours on the Growth of Modular Organisms with an Example from Trees." *Philosophical Transactions of the Royal Society of London. Series B, Biological Sciences* 313, no. 1159 (1986): 209–25.
Gadamer, Hans-Georg. "Are the Poets Falling Silent?" In *Hans-Georg Gadamer on Education, Poetry, and History: Applied Hermeneutics*, edited by Dieter Misgeld and Graeme Nicholson, translated by Lawrence Schmidt and Monica Reuss, 73–81. Albany: State University of New York Press, 1992.
———. "Die Gegenwärtigkeit Hölderlins." *Hölderlin Jahrbuch* 23 (1982-1983): 178–81.
———. "Die Vielfalt der Sprachen und das Verstehen der Welt." In *Gesammelte Werke*, 8:339–49. Tübingen, 1986.
———. "Education Is Self-Education." *Journal of Philosophy of Education* 35, no. 4 (2001): 529–38.
———. *Gadamer on Celan: "Who Am I and Who Are You?" And Other Essays*. Translated by Bruce Krajewski and Richard Heinemann. Albany: State University of New York Press, 1997.
———. *Hermeneutische Entwürfe: Vorträge und Aufsätze*. Tübingen: Mohr Siebeck, 2000.
———. *Language and Linguisticality in Gadamer's Hermeneutics*. Edited by Lawrence Kennedy Schmidt. Lanham, MD: Lexington Books, 2000.
———. *The Idea of the Good in Platonic-Aristotelian Philosophy*. Translated by P. Christopher Smith. New Haven, CT: Yale University Press, 1986.
———. "Plato and the Poets." In *Dialogue and Dialectic: Eight Hermeneutical Studies on Plato*, translated by P. Christopher Smith, Reprint edition, 39–72. New Haven, CT: Yale University Press, 1983.
———. *Plato im Dialog*. Tübingen: Mohr Siebeck, 1991.
———. *Plato's Dialectical Ethics: Phenomenological Interpretations Relating to the Philebus*. New Haven, CT: Yale University Press, 1991.
———. *The Relevance of the Beautiful and Other Essays*. Edited by Robert Bernasconi. New York: Cambridge University Press, 1986.
———. *Truth and Method*. Translated by Joel Weinsheimer. New York: Continuum Publishing Group, 2004.
———. "The Verse and the Whole." In *Hans-Georg Gadamer on Education, Poetry, and History: Applied Hermeneutics*, edited by Dieter Misgeld and Graeme

Nicholson, translated by Lawrence Schmidt and Monica Reuss, 83–91. Albany: State University of New York Press, 1992.
Gallagher, Sean. *Hermeneutics and Education*. Albany: State University of New York Press, 1992.
Giesinger, Johannes. "Kant's Account of Moral Education." *Educational Philosophy and Theory*, 2011. https://doi.org/10.1111/j.1469-5812.2011.00754.x.
Gosetti-Ferencei, Jennifer Anna. *Heidegger, Hölderlin, and the Subject of Poetic Language: Toward a New Poetics of Dasein*. New York: Fordham University Press, 2004.
Grondin, Jean. "Gadamer's Experience and Theory of Education." In *Education, Dialogue and Hermeneutics*, edited by Paul Fairfield, 5–20. London: Continuum, 2012.
———. "Play, Festival, and Ritual." In *Language and Linguisticality in Gadamer's Hermeneutics*, edited by Lawrence Kennedy Schmidt, 51–57. Lanham, MD: Lexington, 2000.
Gundert, Hermann. "Zum Spiel bei Platon." In *Beispiele: Festschrift für Eugen Fink zum 60. Geburtstag*, edited by Ludwig Landgrebe, 188–21. Dordrecht: Springer Netherlands, 1965.
Habermas, Jürgen. "A Review of Gadamer's Truth and Method." In *The Hermeneutic Tradition: From Ast to Ricoeur*, edited by Gayle L. Ormiston, Alan D. Schrift, and Thomas McCarthy, translated by Fred Dallmayr, 213–44. Albany: State University of New York Press, 1990.
Hamburger, Käte. "Schiller und Sartre." In *Philosophie der Dichter: Novalis, Schiller, Rilke*, 129–77. Stuttgart: W. Kohlhammer, 1966.
Hegel, Georg Wilhelm Friedrich. *Lectures on the Philosophy of World History, Volume I: Manuscripts of the Introduction and the Lectures of 1822-1823*. Edited by Robert F. Brown and Peter C. Hodgson. New York: Oxford University Press, 2019.
Heidegger, Martin. *Anmerkungen I–V*. Edited by Peter Trawny. Frankfurt am Main: Verlag Vittorio Klostermann, 2015.
———. *Being and Time*. Translated by Joan Stambaugh. Albany: State University of New York Press, 1996.
———. *Elucidations of Hölderlin's Poetry*. Translated by Keith Hoeller. Amherst, MA: Humanity Books, 2000.
———. *Hölderlin's Hymns "Germania" and "The Rhine."* Translated by William McNeill and Julia Ireland. Bloomington: Indiana University Press, 2014.
———. *Poetry, Language, Thought*. Translated by Alfred Hofstadter. New York: Harper & Row, 1971.
———. *Ponderings VII–XI: Black Notebooks 1938–1939*. Translated by Richard Rojcewicz. Bloomington: Indiana University Press, 2017.
———. *Sein und Wahrheit*. Frankfurt am Main: Vittorio Klostermann, 2001.
———. *What Is Called Thinking?* Translated by J. Glenn Gray. New York; London: Harper Perennial, 1976.
Heidegger, Martin, and Eugen Fink. *Heraclitus Seminar, 1966/67*. Translated by Charles H. Seibert. Evanston, IL: Northwestern University Press, 1993.
Hilt, Annette. "Bilder des Nichts—Eugen Finks Frage nach dem Bild vom Menschen." In *Bildung im technischen Zeitalter: Sein, Mensch und Welt nach Eugen*

Fink, edited by Annette Hilt and Cathrin Nielsen, 290–314. Freiburg im Breisgau: Karl Alber, 2005.

Hölderlin, Friedrich. *Essays and Letters*. London: Penguin Books, Limited, 2009.

———. *Hymns and Fragments*. Translated by Richard Sieburth. Princeton, NJ: Princeton University Press, 2016.

———. *Hyperion*. Edited by Friedrich Beissner. 1st ed. Vol. 3. Sämtliche Werke. Stuttgart: Kohlhammer, 2010.

———. *Hyperion and Selected Poems*. Edited by Eric L. Santner. New York: The Continuum Publishing Company, 1990.

———. *Sämtliche Werke*. 5. Edited by Friedrich Beissner. Stuttgart: Kohlhammer, 1974.

Homan, Catherine. "The Play of Being and Nothing: World, Earth, and Cosmos in Eugen Fink." *Philosophy Today* 63, no. 1 (2019): 35–54. https://doi.org/10.5840/philtoday201967255.

hooks, bell. *Teaching to Transgress: Education as the Practice of Freedom*. New York: Routledge, 1994.

Horn, Dara. "Auschwitz Is Not a Metaphor." *The Atlantic*, June 6, 2019. https://www.theatlantic.com/ideas/archive/2019/06/auschwitz-not-long-ago-not-far-away/591082/.

Huizinga, Johan. *Homo Ludens*. Boston: Routledge & Kegan Paul Ltd., 1980.

Huseyinzadegan, Dilek. "For What Can the Kantian Feminist Hope? Constructive Complicity in Appropriations of the Canon." *Feminist Philosophy Quarterly* 4, no. 1 (March 24, 2018).

Janz, Marlies. "Hölderlins Flamme. Zur Bildwerdung der Frau im Hyperion." *Hölderlin Jahrbuch* 22 (1980): 122–42.

Jay, Martin. *Downcast Eyes: The Denigration of Vision in Twentieth-Century French Thought*. Berkeley: University of California Press, 1993.

Kant, Immanuel. "Anthropology from a Pragmatic Point of View." In *Anthropology, History, and Education*. Edited by Günter Zöller and Robert B. Louden, 227–429. New York: Cambridge University Press, 2007.

———. *Critique of Pure Reason*. Translated by Paul Guyer. Cambridge: Cambridge University Press, 1998.

———. *Critique of the Power of Judgment*. Translated by Paul Guyer. Cambridge: Cambridge University Press, 2000.

———. *Groundwork of the Metaphysics of Morals*. Translated by Mary Gregor. New York: Cambridge University Press, 1998.

———. "Lectures on Pedagogy." In *Anthropology, History, and Education*. Edited by Günter Zöller and Robert B. Louden. Translated by Robert B. Louden, 434–85. New York: Cambridge University Press, 2007.

———. "Lectures on Physical Geography." In *Natural Science*. Edited by Eric Watkins. Translated by Martin Schönfeld, Jeffrey B. Edwards, Olaf Reinhardt, and Lewis White Beck. Cambridge: Cambridge University Press, 2012, 434–679.

———. *The Metaphysics of Morals*. Translated by Mary Gregor. New York: Cambridge University Press, 1996.

Kidd, Stephen E. "Play in Aristotle." *Classical Philology* 111, no. 4 (October 1, 2016): 353–71.

Larmore, Charles. "Hölderlin and Novalis." In *The Cambridge Companion to German Idealism*, edited by Karl Ameriks, 141–60. Cambridge University Press, 2000.
Link, Jürgen. *Hölderlin-Rousseau: inventive Rückkehr*. Wiesbaden: Westdeutscher Verlag, 1999.
Luchte, James. *Mortal Thought: Hölderlin and Philosophy*. New York: Bloomsbury Publishing, 2016.
Lugones, María. *Pilgrimages/Peregrinajes: Theorizing Coalition Against Multiple Oppressions*. Lanham, MD: Rowman & Littlefield Publishers, 2003.
Makkreel, Rudolf A. *Imagination and Interpretation in Kant: The Hermeneutical Import of the Critique of Judgment*. Chicago: The University of Chicago Press, 1990.
Manger, Klaus. "Die Königszäsur · Zu Hölderlins Gegenwart in Celans Gedicht." *Hölderlin Jahrbuch* 23 (1982-1983): 156–65.
May, Markus, Peter Goßens, and Jürgen Lehmann, eds. *Celan-Handbuch: Leben – Werk – Wirkung*. 2nd ed. Stuttgart: J.B. Metzler, 2012.
Mensch, Jennifer. "Caught Between Character and Race: 'Temperament' in Kant's Lectures on Anthropology." *Australian Feminist Law Journal* 43, no. 1 (January 2, 2017): 125–44.
———. "Kant and the Skull Collectors: German Anthropology from Blumenbach to Kant." In *Kant and His German Contemporaries. Volume 1, Logic, Mind, Epistemology, Science and Ethics*, edited by Corey W. Dyck and Falk Wunderlich, 192–210, 2018.
Michelfelder, Diane P., and Richard E. Palmer, eds. *Dialogue and Deconstruction: The Gadamer-Derrida Encounter*. Albany: State University of New York Press, 1989.
Miller, Elaine P. *The Vegetative Soul: From Philosophy of Nature to Subjectivity in the Feminine*. Albany: State University of New York Press, 2002.
Mills, Charles. "Kant's *Untermenschen*." In *Race and Racism in Modern Philosophy*, edited by Andrew Valls, 169–93. Ithaca, NY: Cornell University Press, 2005.
Nagel, Mechthild. *Masking the Abject: A Genealogy of Play*. Lanham, MD: Lexington Books, 2002.
Nancy, Jean-Luc. *The Experience of Freedom*. Translated by Bridget McDonald. Stanford, CT: Stanford University Press, 1993.
Nielsen, Cynthia R. "On Poietic Remembering and Forgetting: Hermeneutic Recollection and Diotima's Historico-Hermeneutic Leanings." *Symposium* 22, no. 2 (2018): 107–34.
Nietzsche, Friedrich. *The Anti-Christ, Ecce Homo, Twilight of the Idols: And Other Writings*. Edited by Aaron Ridley and Judith Norman. Translated by Judith Norman. New York: Cambridge University Press, 2005.
———. *The Birth of Tragedy and Other Writings*. Edited by Raymond Geuss and Ronald Speirs. Translated by Ronald Speirs. New York: Cambridge University Press, 1999.
———. *The Gay Science*. Translated by Walter Kaufmann. New York: Vintage Books, 1974.
———. "Philosophy in the Tragic Age of the Greeks." In *The Nietzsche Reader*, edited by Keith Ansell Pearson and Duncan Large, 101–13. Malden, MA: Wiley-Blackwell, 2006.

———. *Thus Spoke Zarathustra*. Edited by Robert Pippin. Translated by Adrian Del Caro. New York: Cambridge University Press, 2006.

———. *The Will to Power*. Translated by Walter Kaufmann. New York: Vintage Books, 1968.

Nightingale, Andrea Wilson. "Liberal Education in Plato's Republic and Aristotle's Politics." *Education in Greek and Roman Antiquity*, January 1, 2001, 133–73.

Odenstedt, Anders. *Gadamer on Tradition—Historical Context and the Limits of Reflection*. Cham: Springer Verlag, 2017.

Ortega, Mariana. *In-Between: Latina Feminist Phenomenology, Multiplicity, and the Self*. Albany: State University of New York Press, 2016.

Palmer, Richard E., ed. *The Gadamer Reader: A Bouquet of the Later Writings*. Evanston, IL: Northwestern University Press, 2007.

Plato. *Complete Works*. Edited by John M. Cooper. Indianapolis: Hackett Publishing Company, Inc., 1997.

Pöggeler, Otto. "Ach, die Kunst!: die Frage nach dem Ort der Dichtung." In *Über Paul Celan*, edited by Dietlind Meinecke, 77–94. Frankfurt am Main: Suhrkamp, 1970.

———. *Der Stein hinterm Aug: Studien zu Celans Gedichten*. Munich: Fink, 2000.

———. *Spur des Worts*. Freiburg im Breisgau: Karl Alber, 1986.

Pugh, David. *Dialectic of Love: Platonism in Schiller's Aesthetics*. Montreal: McGill-Queen's Press, 1997.

Rancière, Jacques. "Schiller and the Aesthetic Promise." In *Aesthetic Reason and Imaginative Freedom: Friedrich Schiller and Philosophy*, edited by María del Rosario Acosta López and Jeffrey L. Powell, 123–36. Albany: State University of New York Press, 2018.

Richards, Robert J. "Kant and Blumenbach on the Bildungstrieb: A Historical Misunderstanding." *Studies in History and Philosophy of Biological and Biomedical Sciences* 31, no. 1 (2000): 11–32.

Risser, James. *Hermeneutics and the Voice of the Other: Re-Reading Gadamer's Philosophical Hermeneutics*. Albany: State University of New York Press, 1997.

Robinson, T. M., ed. *Heraclitus: Fragments*. University of Toronto Press, 1987.

Roochnik, David. "The 'Serious Play' of Book 7 of Plato's Laws." In *Plato's Laws: Force and Truth in Politics*, edited by Gregory Recco and Eric Sanday, 144–53. Bloomington: Indiana University Press, 2013.

Rousseau, Jean-Jacques. *Emile; or, Education*. Translated by Barbara Foxley. New York: J.M. Dent & Sons, Ltd.; E.P. Dutton & Co., 1911.

Schiller, Friedrich. "'Kallias, or Concerning Beauty: Letters to Gottfried Körner' (1793)." In *Classic and Romantic German Aesthetics*, edited by J.M. Bernstein, 145–83. New York: Cambridge University Press, 2003.

———. "On Naive and Sentimental Poetry." In *Essays*, edited by Walter Hinderer and Daniel O. Dahlstrom, translated by Daniel O. Dahlstrom, 179–260. New York: Continuum Publishing Group, 2005.

———. *On the Aesthetic Education of Man in a Series of Letters*. Translated by Elizabeth M. Wilkinson. New York: Oxford University Press, 1982.

Schmidt, Dennis. *Lyrical and Ethical Subjects: Essays on the Periphery of the Word, Freedom, and History*. Albany: State University of New York Press, 2005.

———. *On Germans and Other Greeks: Tragedy and Ethical Life*. Bloomington: Indiana University Press, 2001.

Schotten, C Heike. "Nietzsche, Anzaldúa, and Playful 'World'-Travel." *Human Architecture: Journal of the Sociology of Self-Knowledge* 4, no. 3 (2006): 18.

Schrift, Alan. *Nietzsche and the Question of Interpretation*. New York: Routledge, 1990.

Shaftesbury, Anthony Ashley Cooper Third Earl of. *Characteristics of Men, Manners, Opinions, Times*. Edited by Lawrence E. Klein. New York: Cambridge University Press, 1999.

Sophocles. *The Oedipus at Colonus of Sophocles*. Translated by Sir Richard Jebb. New York: Cambridge University Press, 1889.

Spariosu, Mihai. *Dionysus Reborn: Play and the Aesthetic Dimension in Modern Philosophical and Scientific Discourse*. Ithaca, NY: Cornell University Press, 1989.

———. *God of Many Names: Play, Poetry, and Power in Hellenic Thought from Homer to Aristotle*. Durham, NC: Duke University Press, 1991.

———. *Modernism and Exile: Liminality and the Utopian Imagination*. New York: Palgrave MacMillan, 2015.

———. *The Wreath of Wild Olive: Play, Liminality, and the Study of Literature*. Albany: State University of New York Press, 1997.

Sullivan, Shannon. "White World-Traveling." *The Journal of Speculative Philosophy* 18, no. 4 (2004): 300–304.

Sutton-Smith, Brian. *The Ambiguity of Play*. Cambridge: Harvard University Press, 1997.

Tobias, Rochelle. "The Ground Gives Way: Intimations of the Sacred in Celan's 'Gespräch im Gebirg.'" *MLN* 114, no. 3 (April 1, 1999): 567–89.

Trawny, Peter. "Heidegger and the Shoah." In *Reading Heidegger's Black Notebooks 1931-1941*, edited by Ingo Farin and Jeff Malpas, 169–79. Cambridge, MA: The MIT Press, 2016.

Turner, Victor. *Dramas, Fields, and Metaphors: Symbolic Action in Human Society*. Ithaca, NY: Cornell University Press, 1975.

———. *From Ritual to Theatre: The Human Seriousness of Play*. Performing Arts Journal Publications, 1982.

Vallega, Alejandro A. *Sense and Finitude: Encounters at the Limits of Language, Art, and the Political*. Albany: State University of New York Press, 2009.

Vilhauer, Monica. *Gadamer's Ethics of Play*. Lanham, MD: Lexington, 2010.

Waibel, Violetta L. "Hölderlin's Idea of 'Bildungstrieb': A Model from Yesteryear?" *Educational Philosophy and Theory* 50, no. 6–7 (May 12, 2018): 640–51. https://doi.org/10.1080/00131857.2017.1373346.

Warminski, Andrzej. *Readings in Interpretation: Hölderlin, Hegel, Heidegger*. Minneapolis: University of Minnesota Press, 1987.

Wiercinski, Andrzej. "Hermeneutic Education to Understanding: Self-Education and the Willingness to Risk Failure." In *Education, Dialogue and Hermeneutics*, edited by Paul Fairfield, Reprint edition., 107–24. London: Continuum, 2012.

Yancy, George. "Geneva Smitherman: The Social Ontology of African-American Language, the Power of Nommo, and the Dynamics of Resistance and Identity Through Language." *The Journal of Speculative Philosophy* 18, no. 4 (2004): 273–99.

Ziarek, Krysztof. "Semiosis of Listening: The Other in Heidegger's Writings on Hölderlin and Celan's 'The Meridian.'" *Research in Phenomenology* 24 (1994): 113–32.

Index

the Absolute, 34-36, 41-44, 55n39, 98, 103-104, 135-37
Acosta, María del Rosario, 127-28n60
Adorno, Theodor, 83
aesthetic education, 5-6, 11-12, 15, 21-22, 27, 29-31, 36, 38, 43
aesthetic experience, 1-2, 4, 16, 22-23, 27, 30-31, 35, 96, 118-19, 122, 146
African American Language, 171-73
Alcoff, Linda Martín, 173-74
alienation, 27, 45-46
annihilation, 13-14, 64-66, 68, 74, 80, 82-83, 88, 131, 143
"Anthropology from a Pragmatic Point of View" (Kant), 25
anti-Semitism, 13-14, 25, 72, 85, 170, 174-75
Antigone (Sophocles), 37-38
Anzaldúa, Gloria, 11, 15, 17, 166-68, 170; *Borderlands: La Frontera = The New Mestiza*, 166-67
"Are the Poets Falling Silent?" (Gadamer), 8, 60
Aristotle: *as if* in, 116; on education, 113; on imitation, 114-16; *Nicomachean Ethics*, 113, 115, 126n39; on play, 113-16; on play vs. leisure, 113; *Poetics*, 113-16; *Politics*, 113, 126n39; on recognition and transformation, 115-16; on tragedy, 114-16; on virtue, 115-16.
art: Gadamer on, 10-11, 78, 89, 93n36, 96-97, 110-11, 116, 118, 123, 141-51, 154, 162n42, 165-66, 174; Hölderlin on, 1, 3-4, 6, 23, 41-45, 49, 51, 55n42, 57n68; Kant on, 16, 21-22, 26, 54n25, 118; Nietzsche on, 130, 132-33, 159n7; Plato on, 106, 110-11; Schiller on, 16, 21-22, 28-31, 118-23; Shaftesbury on, 23, 32-33.
"Ashglory" (Celan), 76-77
Auschwitz, 12, 62, 74, 77, 83-85

Babich, Babette, 129
Bambach, Charles, 71, 92n27, 94n57, 159n2
bearing witness, 8, 12-17, 23, 95, 115, 149; poetry and, 6, 16, 61-63, 75-78, 86-89.
beauty: the Absolute and, 41, 44, 45, 137; attunement to, 21, 32, 38; beautiful games and, 107-8; freedom and, 27-30, 120-21; as harmonizing, 28, 32, 41, 120; Hölderlin on, 38, 41-44, 54n25; Kant on, 11, 22, 52n5, 119; life and, 23, 42, 43, 46; morality and, 11, 119-23; nature and, 29-34,

44-46, 57n68, 120-23; play and, 22, 28, 107-8, 120-21, 125n14; Schiller on, 2, 22, 27-32, 119-23; Shaftesbury on, 32-33; as symbol of morality, 29, 30, 119.
Beiser, Frederick, 55n41, 127n55
Bernasconi, Robert, 25, 52n10, 156
Bertolini, Simona, 161n21
Bildung, 3-4, 16, 18n4, 21, 24, 27, 32, 38, 43, 61, 129, 139, 141-44, 149-55, 161nn22-23, 165-66
Bildungsroman, 36, 38-39
Bildungstrieb, 3, 6, 23, 39-40, 42-44, 51, 52n5, 52-53n10, 54n25, 128n62
Birth of Tragedy (Nietzsche), 57n54, 131-32
Black Notebooks (Heidegger), 13-14, 16, 84
Blumenbach, Johann Friedrich, 52n5, 52-53n10
Böhlendorff, Casimir Ulrich, 4, 13
borderlands, 166-68
Borderlands: La Frontera = The New Mestiza (Anzaldúa), 166-67
Böschenstein, Bernhard, 74
Bruns, Gerald, 8, 175

Caputo, John, 155-56, 165
Carson, Anne, 68, 71
Celan, Paul, 14, 16-17, 92n34, 93n43, 94n57, 95-96, 103, 129-30, 149, 175, 179n36; 20th of January and, 64-65, 69, 71-72; ashes of burned out meaning and, 64, 70, 83; "Ashglory", 76-77; on babbling, 71, 74; on breath, 7, 12, 76-86, 91; on conversation and dialogue, 60, 70, 72-73, 78, 85-89; "Conversation in the Mountains", 72-74; "Edgar Jené and the Dream about the Dream", 63-64, 67; on encounter with the other, 60-61, 63-65, 67-68, 70, 72-74, 77-79, 81-91; exile and, 80, 83, 85; and the German language, 60, 62, 71, 74, 79; on hope, 60, 65, 81-90; I and You, 60, 65-67, 70, 73, 76-79, 85-88, 95-96; "I drink wine", 83-84; "In the rivers north of the future", 85-88, 89, 129; Judaism and, 60, 72-73, 82, 84-85; on keeping Yes and No together, 60, 66, 68, 74, 77, 84, 86, 88, 95, 129; on listening and hearing, 12, 63, 73-74, 77-78, 81, 86; "The Meridian", 7, 60, 62-67, 70, 76-78, 82, 86, 88; as mindful of dates, 63-65, 69, 71-72, 76, 79, 82, 87; as never fully at home, 62-63, 65, 79-80, 82-83, 85; on the poem's relation to time, 60-61, 63, 68, 76, 80, 86-88, 90; on poems as *unterwegs*, 60, 62, 64-65, 76, 78, 80, 82, 88; poetic use of eyes and blindness by, 69-73, 77, 79-82, 92n27; on poetry and bearing witness, 61-63, 75-78, 86-89; on poetry and memory, 60-62, 64, 68, 71, 73-74, 78-82, 87; on poetry as address, 7-8, 61, 63, 69-70, 74, 76-78, 90-91; relation to Heidegger, 79-85; relation to Hölderlin, 70, 72, 74-75, 81, 83; on silence and speaking, 60, 63-64, 69-73, 75, 77, 83, 85; "Speech on the Occasion of Receiving the Literature Prize of the Free Hanseatic City of Bremen", 7, 12, 60, 79, 83, 86; "Sprachgitter", 69-70, 86, 170; "Sprich Auch Du", 66-69, 87, 95; on the still here, 7, 12, 60, 74, 76, 78, 82-83, 87; on the strange, 60, 62, 64-65, 67-68, 70, 79, 86; "Todtnauberg", 81-84; topological research and, 7, 60, 76, 80-81, 87-88, 91n5; "Tübingen, January", 70-74, 87; on utopia, 63-64, 87-89, 91n5; "Weggebeizt", 75-77.
Characteristicks of Men, Manners, Opinions, Times (Shaftesbury), 21, 32
Cocalis, Susan, 38
community, 3, 5, 22-23, 26-27, 31, 33, 51, 60, 90, 96, 101-2, 120, 123, 150, 161n21

comportment, 14, 16, 89, 91, 103, 120, 130-31, 145, 158, 176
conversation, 4, 17, 38, 51, 129-30, 132, 158-59, 173, 175-77; Celan on, 60, 70, 72-73, 78, 87; education and, 11-12, 130; Fink on, 140-43, 158-59; Gadamer on, 10-11, 14, 90, 99, 144-50, 152-53, 155-56, 158-59, 176; Heidegger on, 6, 11, 81-84; Hölderlin on, 81, 83;
play and, 17, 100-101; poetry and, 6, 8, 38, 60, 70, 78, 90.
"Conversation in the Mountains" (Celan), 72-74
cosmos, 12, 102-3, 135-38, 142, 160n12
Critique of Judgment (Kant), 2, 26, 29, 36, 52n5, 52n10, 118

Davey, Nicholas, 150, 152, 158, 175
death, 22-23, 47-51, 63, 66, 68, 77, 86-87, 100, 115, 140, 161n25, 173
Demnig, Gunter, 174
Derrida, Jacques, 65, 76-77, 156, 157
di Cesare, Donatella, 14, 25
dialogue, 36, 46, 51, 61, 84, 123, 129-31, 173-76; Celan on, 60, 85-86, 88-89; Gadamer on, 11, 14, 98-99, 109-112, 126n30, 143-44, 149, 151, 157, 176; Platonic, 52n9, 109-112, 126n30.
Dilthey, Wilhelm, 38-39, 146, 151, 162n37
Diotima, 16, 24, 37, 40-42, 46-51, 57n64, 57n67. *See also Hyperion* (Hölderlin)
divine, 36, 39, 41-43, 46, 49-50, 54n25, 55n42, 57n44, 67, 84, 87, 91-92n15, 92n34, 93n44, 107-8, 113, 125nn13-15, 133, 139, 142
dwelling, 62-63, 89, 131, 142, 152, 172; as poetic, 3-4, 6-8, 18n5, 80, 83, 91-92n15.

Ebel, Johann Gottfried, 37
"Edgar Jené and the Dream about the Dream" (Celan), 63-64, 67

education: as becoming who we are, 28-29, 37, 129-31, 142-45, 155, 159; as *Bildung*, 3, 16, 61, 129, 139, 142, 149-55; as cultivation, 5, 11, 22, 31, 37, 38; Fink on, 11, 17, 130, 138-43, 158, 161n22; Gadamer on, 11, 17. 130, 144, 149-52, 155, 158, 161n2; Hölderlin on, 1, 35-39; Kant on, 21, 24-26; listening and, 11-12, 130, 142, 149, 155, 165, 176; Plato on, 97, 104-12; play and, 5, 11, 17, 30-31, 97-98, 104-12, 124, 130-31, 138, 142-43, 150-51, 155, 176; Schiller on, 27-31, 120, 122. *See also* aesthetic education; *Bildung*; poetic education.
Elucidations on Hölderlin's Poetry (Heidegger), 6, 11, 80-83, 87
ens cosmologicum, 12, 102-103, 124n7, 130, 135, 138, 158
Erziehung, 18n4, 27, 141, 152, 161n22
exile, 80, 83, 85, 168, 172
Existenz und Coexistenz (Fink), 140-41, 161n24
Eze, Emmanuel, 25

Fagen, Robert, 99-100
familiar and foreign, 3-4, 16-17, 23, 35-36, 40, 42, 61-62, 78, 130-132, 137, 140, 144, 146, 151, 166-67, 176
feeling, 2, 4, 11, 26-27, 30-32, 33-34, 45, 78, 115, 175-76
Fichte, Johann Gottlieb, 35, 55n39, 55n41
finitude, 6, 13, 16, 22, 27, 47, 96, 134-35; attunement to infinite and, 3-6, 12, 16, 36-37, 44-45, 61-63, 86, 91-92n15, 103-4, 111, 131, 135-38, 140-43, 149, 158, 159n2; Fink on, 12, 98, 103-4, 135-38, 140-42, 158, 161n25; Gadamer on, 59, 61, 90, 115, 143, 158; Hölderlin on, 3-6, 23, 36-37, 44-45, 47, 49-51, 91-92n15; poetry and, 44-45, 61-63, 67, 86, 90-9.
Fink, Eugen, 5, 9, 14, 17, 32; on contemporary pedagogy as nihilistic,

11, 138-39; on conversation, 140-43, 158-59; on the cosmological difference, 136-37; criticisms of Plato by, 108-9, 159n6; on earth as concealing, 102, 137-38, 140, 142-43, 157-58; on earth as site of alterity, 137-38; on education, 11, 17, 130, 138-43, 158, 161n22; on existence as coexistence, 141-42; *Existenz und Coexistenz*, 140-41, 161n24; on finitude, 12, 98, 103-4, 135-38, 140-42, 158, 161n25; on freedom, 101-2, 125n13, 138-43; on human as *Weltwesen* and *ens cosmologicum*, 12, 102, 103, 124n7, 130, 135-39, 141, 158; on imitation and mirroring, 98, 100, 108-10, 135-34, 142; on Kant, 136; *Natur, Freiheit, Welt*, 138-43; on nature as *physis*, 137, 140, 150, 161n22; on Nietzsche, 135, 137, 141-42, 159n7, 160n12; "Nietzsche's Metaphysics of Play (1946)", 131, 137, 159n6; *Nietzsche's Philosophy*, 160n12; on non-metaphysical thinking, 98, 135; on Plato, 108-109; on play as basic human phenomenon, 98, 100; on play of being and nothing, 103, 135, 137-38; on play as non-actual, 100-103, 108-9, 123; on play as symbol of the world, 102-3, 124n7, 135-36, 138; *Play as Symbol of the World*, 100-103, 108-9, 125n13, 135-36; on recognition, 108, 110, 137, 140-41, 158; rejection of rational animal, 102, 135, 137, 139, 161n23; on the relationship between education and nature, 138-41; *Sein und Mensch*, 137; *Welt und Endlichkeit*, 98, 102, 135-38; on understanding, 102-3, 136-37, 139; on world as granting appearance, 5, 100, 102-3, 131, 135-38, 140-43, 156-58, 160n20; on world as groundless, 102-3, 123, 137-39, 141; on world as totality or Absolute, 12, 102-4, 123, 131, 135-42, 160n2, 162n34; "Zur Bildungstheorie der technischen Bildung", 141.

Fleming, Marie, 156

forgetting, 2, 42, 62, 98, 100, 110, 131, 134, 147-48, 163n41, 170

form drive, 27, 29, 35, 119, 121-22

free play, 2, 4, 26, 29, 118, 119, 122, 168

freedom, 17, 22, 101-4, 176; Fink on, 101-2, 125n13, 138-43; Gadamer on, 87-90, 143, 148, 150, 152-53, 155; Hölderlin on, 1-5, 23, 43; Kant on, 24, 26-27, 52n9, 54n25, 117-18; play and, 2, 4-5, 9-11,17, 26-31, 54n30, 101-4, 108, 112, 115, 117-24, 125n13, 133, 142-43, 148, 155, 168; poetry and, 7-8, 64, 78, 82, 87-90, 175; Schiller on, 24, 27-32, 54n30, 118-23, 127n56.

friendship, 6, 8, 46, 86, 89, 176-77

Gadamer, Hans-Georg, 5, 21, 32, 33; on aesthetic consciousness, 96-97, 110-11, 114, 146, 148-49; "Are the Poets Falling Silent?", 8, 60, 90; on Aristotle, 114-16; on art, 10-11, 78, 89, 93n36, 96-97, 110-11, 116, 118, 123, 141-51, 154, 162n42, 165-66, 174; on being and language, 10, 12, 89-90, 112, 143-44, 153-55, 166; on *Bildung* and cultivation, 132, 144, 149-55; on *Bildung* and language, 152-55; on *Bildung* and openness to the other, 144, 150-55, 166; on Celan, 75-76, 85-90; criticisms of, 15, 155-56, 165, 173-74, 178n18; on dialogue and conversation, 10-11, 14, 90, 98-99, 109-112, 126n30, 143-59, 176; on *Erlebnis* and *Erfahrung*, 146, 162n37; on finitude, 59, 61, 90, 115, 143, 158; on the fusion of horizons, 15, 154-56, 170, 173; on hermeneutics, 9, 15, 93n43, 98-

99, 116, 143, 146-47, 149, 151, 155, 166, 179n38; on historically effected consciousness, 14, 153-54; on Hölderlin, 59-60, 72; *The Idea of the Good in Platonic-Aristotelian Philosophy*, 98, 111, 126n30; on interpretation, 10, 14-15, 89, 112, 116, 146-47, 153-55, 175n18; on Kant, 96, 118, 148; on language and memory, 16, 61, 90, 110, 112; on the limits of language, 59-60, 72, 75, 89, 143; on mimesis and imitation, 100, 110-11, 113-16, 126n30, 147, 163n42; philosophy as conversation, 14-15, 98-99, 110-12; on Plato, 109-112, 126n30; *Plato's Dialectical Ethics*, 110; on play, 9-11, 17, 96-97, 100-102, 111-12, 144-49, 155, 157, 166, 176, 178n18; on the play of art, 10-11, 144-49; on poetry, 8, 10, 16-17, 59-61, 72, 75-76, 78, 85-90, 93n43, 112; on prejudices, 14-15, 151, 153, 157; on question and answer, 43, 101, 109-12, 131, 149, 151, 155-58, 176; on recognition, 89-90, 99, 111-12, 114-16, 145-52, 154, 157-58, 174, 175; on the relation to the world, 143-49, 152-56, 162n32, 162n34, 170; *The Relevance of the Beautiful*, 10, 78, 89, 93n36, 96, 115, 118, 144-45, 148, 163n42; on the role of the spectator, 9-10, 96-97, 114, 145, 147-48, 162n40, 163n42; on scientific approach to education and nihilism, 149-50; on symbols, 78, 86; on tact, 175-76; on tradition, 98-99, 115, 125n23, 150-57, 166; on transformation, 9-10, 97, 100, 111, 116, 144-55; on transformation into structure and art, 145-47, 154; on *Truth and Method*, 9, 11, 59, 96-97, 114-16, 129, 143, 145-54, 165-66, 175; on understanding, 14-15, 89-90, 110-11, 116-18, 144, 146-47, 149-59, 162n40, 173, 175-76; "Die Vielfalt der Sprachen und das Verstehen der Welt", 143.
Gallagher, Sean, 155
The Gay Science (Nietzsche), 129, 133, 160n13
Gods. *See* Divine
Gontard, Susette, 47
Grondin, Jean, 12, 163n47
"The Ground for the *Empedocles*" (Hölderlin), 44, 50, 55n42, 57n70
groundlessness, 3, 9-11, 17, 23, 43, 60-61, 72-73, 88, 100, 102-3, 112, 117, 123-24, 137-39, 141

Habermas, Jürgen, 155
harmony, 6, 46, 62, 68, 109, 112; Hölderlin on, 2-3, 23, 36-37, 40-46, 48-51, 68; Schiller on, 4, 27-31, 54n25, 119-23; Shaftesbury on, 21, 32-34.
heart, 21, 31, 40, 42, 48, 69-70, 80-85, 88, 91n15, 177
Hegel, Georg Wilhelm Friedrich, 18n2, 144, 151-52, 160n12, 161n23, 163n46, 165
Heidegger, Martin, 6-7, 19n18, 72, 93n45, 94n57, 99, 131, 136, 140, 159n6; anti-Semitism and, 13-14, 19n14; *Being and Time*, 69, 72, 161n20, 161n25; *Black Notebooks*, 13-14, 16, 84; on conversation, 6, 11, 81-82; *Elucidations on Hölderlin's Philosophy*, 6, 11, 80-83, 87; on Hölderlin, 6-7, 13, 79-81, 83, 87; on idle talk, 72; on the ontological difference, 136; on poetic dwelling, 6-8, 18n5, 80, 83; "...Poetically Man Dwells...", 6, 18n5; relation to Celan, 79-85.
hen kai pan, 35-36, 41, 49
Heraclitus, 13, 35-36, 44, 74
Herder, Johann Gottfried, 38, 150
hermeneutics, 11, 13-15, 97-98, 155-59, 165-66, 173-74, 178n18; Gadamer on, 9, 15, 93n43, 98-99, 116, 143, 146-47, 149, 151, 155, 166, 179n38.

Hilt, Annette, 141
Hölderlin, Friedrich, 9, 18n4, 59-62, 66-68, 70-72, 74-75, 79-81, 83-84, 87, 92n27, 93n44, 98, 101-2, 122, 129, 137, 141, 155, 158, 159n2, 176; on the Absolute, 34-36, 41-44, 55n39, 62; the Absolute, intellectual intuition of 3, 24-36, 41, 44-45; the Absolute, language and, 45, 50; on the ancients, 35, 43-44, 56n52; on *Bildungstrieb*, 3, 6, 23, 39, 40, 42-44, 51, 53n10; criticism of play by, 2, 5, 16; on the eccentric path of existence, 39-40, 42-43, 61, 79; on education, 1-2, 34-38; on finitude, 6, 23, 36, 47, 48-51; on giving form to what is formless, 1, 3, 23, 39, 43-44, 47, 49-51; *Hyperion*, 16, 23-24, 37, 38-51, 56n52, 57n59, 57n64, 57n67; "In Lovely Blueness", 3, 68, 91n15; on poetry, 1, 5, 18n2, 23, 36-37, 43-46, 48, 50-51; on preserving tensions, 23, 36, 39, 41, 44-45, 55n42, 62, 68; "The Oldest System of German Idealism", 18n3; "On the Procedure of the Poetic Spirit", 45; on the relation between humans and nature, 3, 6, 16, 23, 38-51, 57n68; on the relationship between poetry and philosophy, 18n2, 35, 44; on the use of the aorgic and organic, 44, 50-51, 55n42; tragedy and, 23, 36, 38, 42, 50-51; on what is our ownmost, 4, 13, 35, 67.
Hölderlin's Hymns "Germania" and "The Rhine" (Heidegger), 13
Holocaust. See Shoah
home: being at home, 8, 42, 44-45, 60, 62-63, 65, 80, 82, 88-90, 112, 144, 151-52, 167-68, 172; homecoming and, 8, 36, 62, 78-79; homeland and, 40, 59; homelessness and, 80, 83, 88.
hooks, bell, 11, 15, 17, 172; *Teaching to Transgress*, 172.
hospitality, 75, 78-79, 85, 94n57, 173

Huizinga, Johan, 125n14, 178n18
Humboldt, Wilhelm von, 38
Huseyinzadegan, Dilek, 25
Hyperion (Hölderlin), 16, 23-24, 37-40, 56n52, 57n59, 57n64, 57n67; art as rejuvenation in, 42, 46; attunement to time in, 47-51; childhood and, 42-43; death and, 40, 42, 48-51; Diotima as poet in, 48-51; eternal rhythm, 41, 49-50 feminist model of subjectivity in, 48-51; fermentation in, 42, 48; harmony in, 41-43; love in, 42-43, 46, 49; orientation to nature in, 42-44, 46, 48; poetry as prior to philosophy in, 43-44; role of silence in, 49-50; tragedy and, 42, 50-51, 57n64, 57n67; vegetative metaphors in, 41-42, 46, 48, 50-51.

I and You, 7, 17, 66-68, 73, 76-79, 86-90, 95-96, 129-30, 143, 159
The Idea of the Good in Platonic-Aristotelian Philosophy (Gadamer), 98, 111, 126n30
"I drink wine" (Celan), 83-84
imagination, 26, 31, 118, 137
in-between, the, 7, 11, 15, 17, 104, 112, 130, 139, 142-143, 148, 165-70, 176, 177n8, 177n12
individuation, 39, 51, 65, 87, 131, 142
"In Lovely Blueness" (Hölderlin), 3, 68, 91
"In the rivers north of the future" (Celan), 85-88, 89, 129
intuition, 3, 34-36, 41, 44-45, 88, 119, 131, 136

Jacobi, Friedrich Heinrich, 35
Janz, Marlies, 47-48, 50
Judaism, 13-14, 25, 72-73, 82, 84-85
judgment, 2, 6, 16, 21, 33, 54n30, 61, 114, 118, 148, 167

Kalb, Fritz von, 37, 55n44

Index   197

"'Kallias, or Concerning Beauty: Letters to Gottfried Körner' (1793)" (Schiller), 29, 119, 56n45, 122-23, 128n62, 56n45, 122

Kant, Immanuel, 1-5, 12, 30-31, 38, 44, 53n21, 56n52, 96-97, 122-23, 136, 145, 148-49, 174; aesthetic judgments, 26, 54n30, 118, 148; "Anthropology from a Pragmatic Point of View", 25; on art, 16, 21-22, 26, 54n25, 118; *as if* and, 117, 127n42; on beauty, 11, 22, 52n5, 119; on *Bildungstrieb*, 52n5, 52n10, 54n25; categorical imperative, 52n9, 117; *Critique of Judgment*, 2, 26, 29, 36, 52n5, 52n10, 118; on education, 21, 24-26; on freedom, 24, 26-27, 52n9, 54n25, 117-18; "Lectures on Physical Geography", 25; morality, 1, 24-26, 117-18; "Of the Different Races of Human Beings", 25; on play, 4, 22, 26-27, 117-19; on race, 25-26, 53n10; on taste, 26, 118.

Körner, Christian Gottfried, 29, 120

language: as continuing to speak, 12, 17, 59-67, 75-80, 83, 85, 87, 89-90, 112, 154, 158, 160n14, 172; as conversation, 8, 11, 38, 85, 110, 134, 140-43, 153, 155, 158, 175; as corporeal, 8, 61, 78, 83-84, 176; existence and, 10, 15-17, 45, 48, 50, 74, 79, 112, 131, 134, 140-43, 151, 153, 162n34, 166, 172, 175; limits of, 7, 22-23, 37, 39, 59-67, 75-80, 83, 87, 89-90, 171; mother tongue and language of nurture in, 85, 171; oppression and, 12, 17, 60, 62, 64, 79, 82, 171; as resistance, 8, 172-73; tradition and, 16-17, 166.

"Lectures on Physical Geography" (Kant), 25

Levi, Primo, 74, 90

limen, 95, 122, 168

liminality, 7, 15, 17, 95, 97, 99, 103-4, 112, 115-16, 124, 129-31, 140, 142, 166-70, 172, 174, 177n8, 177n12

limits, 5-7, 9, 22-23, 27, 36, 39, 45, 59-60, 62, 68, 75, 77-78, 86-88, 95-96, 125n23, 130, 143-44, 149, 159n2, 172, 175-76

linguisticality, 7, 12, 78

listening, 4-5, 8, 11-12, 14-17, 24, 51, 63, 70, 78, 90, 112, 130, 142, 145, 149, 155, 157, 165, 167, 172-76

love, 33, 40, 42-43, 46, 49-50, 79, 90, 100, 168-69, 176-77

Loyola, Ignatius of, 39

Luchte, James, 57n64

Lugones, María, 15, 17, 168-71, 176, 178n18

Luxemburg, Rosa, 71

Makkreel, Rudolf, 26

mastery, 5, 8, 11, 22-23, 30-31, 43, 61, 79, 97-99, 112, 114-115, 126n30, 130, 150

measure, 6-7, 13, 18n5, 32, 66-68, 80, 86, 88-91, 91n15, 92n27, 130, 140-42, 145, 159n2

Mensch, Jennifer, 25

meridian, 7-8, 65, 67, 86, 88, 96, 129, 176

"The Meridian" (Celan), 7, 60, 62-67, 70, 76-78, 82, 86, 88

mestiza, 166-67

metaphysics, 5, 13, 15, 17, 34, 69, 79, 98-99, 102, 104, 108, 130-32, 135, 137, 139, 158, 159n6

Miller, Elaine, 49-50

Mills, Charles, 25

mirroring, 10, 42, 48, 89-90, 98, 100, 108-10, 132, 134-36, 147-48

moral development, 11, 21-22, 24 32, 37, 43, 104-21

morality, 1-2, 11, 21-22, 24-32, 37-38, 43, 52n9, 56n45, 108-10, 117-23, 133, 143

mortals, 39, 68, 79-80, 93n45

mortality, 42, 62, 65, 68, 80
Moses, 1, 92n34
music, 32-33, 41-42, 56n50, 62, 104-5, 109, 113, 131, 146, 163n41, 171, 176

Nagel, Mechthild, 126n39
names and naming, 41-42, 51, 72-74, 78-82, 93n4, 166-67, 174
National Socialism, 14, 59-60, 62, 64, 71, 74, 84-85, 88
Natur, Freiheit, Welt (Fink), 138-43
nature, 26, 52n5, 53n10, 54n25, 72-73, 159n7, 161n23; beauty, art, and, 29-34, 44-46, 57n68, 120-23; human relation to, 3, 6, 16, 21-24, 29-34, 38-47, 49-51, 55-56n46, 90, 98, 102, 120-23, 128n62, 131-32, 136, 158; as *physis*, 137, 140, 150; state of nature, 34, 55n45.
nepantla, 15, 67
Nicomachean Ethics (Aristotle), 113, 115, 126n39
Nielsen, Cynthia, 163n41
Niethammer, Immanuel, 1, 34
Nietzsche, Friedrich, 11, 17, 99, 104, 137, 141-42, 160n14; on the Apollonian and Dionysian, 131-33, 142, 159n7; on art, 130, 132-33, 159n7; *The Birth of Tragedy*, 57n54, 131-32; *The Gay Science*, 129, 133, 160n13; on Heraclitus, 132-33; *Philosophy in the Tragic Age of the Greeks*, 132; on play, 17, 130-35, 142, 148, 157-58, 159n7, 170; on recognition, 132-34; on self-styling, 133-34, 170; *Thus Spoke Zarathustra*, 134, 170; *The Will to Power*, 133-35, 142, 160n12.
Nietzsche's Philosophy (Fink), 131, 137
"Nietzsche's Metaphysics of Play (1946)" (Fink), 131, 137, 159n6
"Notes on Antigone" (Hölderlin), 18n2, 35

"Observations on the Feeling of the Beautiful and the Sublime" (Kant), 25

Oedipus, 37, 47, 57n54, 92n27
"Of the Different Races of Human Beings" (Kant), 25
"The Oldest System of German Idealism" (Hölderlin), 18n3
On the Aesthetic Education of Man in a Series of Letters (Schiller), 2, 27-31, 54n25, 120-23, 127n56
"On the Procedure of the Poetic Spirit" (Hölderlin), 45
openness to the other, 5-8, 10, 12, 15-17, 23, 30, 41-42, 50, 60-68, 73-91, 94n57, 95-97, 101-4, 110-11, 114-15, 131-33, 136-44, 147-58, 165-177, 177-78n13

Philosophy in the Tragic Age of the Greeks (Nietzsche), 132
Plato, 13, 17, 37, 52n9, 69, 118, 120-21, 124n11, 125n14, 125n21, 125n23, 126n30, 127n42, 131, 139, 159n6; on the dangers of art and poetry, 105-7, 109-12; dialogues as self-aware in, 109-12; on education and *paideia*, 97, 104-12; on imitation, 105-11; *Laws*, 97, 104-5, 107, 109, 121; on play and *paidia*, 17, 97, 104-112; as poet, 111-12; *Republic*, 97, 105-7, 109-11, 121; *Symposium*, 37.
Plato's Dialectical Ethics, Gadamer, 2
play, 2, 35-36, 49-51, 54n25, 54n30, 59, 61-62, 73-74, 159n6-7, 163n42, 166, 168-70, 173-74, 176-77, 177n12-13; as ambiguous, 9-10, 17, 96-97, 99-100, 103-4, 125n13, 168-69; *as if* and, 9, 26, 99-102, 116-18, 127n42; Aristotle on, 17, 113-14; art and, 118-23, 130-33, 144-49; as autotelic, 9, 96, 98, 100-101, 112, 124n3, 126n39, 134, 150; between being and nothing in, 35, 102-3, 131, 135-37; childhood and, 9, 17, 96-97, 104-6, 110, 113, 125n14, 132-34, 142, 147; cognitive element of, 27, 31, 54n30, 106, 118, 148; conversation and, 17, 100-101; definition of, 9, 99-104;

education and, 5, 11, 17, 30-31, 97-98, 104-12, 124, 130-31, 138, 142-43, 150-51, 155, 176; Fink on, 9, 12, 17, 97-98, 100-104, 108-9, 123, 124n7, 125n13, 125n15, 130-31, 135-38, 141-43, 157-58, 159nn6-7, 160n12; freedom and, 2, 4-5, 9-11, 17, 26-31, 54n30, 101-4, 108, 112, 115, 117-24, 125n13, 133, 142-43, 148, 155, 168; Gadamer on, 9-11, 17, 96-97, 100-102, 111-12, 144-49, 155, 157, 166, 176, 178n18 as groundless, 9, 17, 100-103; imitation and mimesis, 100, 105-8, 110-11, 113-14, 124-25n11, 126n39, 147, 163n42 Kant on, 4, 22, 26-27, 117-19; Nietzsche on, 17, 130-35, 142, 148, 157-58, 159n7, 170; as non-actual, 100-103, 108-9, 123; Plato on, 17, 97, 104-112; playfulness and world-traveling, 168-70, 178n18; playspace of, 9, 10, 17, 100, 103, 118, 124, 132, 138, 142-43, 147, 153; relation to everyday in, 2, 4-5, 10, 100, 104, 112, 118, 131, 176; as resistance, 10, 17, 97, 99, 103-4, 115, 122, 130-31, 138, 159n6, 166, 168, 170; Schiller on, 4, 22, 27-32, 117, 119-23; as serious, 2, 4-5, 9-10, 16-17, 30, 97, 99-100, 105-12, 117, 122, 125n14, 133, 145, 176; as to-and-fro movement, 9, 17, 96; tragedy and, 98, 114-15, 126n39, 131-32, 142; as transformative, 9, 17, 97, 100-101, 112-13, 116, 131, 145, 147-48, 155, 170, 176; world and, 102-3, 131-32, 134-38, 141-49, 155, 157-59, 169-70.
play drive, 27, 28, 54n25, 54n30, 119
Play as Symbol of the World (Fink), 100-103, 108-9, 125n13, 135-36
poet, 3, 6-8, 23, 32-33, 37, 39, 45-48, 50-51, 59, 61-62, 67-68, 75, 78-90, 106, 110-12, 114-15, 123, 166, 176, 179n6
"...Poetically Man Dwells..." (Heidegger), 6, 18n5

poetic conversation, 6, 90, 176
poetic education: as attunement, cultivation, or formation, 6, 8, 23, 38, 51, 61, 97-98, 124, 129-30, 148-49, 174-76; groundlessness and, 3, 61, 175; listening and, 12, 17, 23-24, 51, 130, 144, 151-52, 159, 176; nature and, 6, 23, 158; play and, 5, 9, 17, 112, 124, 130, 143-44, 175-76; tradition and, 5, 165, 176; tragedy and, 36, 47, 51.
poetic speaking, 7-8, 16-17, 35, 44-46, 50-51, 59-61, 63-85, 87, 90-91, 111-12
poetic versus unpoetic, 6, 18n5
Poetics (Aristotle), 113-16
poetry: as act of remembrance, 6, 12, 16, 61, 64, 78-81, 89; as bearing witness, 6, 8, 16, 61-63, 75-78, 86-89; as corporeal, 8, 61, 78, 83-84; as encounter, 8, 60-61, 63-65, 67-68, 70, 72-74, 77-79, 81-91; freedom and, 7-8, 64, 78, 82, 87-90, 175; Gadamer on, 8, 10, 16-17, 59-61, 72, 75-76, 78, 85-90, 93n43, 112; Hölderlin on, 37, 43-46, 50, 62, 74-75; as liminal, 7, 95-97; limits of what can be said and, 6, 23, 46, 51, 59-67, 75-80, 83, 87, 89-90; listening and, 12, 63, 73-74, 77-78, 81, 86; as measure, 7, 13, 18n4; philosophy and, 1, 3, 5, 16, 18n2, 36, 43-44, 50-51, 61, 63, 111-12; relation to finite and infinite in, 16, 23, 45, 61; relation to limits and, 45, 61; as resisting totalization, 8, 16, 61, 67, 71-72, 75, 96, 130; responsibility and, 8, 69, 76-77; as teacher of humanity, 3, 5, 16, 61, 90-91; tragedy and, 23, 36, 50-51, 114-15; uncanny and, 8, 64-65, 83, 89; utopia and, 2, 16, 63-64, 87-89, 91n5.
Pöggeler, Otto, 85-86, 88, 91n5
Politics (Aristotle), 113, 126n39

recognition, 6, 23, 27-28, 33, 41-42, 45-47, 52n9, 62-68, 73, 78-79, 85, 104,

113-14, 118, 123, 168, 171-72; Fink on, 137, 10-41; Gadamer on, 111-12, 114-16, 145-48, 151-54, 157-58, 175; Nietzsche on, 132-34.
regulative idea, 22, 31, 35, 52
The Relevance of the Beautiful (Gadamer), 10, 78, 89, 93n36, 96, 115, 118, 144-45, 148, 163n42
responsibility, 8, 9-12, 14, 31, 37, 130, 159, 174-76; as playful, 12, 101-2; poetry and, 8, 69, 76-77.
rhythm, 18n2, 41, 49-50, 78, 90, 105, 113
Risser, James, 156-57, 162n38, 175
rivers, 42, 71-72, 74, 76, 85-88, 94n63, 96, 129, 133, 167
Rousseau, Jean-Jacques, 38, 43, 55-56n45, 56n51, 121

Schelling, Friedrich Wilhelm Joseph von, 18n2
Schiller, Friedrich, 1-2, 34-39, 44, 53n10, 97, 127-28n60, 148, 151, 159n7, 174; on the aesthetic and the political, 27, 29-30, 119-23; on the aesthetic state, 11, 22, 31, 54n25, 120-21; on art, 16, 21-22, 28-31, 118-23; on beauty and nature, 29-30, 119-24; on drives, 3, 27-29, 31, 119, 121-22, 127n55; on education, 27-31, 120, 122; on freedom, 24, 27-32, 54n30, 118-23, 127n56; on harmony, 4, 27-31, 54n25, 119-23; "'Kallias, or Concerning Beauty: Letters to Gottfried Körner' (1793)", 29, 119; *On the Aesthetic Education of Man in a Series of Letters*, 2, 27-31, 54n25, 120-23, 127n56; "On Naive and Sentimental Poetry", 56n45, 122-23, 128n62; on Plato, 120-21; on play, 4, 22, 27-32, 54n25, 119; relation to Kant, 27, 118-24; on taste, 29, 31, 119-20; on tradition, 122-23.
Schmidt, Dennis, 27, 57n67, 112, 132
Schotten, C. Heike, 170
Sein und Mensch (Fink), 137

self-consciousness, 9, 54n39, 55n41, 96, 98, 140, 161n24
sense drive, 27, 29
sensus communis, 21-22, 26, 32-33, 52n9, 96, 118, 144
Shaftesbury, Third Earl of, 16, 21-23, 32-35, 38, 51, 96
Shoah, the, 12, 14, 16, 72, 82, 84, 174
silence, 12, 16, 24, 41, 48-51, 59-60, 63-64, 84-85, 172. *See also* Celan, Paul, on silence and speaking
singularity, 40, 64-65, 73, 75-77, 79
social contract theory, 34, 51, 56n45, 121
Spariosu, Mihai, 54n30, 104, 124n11, 127n42, 168, 177n11, 177n13
"Speech on the Occasion of Receiving the Literature Prize of the Free Hanseatic City of Bremen" (Celan), 7, 12, 60, 79, 83, 86
Spinoza, Baruch, 35, 55n41
"Sprachgitter" (Celan), 69-70, 86, 170
"Sprich Auch Du" (Celan), 66-69, 87, 95
Standard American English, 171-73
Stolpersteine, 174
Sullivan, Shannon, 173
Sutton-Smith, Brian, 99, 126n35
symbol, 29-30, 78, 86, 90, 102-3, 119, 124n7, 135-36, 138
Symposium (Plato), 37

tact, 120, 175-76, 179n36
taste, 2, 5, 21, 26, 29, 31, 33, 96, 114, 118-20, 124, 126n30, 148-9, 165
Teaching to Transgress (hooks), 172
threshold, 95-98, 129, 167
Threshold to Threshold (Celan), 95
Thus Spoke Zarathustra (Nietzsche), 134, 170
to and fro movement, 9, 12, 17, 96, 98, 108, 143, 158, 176
Tobias, Rochelle, 73
"Todtnauberg" (Celan), 81-84
totalization, 8, 13, 16, 59, 72, 75, 83, 85, 88-89, 96, 99, 121-22, 130, 137-38, 153, 168, 172

tradition, 135, 151-58, 160n12, 165-66, 169-74; concerns regarding, 13-15, 99, 155-57, 165-66, 172-74; as dynamic, 4, 14, 99, 110, 123, 150, 153-4, 156-59, 173; Gadamer on, 98-99, 115, 125n23, 150-57, 166.

tragedy, 22, 36-38, 42, 57n64, 57n67, 98, 126n39, 131-32, 142, 159n2; poetry and, 23, 36, 50-51, 114-15.

transformation, 8-11, 17, 24, 27, 30-31, 50-51, 57n68, 61, 68, 97, 100-101, 111-12, 114-16, 123, 129, 131, 144-55, 166, 170-73, 176, 177n12

truth, 32, 63-64, 67, 69, 77, 79, 81, 89, 92n27, 106-7, 112, 118, 141, 147-50, 157

Truth and Method (Gadamer), 9, 11, 59, 96-97, 114-16, 129, 143, 145-54, 165-66, 175

"Tübingen, January", Celan, 70-74, 87

Turner, Victor, 177n12

unity, primordial, 2, 3, 5, 23, 35-38, 62, 122

utopia, 21-22, 36, 63-64, 87-89, 91n5, 96, 111-12, 120, 168-69; poetry and, 2, 16, 63-64, 87-89, 91n5.

"Die Vielfalt der Sprachen und das Verstehen der Welt" (Gadamer), 143

Vilhauer, Monica, 157

virtue, 17, 32-34, 105-8, 110, 113-17

vulnerability, 12, 23-24, 30-31, 43, 50-51, 65, 86, 115, 137, 152, 158, 167, 175-76

Waibel, Violetta, 54n25

"Weggebeizt" (Celan), 75-77

Welt und Endlichkeit (Fink), 98, 102, 135-38

The Will to Power (Nietzsche), 133-34, 160n12

Wierciński, Andrzej, 155, 158

Yancy, George, 170-73

"Zur Bildungstheorie der technischen Bildung" (Fink), 141

About the Author

Catherine Homan is assistant professor of philosophy at Mount Mary University in Milwaukee, Wisconsin. She holds a PhD in philosophy from Emory University. She was a visiting assistant professor at Siena College. Her primary areas of research include nineteenth and twentieth century continental philosophy, philosophy of art, and philosophy of play. She has published multiple articles on Eugen Fink as well as translations. Her work has appeared in *Philosophy Today*, *The Journal of Speculative Philosophy*, *The Philosophy of Play*, and *Teaching Philosophy*.

www.ingramcontent.com/pod-product-compliance
Lightning Source LLC
Chambersburg PA
CBHW050905300426
44111CB00010B/1385